QuickCook

QuickCook
Hot & Spicy

Recipes by Sunil Vijayakar

Every dish, three ways—you choose!
30 minutes | 20 minutes | 10 minutes

An Hachette UK Company
www.hachette.co.uk

First published in Great Britain in 2012 by Hamlyn,
a division of Octopus Publishing Group Ltd
Endeavour House, 189 Shaftesbury Avenue
London WC2H 8JY
www.octopusbooks.co.uk

Distributed in the US by Hachette Book Group USA
237 Park Avenue, New York, NY 10017 USA
www.octopusbooksusa.com

Distributed in Canada by Canadian Manda Group
165 Dufferin Street, Toronto, Ontario, Canada M6K 3H6

ISBN 978-0-6006-2507-0

Printed and bound in China

10 9 8 7 6 5 4 3 2 1

Standard level spoon and cup measurements are level unless otherwise indicated.

Ovens should be preheated to the specified temperature. If using a convection oven,
follow the manufacturer's instructions for adjusting the time and temperature.
Broilers should also be preheated.

This book includes dishes made with nuts and nut derivatives. It is advisable for
those with known allergic reactions to nuts and nut derivatives and those who may
be potentially vulnerable to these allergies, such as pregnant and nursing mothers,
people with weakened immune systems, the elderly, babies, and children, to avoid
dishes made with nuts and nut oils.

It is also prudent to check the labels of prepared ingredients for the possible inclusion
of nut derivatives.

The U.S. Food and Drug Administration advises that eggs should not be consumed
raw. This book contains some dishes made with raw or lightly cooked eggs. It
is prudent for vulnerable people, such as pregnant and nursing mothers, people
with weakened immune systems, the elderly, babies, and young children to avoid
uncooked or lightly cooked dishes made with eggs.

Contents

Introduction 6

Poultry 20
Recipes listed by cooking time 22

Meat 72
Recipes listed by cooking time 74

Fish and Seafood 124
Recipes listed by cooking time 126

Vegetarian 176
Recipes listed by cooking time 178

Beans, Peas, and Grains 228
Recipes listed by cooking time 230

Index 280

Introduction

30 20 10—Quick, Quicker, Quickest

This book offers a new and flexible approach to planning a meal for busy cooks, letting you choose the recipe option that best fits the time you have available. Inside you will find 360 dishes that will inspire and motivate you to cook every day of the year. All the recipes take a maximum of 30 minutes to cook. Some take as little as 20 minutes and, amazingly, many take only 10 minutes. With a little preparation, you can easily try out one new recipe from this book each night, and slowly you will be able to build a wide and exciting portfolio of recipes to suit your needs.

How Does it Work?

Every recipe in the QuickCook series can be cooked one of three ways—a 30-minute version, a 20-minute version, or a superquick and easy 10-minute version. At the beginning of each chapter, you'll find recipes listed by time. Choose a dish based on how much time you have and turn to that page.

You'll find the main recipe in the middle of the page, accompanied by a beautiful photograph, as well as two time-variation recipes below.

If you enjoy your chosen dish, why not go back and cook the other time-variation options at a later date? So if you liked the 20-minute Spicy Vietnamese Chicken, but only have 10 minutes to spare this time around, you'll find a way to cook a similar dish using quick ingredients or clever shortcuts.

If you love the ingredients and flavors of the 10-minute Spiced Crayfish and Arugula Sandwiches, why not try something more substantial, such as the 20-minute Crayfish, Vegetable, and Coconut Stir-Fry, or be inspired to make a more elaborate version, such as the Caribbean Crayfish and Coconut Curry? Or browse through all 360 delicious recipes, find something that catches your eye—then cook the version that fits your time frame.

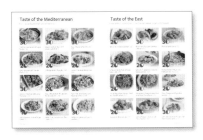

Alternatively, for easy inspiration, turn to the gallery on pages 12–19 to get instant ideas for cooking for different occasions, for diverse flavors and palates, from the fearlessly fiery to family favorites.

QuickCook online

To make life even easier, you can use the special code on each recipe page to e-mail yourself a recipe card for printing, or e-mail a text-only shopping list to your phone.

HOT-FISH-RAT

QuickCook Hot & Spicy

Spices are essential culinary ingredients, used in every nation's cuisine to stimulate the appetite and titillate the palate. Prized for centuries, they led to trade routes that spanned the globe.

Today, we can create and sample exotic spiced dishes, with diverse flavors, colors, and textures from all over the world, in our kitchens. From the islands of the Caribbean, to Southeast Asia, China, India, Mexico, South America, and even Africa, "hot and spicy" conjures delightful and varied cuisines at every turn.

In this book, we have recipes from all over the globe that use spices to their best advantage, and that are both quick and easy to cook. With this book, and a few essential ingredients, you can cook up a storm in the kitchen to share with family and friends.

Fresh Aromatics and Wet Spices

Chiles: In general, green chiles are less hot and more "earthy," while red chiles are hotter and fiery. If you want a chile flavor with less heat, remove the pith and seeds before chopping.

Curry Leaves: These highly aromatic leaves are used fresh in Indian and Southeast Asian cooking. Fresh curry leaves freeze well and can be used straight from the freezer.

Cilantro: Often the delicate leaves are used to flavor dishes, but the stems are also used, especially in Thai curry pastes.

Ginger: Fresh ginger root is peeled before using. It has a fresh, peppery flavor and is used in both savory and sweet recipes.

Kaffir Lime Leaves: These highly aromatic leaves are usually finely shredded when using in a curry or sometimes left whole. They freeze well and can be used straight from the freezer.

Lemon Grass: This green grass is used for its citrus flavor. It can be used by bruising the bottom of the stem or chopping.

Thai Basil: Found in Asian grocery stores, this delicate herb is used as a garnish. You can substitute regular basil, if necessary.

Shallots: These small, sweet, and pungent onions are widely used in Southeast Asian cooking. The easiest way to peel them is to slice them in half and remove the outer skin.

Pantry Essentials: Dry Spices and Ingredients

Cardamom: This spice is usually used whole, in its pod, as an aromatic. You can also use the little black seeds inside the pods, by crushing them and using as part of a spice mixture.

Chile: Whole dried red chiles add the fiery heat to a curry. Dried red pepper flakes tend to have a milder flavor and chili powders made from dried chiles vary in heat.

Cinnamon: This sweet and warming aromatic spice is available as sticks or rolled bark, and in ground powder form.

Cloves: These aromatic dried buds can be used whole or ground.

Coconut Milk: Widely used in Asian cuisine, coconut products are added to curries to produce a rich, creamy texture.

Coriander: These small, pale brown seeds are available whole or ground, and form the base of many curry pastes and mixes.

Crispy Fried Onions: These can be bought from a good Asian supermarket. To make from scratch, gently sauté thinly sliced onions in a large skillet with a little oil over low heat for 15-20 minutes or until golden and caramelized. Drain on paper towels until crisp and dried.

Cumin: Essential in Asian, Mexican, and Middle Eastern cooking, these small brown elongated seeds are used whole or ground and have a warm, pungent aroma. Whole seeds may be dry-roasted and sprinkled over a curry or dish just before serving.

Fennel Seeds: These small, pale green seeds have a subtle anise flavor and are used in some spice mixtures.

Fenugreek Seeds: These square, shiny yellow seeds are used widely in pickles spice mixes for curries.

Thai Fish Sauce: Also widely known as nam pla, this sauce is one of the main ingredients in Thai cooking and is made from the liquid extracted from salted, fermented fish.

Garam Masala: Usually added to a dish at the end of cooking time. A classic mix comprises of ground cardamom, cloves, cumin, peppercorns, cinnamon, and nutmeg.

Chickpea Flour: Also known as besan, this pale yellow flour, made from dried chickpeas, is used for thickening and binding as well as the main ingredient in savory batters.

Mustard Seeds: Black, brown, and yellow, these tiny, round seeds are widely used as a flavoring and are usually sautéed in oil until they "pop" to impart a mellow, nutty flavor.

Nigella Seeds: Also known as black onion seeds, or kalonji, these tiny, matte, black, oval-shape seeds are most frequently used to flavor breads and pickles.

Jaggery: Also known as palm sugar, this is the sugar produced in India from the sap of various types of palm. Sold in cakes or cans, it has a deep, caramel flavor and is light brown. Used in curries to balance the spices.

Saffron: These deep orange strands are the dried stamens from a special crocus and are use to impart a musky fragrance and golden color to rice dishes and desserts.

Shrimp Paste: Also known as kapee, this is a pungent preserve used in Asian cooking, made from pounding shrimp with salt and leaving it to decompose. It is sold in small jars and has a powerful aroma that disappears when cooked.

Star Anise: A flower-shape collection of pods. Dark brown in color, this spice has a decidedly anise flavor.

Tamarind Paste: Used as a souring agent in curries, the paste from this pod is available and can be used straight from the jar. You can also buy it in semidried pulp form, which needs to be soaked in warm water and strained before use. Look for it in Mexican, Asian and Indian grocery stores.

Turmeric: This bright orange-yellow rhizome has a warm, musky flavor and used in small quantities to flavor lentil and rice dishes. It is available as a dried, ground powder.

White Poppy Seeds: These tiny, white poppy seeds are used in Indian cooking, mainly to thicken sauces and curries.

Essential Equipment

Cooking these hot and spicy recipes does not mean investing in any expensive or complicated equipment. Most of what you will need is part of those basic essentials that every kitchen usually has: ladles, spoons, strainers, colanders, cutting boards, knives, etc. However, these other essential items will help you to prepare each meal with more ease.

Blender or Mini Food Processor: These are invaluable for making a smooth, well-blended mixture easily when you have to grind or combine wet and dry spices.

Electric Coffee Grinder: Excellent for grinding dry spices, they are available widely and are inexpensive to buy.

Skillets: Having a selection of skillets, preferably good, nonstick ones, in different sizes makes light work of cooking.

Heat diffuser: This is a disk made from perforated metal, usually with a removable handle, that sits on top of the heat source. When the pan is placed over it, it provides an even, low, well-distributed heat, perfect for slowly cooked recipes and rice dishes. They are available from any good kitchen store, are inexpensive, and will last for years.

Heavy Saucepans: Having a heavy bottom ensures that the food cooked will be heated evenly, without burning or sticking to the bottom of the pan. This is especially useful when cooking ingredients or sauces for a longer period.

Mortar and Pestle: A mortar and pestle is the traditional equipment for combining ground spices or pastes and is always reliable, but it does involve a lot of elbow grease. The ingredients are put in the mortar, then ground with the pestle.

Wok: Essential for fast stir-fries and other dishes.

Recipes to Impress

For the perfect hassle-free dinner party.

Spicy Chicken, Apricot, and Cranberry Couscous 40

Rose Harissa and Chicken Meatball Tagine 54

Spicy Mango and Duck Salad 56

African Curried Beef and Mango Chutney Casserole 76

Lamb Chops with Spicy Chickpeas and Spinach 88

Beef and Mixed Peppercorn Stroganoff 94

Spicy Lamb and Vegetable Stew 112

Grilled Piri Piri Squid with Mint and Cilantro 140

Coconut Spiced Clams 154

Creamy Spiced Lobster Tail 156

Mustard and Curry Leaf Halibut 162

Scallop Molee 166

Lighter Bites

Guilt-free food that tastes great.

Green Chicken Skewers with Cucumber and Chili Dip 24

Piquant Chicken and Mixed Pepper Brochettes 36

Chicken, Shrimp, and Lemon Grass Cakes 64

Spicy Beef Koftas with Mint Relish 96

Spicy Beef Enchilada Wraps 104

Chorizo, Spinach, and Egg Salad with Paprika Croutons 106

Thai Pork Larb Salad 118

Spicy Herb and Coconut Salmon Packages 128

Tandoori Jumbo Shrimp Skewers with Mint and Yogurt Dip 148

Spiced Crayfish and Arugula Sandwiches 152

Island-Spiced Corn with Avocado and Tomato 188

Cumin Potatoes with Pomegranate Seeds 194

Taste of the Mediterranean

Warm, sunny flavors from Spain and beyond.

Chicken, Lemon, and Tarragon Risotto 26

Spiced Spanish Turkey Stew with Lemon 38

Spicy Ham and Pea Risotto 108

Spicy Sausage and Tomato Pasta 110

Chile Spaghetti Vongole 130

Lemon Sole with Spicy Salsa 138

Spanish Potatoes with Spicy Tomatoes 224

Spicy Green Bean, Potato, and Pesto Linguine 238

Spicy Smoked Salmon and Asparagus Pasta 244

Spicy Bean and Mixed Pepper Salad 252

Spicy Tuna, Tomato, and Olive Pasta 262

Chile and Butternut Squash Risotto 272

Taste of the East

Exotic dishes from Asia, from China to Vietnam, Singapore to Thailand.

Spicy Vietnamese Chicken 44

Thai Green Coconut-Stuffed Chicken 50

Thai Fish Ball Curry 150

Chinese-Style Green Beans with Chile 206

Spicy Tofu with Bok Choy and Scallions 220

Malaysian Red Pepper and Cabbage Stir-Fry 222

Warm Edemame, Ginger, Chile, and Noodle Salad 232

Vietnamese Herbed Chicken Rice with Nuoc Cham Sauce 234

Spicy Shrimp and Vegetable Noodles 236

Singapore Rice Noodles 256

Spiced Shrimp, Coconut, and Banh Pho Pot 260

Burmese Coconut Chicken and Rice Noodle Curry 276

A Hint of Heat

Warm, comforting dishes that never fail to satisfy.

 **1**

Spicy Chicken and Mango Noodles 34

 **3**

Burmese Lemon Grass and Chile Pork 80

 **3**

Spicy Chile Dogs 98

 **2**

Veal and Scallion Kebabs with Sweet Chili Dip 116

 **3**

Chile and Cilantro Crab Cakes 134

 **2**

Garlicky Chile and Tomato Shrimp 168

 **2**

Sumac, Chile, and Lemon-Spiced Monkfish Kebabs 170

 **3**

Turmeric Mackerel Skewers with Chile Rice Noodles 174

 **3**

Eggplant, Tomato, and Chile Curry 180

 **3**

Chile, Cherry Tomato, and Goat Cheese Tart 182

 **3**

Spiced Fava Bean and Dill Pilaf 268

 **3**

Chile and Zucchini Pennette 270

Hot, Hot, Hot

For fearless diners, these recipes really pack a punch.

Thai Red Duck Curry 48

Haddock, Tomato, and Tamarind Fish Curry 136

Spicy Monkfish and Mixed Pepper Stew 144

Spicy Shrimp and Tomato Curry 146

Hot, Sweet, and Sour Salmon 160

Creamy Beet, Green Bean, and Tomato Curry 184

Mango and Coconut Curry 186

Sweet Potato and Litchi Curry 190

Carrot, Pea, and Potato Curry 204

Butternut Squash and Red Pepper Curry 212

Spiced Okra, Tomato, and Coconut 218

Spicy Chickpea Curry 274

Mild to Medium

A subtle hint of spice to tempt every palate.

Thai Green Chicken Curry 46

Curried Chicken and Peas 62

Pork, Red Pepper, and Pea Curry 90

West Indian Curried Beef and Black Bean Stew 120

Creamy Curried Mussel Soup 132

Shrimp, Lemon Grass, and Mango Curry 164

Yellow Fish, Potato, and Tomato Curry 172

Spinach, Tomato, and Paneer Curry 202

Curried Mushrooms and Tomatoes 208

Middle Eastern Zucchini, Tomato, and Mint Curry 214

Thai Massaman Pumpkin Curry 226

Carrot and Black Bean Curry 242

Food for Friends

Wholesome, hearty meals perfect for a get-together.

Cold Roasted Chicken with Spicy Salsa Verde 28

Sweet and Spicy Chicken Noodles 52

Spicy Chicken, Mushroom, and Spinach Pancakes 58

Chicken, Chile, and Rosemary Soup 60

Curried Chicken and Grape Salad 66

Chinese Turkey Chow Mein 70

Chinese Beef with Tofu and Vegetables 78

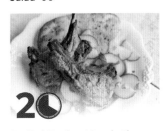

Broiled Tandoori Lamb Chops 84

Hot and Spicy Steak and Arugula Ciabattas 86

Spicy Lamb and Herb Skewers 100

Spicy Eggs with Merguez Sausages and Tomato 102

Five-Spice Pork Chops with Green Beans 122

QuickCook
Poultry

Recipes listed by cooking time

30

Green Chicken Skewers with Cucumber and Chile Dip   24

Chicken, Lemon, and Tarragon Risotto   26

Poached Chicken with Spicy Salsa Verde   28

Grilled Chicken with Chile and Arugula Pesto   30

Harissa-Spiced Turkey and Bell Pepper Kebabs   32

Chicken and Mango Curry   34

Piquant Chicken and Bell Pepper Stew   36

Spiced Spanish Turkey Stew with Lemon   38

Fruity Chicken Moroccan Stew 40

Spiced Chicken Stew with Preserved Lemon   42

Vietnamese Broiled Chicken 44

Thai Green Chicken Curry 46

Thai Red Duck Curry   48

Thai Green Coconut-Stuffed Chicken   50

Sweet and Spicy Chicken Drumsticks   52

Rose Harissa and Chicken Meatball Moroccan Stew 54

Spicy Mango and Duck Noodles   56

Spiced Chicken, Mushroom, and Spinach Pilaf   58

Rosemary and Chile-Stuffed Chicken   60

Curried Chicken and Peas 62

Chicken, Shrimp, and Lemon Grass Cakes   64

Broiled Chicken with Curry Mayonnaise   66

Duck Tikka Kebabs   68

Chinese Turkey Chow Mein   70

20

Green Chicken Stir-Fry   24

Broiled Chicken with Chile, Lemon, and Tarragon Butter   26

Pan-Fried Chicken with Spicy Salsa Verde   28

Chicken with Chile and Arugula Pesto Linguine   30

Turkey, Bell Pepper, and Harissa Stir-Fry   32

Spicy Chicken and Mango Kebabs   34

Piquant Chicken and Mixed Pepper Brochettes   36

Turkey, Chile, and Lemon Stir-Fry   38

Spicy Chicken, Apricot, and Cranberry Couscous   40

Spicy Chicken and Preserved Lemon Skewers   42

Spicy Vietnamese Chicken 44

Broiled Thai Green Chicken 46

Broiled Thai Red Duck   48

Thai Green Chicken Fried Rice   50

Sweet and Spicy Chicken Noodles   52

Broiled Rose Harissa
Chicken   54

Mango and Duck Curry   56

Spicy Chicken, Mushroom,
and Spinach Crepes   58

Creamy Chicken, Chile, and
Rosemary Pasta   60

Spicy Chicken and Pea Sauce
with Pasta   62

Chicken, Shrimp, and Lemon
Grass Skewers   64

Curried Chicken Pasta Salad
                                66

Tikka-Spiced Duck Omelet
                                68

Glazed Chinese-Style
Turkey Cutlets   70

Warm Green Chicken and
Rice Salad   24

Chicken, Lemon, and
Tarragon Baguettes   26

Cold Roasted Chicken with
Spicy Salsa Verde   28

Chicken Salad with Chile
and Arugula Pesto   30

Turkey Ciabattas with
Harissa Mayo   32

Spicy Chicken and Mango
Noodles   34

Piquant Chicken and Roasted
Pepper Salad   36

Quick Turkey, Lemon, and
Chile Rice   38

Spicy Chicken and Fruit
Couscous Salad   40

Spicy Lemon Chicken
Salad   42

Vietnamese Chicken Soup 44

Thai Green Chicken
Stir-Fry   46

Thai-Style Red Duck Salad
                                48

Quick Thai Green
Chicken Curry   50

Sweet and Spicy Chicken
and Pea Rice   52

Quick Rose Harissa and
Chicken Sauté   54

Spicy Mango and Duck
Salad   56

Chicken, Mushroom, and
Spinach Salad with Spicy
Yogurt Dressing   58

Chicken, Chile, and Rosemary
Soup   60

Quick Chicken and
Pea Curry   62

Chicken, Shrimp, and
Lemon Grass Stir-Fry   64

Curried Chicken and
Grape Salad   66

Duck and Vegetable Tikka
Stir-Fry   68

Chinese Turkey and Noodle
Salad   70

Green Chicken Skewers with Cucumber and Chile Dip

Serves 4

1¾ lb boneless, skinless chicken thighs, cut into bite-size pieces
¾ cup chopped cilantro
⅔ cup chopped mint leaves
1 teaspoon coarse black pepper
juice of 2 lemons
1 teaspoon light brown sugar
2 teaspoons peeled and finely grated fresh ginger root
2 garlic cloves, crushed
1 cup plain yogurt
lemon wedges, to serve

For the dip

½ cup rice or wine vinegar
2 tablespoons sugar
1 red chile, finely diced
½ red onion, finely diced
⅓ cup finely diced cucumber

- Put the chicken in a shallow nonmetallic bowl. Put the herbs, pepper, lemon juice, sugar, ginger, garlic, and yogurt in a food processor or blender and blend until smooth. Pour the mixture over the chicken and toss to coat evenly, then cover and let marinate for 10–15 minutes.

- Meanwhile, make the dip. Heat the vinegar and sugar in a small saucepan until the sugar has dissolved, then increase the heat and boil for 3 minutes, until slightly syrupy. Remove from the heat and stir in the red chile and red onion. Let cool. When cool, stir in the cucumber and set aside.

- Thread the chicken onto 12 metal skewers, then cook under a preheated medium-hot broiler for 4–5 minutes on each side or until cooked through.

- Transfer the skewers to 4 serving plates and drizzle a little of the dip over them. Serve with the remaining dip and lemon wedges to squeeze over the chicken.

Warm Green Chicken and Rice Salad

Heat a large nonstick wok, add 4 cups cold, cooked long-grain rice and stir-fry over high heat for 3–4 minutes, until piping hot. Remove from the heat. Stir in 3 cups diced, cooked skinless chicken breasts, 1 seeded, finely chopped red chile, and a large handful each of chopped mint and cilantro. Transfer to a large bowl, squeeze the juice of 1 lime over the mixture, season, and toss to mix well.

Green Chicken Stir-Fry

Prepare 1 (10 oz) package of rice noodles according to the package directions. Meanwhile, heat 2 tablespoons sunflower oil in a large wok or skillet until hot, add 8 sliced scallions, 2 chopped garlic cloves, and 2 teaspoons peeled and grated fresh ginger root, and stir-fry over medium-high heat for 2–3 minutes. Add 1¼ lb boneless, skinless chicken breasts, thinly sliced, and stir-fry for an additional 5–6 minutes or

until just cooked through. Add cooked rice noodles and stir-fry for another 2–3 minutes or until piping hot. Remove from the heat and stir in a large handful each of finely chopped mint and cilantro. Serve immediately.

3 Chicken, Lemon, and Tarragon Risotto

Serves 4

4 tablespoons unsalted butter
1 tablespoon olive oil
1 onion, finely chopped
1 red chile, seeded and
  finely chopped
2 garlic cloves, finely chopped
1 celery stick, finely chopped
1 carrot, peeled and finely chopped
1½ cups risotto rice
½ cup dry white wine
3 cooked chicken breasts, skin
  removed and diced
3¾ cups hot vegetable stock
1 cup finely grated Parmesan
  cheese
finely grated rind of 1 lemon
⅓ cup finely chopped tarragon
salt and pepper

- Heat the butter and oil in a large skillet, add the onion, chile, garlic, celery, and carrot, and cook over medium heat for 3–4 minutes, until softened. Add the rice and stir for 1 minute or until the grains are well coated. Pour in the wine and stir until it has been absorbed, then stir in the chicken.

- Add 1 ladle of hot stock and simmer, stirring until it has been absorbed. Repeat with another ladle of stock, then continue to add the stock at intervals and cook as before, for an additional 18–20 minutes or until the liquid has been absorbed and the rice is tender but still firm (al dente). Reserve 1 ladle of stock.

- Add the reserved stock, Parmesan, lemon rind, and tarragon, season, and mix well. Remove from the heat, cover, and let stand for 2 minutes.

- Spoon into warm bowls, season, and serve immediately.

---

1 **Chicken, Lemon, and Tarragon Baguettes**

Slice 2 warm medium baguettes into half horizontally and spread each with 2 tablespoons prepared tarragon mayonnaise. Divide 2 store-bought, cooked chicken breasts, skin removed and sliced, between the baguette bottoms, then sprinkle over the finely grated rind of ½ lemon and season. Top with the baguette lids, then cut each in half and serve.

2 **Broiled Chicken with Chile, Lemon, and Tarragon Butter**

Mix together 1¼ sticks softened butter, 1 seeded and finely diced red chile, the finely grated rind and juice of 1 lemon, 1 crushed garlic clove and ¼ cup finely chopped tarragon in a bowl. Meanwhile, season 4 large, boneless chicken breasts with skin and cook under a preheated hot broiler for 6–8 minutes on each side or until cooked

through. Serve with the flavored butter and a crisp green salad.

Cold Roasted Chicken with Spicy Salsa Verde

Serves 4

1 (3 lb) rotisserie chicken

For the spicy salsa verde

2 tablespoons red wine vinegar

⅔ cup chopped flat-leaf parsley leaves

½ cup chopped basil or mint leaves

2 garlic cloves, crushed

2 red chiles, seeded and finely chopped

4 anchovy fillets in oil, drained and chopped

2 tablespoons salted capers, rinsed

½ cup extra-virgin olive oil, plus extra if needed

pepper

- To make the spicy salsa verde, pour the vinegar into the bowl of a mini food processor, then add the herbs and pulse to form a coarse paste. Add the garlic, red chiles, anchovies, and capers and process again to a coarse paste. Gradually add the oil with the motor running, but do not overprocess. Season with pepper.

- To serve, cut the chicken into separate pieces and transfer to 4 plates. Spoon the spicy salsa verde over the chicken and serve.

Pan-Fried Chicken with Spicy Salsa Verde

Make the salsa verde as above. Lay 4 large, boneless chicken breasts with skin, between 2 sheets of plastic wrap and flatten with a rolling pin or meat mallet until ½ inch thick. Season and drizzle with 2 tablespoons olive oil. Heat a large, nonstick skillet until hot, add the chicken breasts, skin-side down, and cook for 4–5 minutes on each side or until cooked through. Serve with the salsa verde.

Poached Chicken with Spicy Salsa Verde

Put 4 large boneless, skinless chicken breasts in a large saucepan and pour 3½ cups hot chicken stock over the chicken. Add 1 bay leaf, 1 chopped carrot, 2 chopped celery sticks, and 1 quartered onion. Bring to a boil, then reduce the heat to medium and cook, uncovered, for 20 minutes or until the chicken is cooked all the way through. Meanwhile, make the salsa verde as above. Remove the chicken from the pan with a slotted spoon and drain on paper towels. Slice the chicken and serve with the salsa verde.

Grilled Chicken with Chile and Arugula Pesto

Serves 4

20 small tomatoes on the vine
4 large boneless, skinless
  chicken breasts
olive oil, for brushing
salt and pepper

For the pesto

4 garlic cloves, crushed
2 red chiles, seeded and
  finely chopped
¾ cup basil leaves
2 cups arugula leaves
½ cup grated Parmesan cheese
¾ cup pine nuts, toasted
⅔ cup extra-virgin olive oil, plus
  extra if needed

- Brush the tomatoes with oil and season well. Place on a nonstick baking sheet and cook in a preheated oven, at 425°F, for 10–12 minutes.

- Meanwhile, lay a chicken breast between 2 sheets of plastic wrap and flatten slightly with a rolling pin or meat mallet. Repeat with the remaining chicken breasts. Brush lightly with oil and season. Heat a ridged grill pan until smoking hot, add the chicken, and cook for 5–6 minutes on each side or until cooked through. Remove the chicken and let rest for 2–3 minutes.

- While the chicken is cooking, make the pesto. Put all the ingredients in a food processor or blender and blend until fairly smooth, adding a little more oil for a runnier consistency if desired.

- Transfer the chicken to warm serving plates, drizzle the pesto over the chicken, and serve with the roasted vine tomatoes.

Chicken Salad with Chile and Arugula Pesto

Make the pesto as above. Put 4 store-bought cooked chicken breasts, skin removed and thinly sliced, and 12 small tomatoes, halved, in a salad bowl. Drizzle the pesto over the salad, toss to mix well, and serve.

Chicken with Chile and Arugula Pesto Linguine

Cook 12 oz dried linguine in a large saucepan of salted boiling water according to the package directions until al dente. Meanwhile, make the pesto as above and cut 2 large store-bought boneless, skinless,

cooked chicken breasts into ½ inch pieces. Put the chicken and 8 small tomatoes, quartered, in a large bowl. Drain the pasta, then add to the chicken mixture. Add the pesto, toss to mix well, and serve immediately.

30 Harissa-Spiced Turkey and Bell Pepper Kebabs

Serves 4

1 lb turkey cutlets, cut into
  bite-size pieces
¼ cup harissa paste
1 tablespoon finely grated garlic
1 tablespoon peeled and finely
  grated fresh ginger root
juice of 2 lemons
1 red bell pepper, cored, seeded
  and cut into bite-size pieces
1 yellow bell pepper, cored,
  seeded and cut into bite-size
  pieces
1¼ cups couscous
¼ cup finely chopped parsley,
  plus extra to garnish
salt and pepper

- Put the turkey in a large nonmetallic bowl. Mix together the harissa, garlic, ginger, and lemon juice in a small bowl, then season well. Pour the mixture over the turkey, toss to coat evenly, then cover and let marinate for 10 minutes.

- Thread the turkey onto 8 metal skewers, alternating with the red and yellow bell peppers. Cook under a preheated medium-hot broiler for 6–8 minutes on each side or until the edges are lightly charred in places and the turkey is cooked all the way through.

- Meanwhile, put the couscous in a large heatproof bowl and season with salt. Pour enough boiling water over the grains to just cover, then cover with plastic wrap and let stand for 8–10 minutes, or according to the package directions, until the water is absorbed. Gently fork to separate the grains, then set aside and keep warm.

- Spoon the couscous onto 4 serving plates and sprinkle with the parsley. Top each with 2 skewers and serve with extra parsley scattered over the top.

---

10 Turkey Ciabattas with Harissa Mayo

Halve and toast 4 ciabatta rolls. Meanwhile, mix together 1 tablespoon harissa paste, ½ cup mayonnaise, and the juice of ½ lemon in a bowl, then spread over the toasted ciabatta bottoms. Divide ¼ cucumber, thinly sliced, 4 plum tomatoes, thinly sliced, and 1 lb store-bought cooked, sliced turkey breast among the bottoms and top with the ciabatta lids. Serve with fries.

20 Turkey, Bell Pepper, and Harissa Stir-Fry

Core, seed, and thinly slice 1 red bell pepper and 1 yellow bell pepper. Heat 2 tablespoons sunflower oil in a large wok or skillet until hot, add the peppers and 1 lb turkey cutlets, thinly sliced, and stir-fry over high heat for 6–8 minutes or until the turkey is just cooked through. Add 1 thinly sliced red onion and 8 finely sliced scallions and stir-fry for an additional 3–4 minutes. Mix together 2 tablespoons harissa paste and ¼ cup tomato puree, then add to the wok or skillet and cook for 1–2 minutes or until piping hot. Serve with herbed couscous or rice.

Spicy Chicken and Mango Noodles

Serves 4

2 tablespoons vegetable oil

2 tablespoons hot chili sauce

¼ cup sweet chili sauce

¼ cup dark soy sauce

2 large boneless, skinless chicken breasts, cut into thin strips

1¼ cups fresh mango chunks

1 (12 oz) package stir-fry vegetables, thawed, if frozen

2 (10 oz) packages medium egg noodles, cooked

½ cup dry-roasted peanuts, chopped

salt and pepper

- Mix together the oil, hot chili sauce, sweet chili sauce, and soy sauce in a large bowl. Add the chicken strips, season, and mix together.

- Heat a large nonstick wok or skillet until hot, then add the chicken, reserving the marinade, and stir-fry over high heat for 5 minutes or until lightly browned and cooked through. Add the mango, stir-fry vegetables, noodles, and the reserved marinade and stir-fry for an additional few minutes, until piping hot.

- Mix in the chopped peanuts, then divide among 4 warm bowls. Serve immediately.

Spicy Chicken and Mango Kebabs

Cut 4 large, boneless, skinless chicken breasts into bite-size pieces and place in a bowl with 1 tablespoon hot chili sauce, 2 tablespoons sweet chili sauce, and 2 tablespoons light soy sauce. Stir to mix well. Thread the chicken onto 12 metal skewers, alternating with 2½ cups fresh mango chunks. Cook under a preheated medium-hot broiler for 4–5 minutes on each side or until the chicken is cooked all the way through. Serve with a mixed green salad.

Chicken and Mango Curry

Heat 2 tablespoons sunflower oil in a large wok or skillet until hot, add 1 chopped onion, and stir-fry over medium heat for 4–5 minutes, until softened. Add 2 chopped garlic cloves, 1 teaspoon peeled and grated fresh ginger root, 1 seeded and chopped red chile, and 1 tablespoon medium or hot curry powder and stir-fry for an additional 1–2 minutes, then add 1¼ lb boneless, skinless chicken breasts, cubed, and stir-fry for 1–2 minutes or until lightly browned. Pour in 1 (14 fl oz) can coconut milk and bring to a boil, then reduce the heat to medium and cook, stirring frequently, for 10–12 minutes. Add 2½ cups fresh mango chunks and cook for an additional 3–4 minutes or until the chicken is cooked all the way through. Sprinkle with ¼ cup chopped cilantro leaves and serve immediately with steamed rice.

Piquant Chicken and Mixed Pepper Brochettes

Serves 4

1¾ lb boneless, skinless chicken breasts, cut into bite-size pieces

finely grated rind and juice of 1 lemon

1 red chile, seeded and finely chopped

1 teaspoon hot smoked paprika

½ cup extra-virgin olive oil

1 tablespoon dried oregano

3 garlic cloves, crushed

1 onion, cut into large pieces

1 red bell pepper, cored, seeded, and cut into large pieces

1 yellow bell pepper, cored, seeded, and cut into large pieces

salt and pepper

lemon wedges, to serve (optional)

- Put the chicken in a shallow nonmetallic bowl. Mix together the lemon rind and juice, chile, smoked paprika, oil, oregano, and garlic in a bowl, then season well. Pour the mixture over the chicken and toss to coat evenly.

- Thread the chicken onto 8 metal skewers, alternating with the onion and red or yellow bell peppers. Cook under a preheated medium-hot broiler for 4–5 minutes on each side or until the chicken is cooked all the way through.

- Transfer the brochettes to 4 serving plates and serve with lemon wedges to squeeze over, if desired.

 Piquant Chicken and Roasted Pepper Salad

Put 4 store-bought, cooked chicken breasts, skinned and coarsely shredded, 1 (12 oz) jar mixed roasted peppers, drained, and a handful of arugula leaves in a large salad bowl. Mix together 1 teaspoon chili paste, ⅓ cup extra-virgin olive oil, 1 teaspoon honey, and the juice of 1 large lemon in a bowl, then season. Pour the dressing over the salad, toss to mix well, and serve.

Piquant Chicken and Bell Pepper Stew

Heat 2 tablespoons sunflower oil in a large, heavy saucepan, add 1 chopped red onion, and cook over medium heat for 2–3 minutes, stirring occasionally, until beginning to soften. Add 4 chopped garlic cloves and 1 seeded and chopped red chile and sauté, stirring, for an additional 1–2 minutes. Stir in 4 large, boneless, skinless chicken breasts, thickly sliced, 1 cored, seeded, and thickly sliced red bell pepper, and 1 cored, seeded and thickly sliced yellow bell pepper and cook, stirring, until the chicken is lightly browned, then pour in 2 cups hot chicken stock and bring to a boil. Reduce the heat to medium and cook, uncovered, for 15–20 minutes or until the chicken is cooked all the way through and the bell peppers are tender. Season, then serve with warm crusty bread.

30 Spanish Turkey Stew with Lemon and Chile

Serves 4

1¾ lb turkey cutlets, cut into
  bite-size pieces
2 tablespoons sunflower oil
4 garlic cloves, crushed
1 onion, finely chopped
2 teaspoons dried red pepper flakes
10–12 pearl onions, peeled
2 carrots, peeled and cut into
  bite-size pieces
2 Yukon gold or white round
  potatoes, peeled and cut into
  bite-size pieces
1 tablespoon sweet smoked paprika
3 tablespoons lemon juice
⅓ cup chopped flat-leaf parsley
2 cups hot chicken stock
salt and pepper
crusty bread, to serve

- Put the turkey in a bowl and season well. Heat the oil in a large skillet, add the turkey, and cook over high heat, stirring occasionally, for 2–3 minutes or until browned all over.

- Transfer to a heavy saucepan, stir in the remaining ingredients, and bring to a boil. Reduce the heat to medium and cook, uncovered, for 20 minutes or until the turkey is cooked through and the vegetables are tender.

- Ladle into warm bowls and serve with crusty bread.

 Quick Turkey, Chile, and Lemon Rice

Heat 2 tablespoons sunflower oil in a large skillet until hot, add 4 chopped garlic cloves, 1 seeded and chopped red chile, and ½ small chopped onion. Stir-fry for 1–2 minutes. Add 4 cups cooked rice, 1 tablespoon smoked paprika, and 3 cups cooked, diced turkey breast and stir-fry for an additional 3-4 minutes, until piping hot. Remove from the heat, season, and stir in the grated rind of ½ lemon and ¼ cup chopped flat-leaf parsley.

 Turkey, Chile, and Lemon Stir-Fry

Heat 2 tablespoons sunflower oil in a large wok or skillet until hot, add 2 finely sliced onions, 2 seeded and finely sliced red chiles, 1 teaspoon peeled and grated fresh ginger root, and 3 chopped garlic cloves, and stir-fry over high heat for 4–5 minutes. Add 1¼ lb turkey cutlets, thinly sliced, and stir-fry for an additional 6–8 minutes or until cooked through. Stir in ¼ cup light soy sauce, 2 tablespoons sweet chili sauce, and the finely grated rind and juice of 1 lemon. Season, then serve immediately with steamed rice or noodles.

Spicy Chicken, Apricot, and Cranberry Couscous

Serves 4

1 cup couscous

1 tablespoon hot curry powder

⅓ cup extra-virgin olive oil

3 cups hot chicken stock

¾ cup cashew nuts

finely grated rind and juice of
  1 lemon

1 red chile, seeded and chopped

¼ cup chopped mint leaves

¼ cup chopped cilantro

¾ cup finely chopped
  dried apricots

¾ cup dried cranberries

2 store-bought, cooked, boneless
  chicken breasts, skin removed
  and coarsely shredded

juice of 1 orange

salt and pepper

chopped flat-leaf parsley, to serve

- Put the couscous, curry powder, and oil in a large heatproof bowl. Stir in the stock, then cover with plastic wrap and let stand for 8–10 minutes, or according to the package directions, until the stock is absorbed.

- Meanwhile, heat a small nonstick skillet until hot, add the cashew nuts, and dry-fry, stirring frequently, for 3–4 minutes or until toasted. Remove from the skillet and set aside.

- Gently fork the couscous to separate the grains, then stir in the cashew nuts and all the remaining ingredients. Season, toss to mix well, and serve sprinkled with chopped parsley.

 Spicy Chicken and Fruit Couscous Salad

Put 1 lb store-bought, cooked chicken breasts, skin removed and shredded, and 3 cups cooked couscous in a large bowl. Mix together ¼ cup olive oil, 1 seeded and finely diced red chile, ⅓ cup chopped dried apricots, ⅓ cup dried cranberries, 1 teaspoon hot curry powder, and the juice of 2 limes in a bowl and season. Pour over the salad, toss, and serve.

Fruity Chicken Moroccan Stew

Put 1¾ cups couscous in a large heatproof bowl. Add enough boiling water to just cover the grains, cover with plastic wrap, and let stand for 8–10 minutes, or according to the package directions, until all the water is absorbed. Meanwhile, heat 2 tablespoons olive oil in a large skillet, add 1 tablespoon hot curry powder, 1 chopped onion, 2 chopped garlic cloves, and 1 tablespoon peeled and finely grated fresh ginger root, and cook over high heat, stirring, for 1 minute. Add 1½ lb boneless, skinless chicken thighs, diced, and cook for 1–2 minutes, until browned, then pour 2½ cups hot chicken stock over the mixture and bring to a boil. Stir in 2 cups dried apricots and 1⅓ cups raisins, reduce the heat to medium, and cook, covered, for 20 minutes, until cooked through. Stir in 1 tablespoon harissa paste and a handful of chopped cilantro and season. Serve with the couscous.

30 Spiced Chicken Stew with Preserved Lemon

Serves 4

2 tablespoons olive oil

1¾ lb boneless, skinless chicken breasts, cut into bite-size pieces

1 large onion, thinly sliced

4 garlic cloves, finely chopped

1 teaspoon peeled and finely grated fresh ginger root

1 red chile, seeded and finely chopped

2 teaspoons ground cumin

3 cinnamon sticks

¼ teaspoon ground turmeric

2 large carrots, peeled and cut into bite-size pieces

large pinch of saffron threads

3 cups hot chicken stock

1 tablespoon rose harissa paste

8 green olives, pitted

8 ripe black olives, pitted

6 small preserved lemons, halved

salt and pepper

- Heat the oil in a large, heavy saucepan, add the chicken and onion, and cook over high heat, stirring occasionally, for 2–3 minutes, until browned. Add the garlic, ginger, red chile, cumin, cinnamon sticks, and turmeric and sauté, stirring, for 30 seconds.

- Add the carrots, saffron, and stock and bring to a boil. Reduce the heat to medium and cook, uncovered, for 15–20 minutes or until the chicken is cooked all the way through and the carrots are tender.

- Add the harissa, olives, and preserved lemons, season, and stir to mix well. Ladle into warm bowls and serve immediately.

 Spicy Lemon Chicken Salad

Put 4 store-bought, cooked chicken breasts, skin removed and coarsely shredded, and the leaves from 1 romaine lettuce in a large serving dish. Mix together the juice of 1 lemon, 2 tablespoons finely chopped preserved lemons, 2 teaspoons harissa paste, 1 tablespoon honey, and ⅓ cup olive oil in a bowl. Season and serve with the salad.

 Spicy Chicken and Preserved Lemon Skewers

Mix together 1 tablespoon harissa paste, 2 tablespoons finely chopped preserved lemons, the juice of 2 lemons, and 1 tablespoon honey in a large nonmetallic bowl. Add 1¾ lb boneless, skinless chicken breasts, cubed, and toss to coat evenly. Season, then cover and let marinate for a few minutes.

When ready to cook, thread the chicken onto 8 metal skewers and cook under medium-hot broiler for 6–8 minutes on each side or until cooked all the way through. Serve with couscous or steamed rice.

Spicy Vietnamese Chicken

Serves 4

3 tablespoons sunflower oil

1¾ lb boneless, skinless chicken breasts, cut into strips

12 scallions, cut into 1 inch lengths

4 garlic cloves, finely chopped

1 red chile, seeded and finely sliced

2 star anise

3 inch length of trimmed lemon grass stalk, finely chopped

1 teaspoon crushed cardamom seeds

1 cinnamon stick

3 cups sliced snow peas

1 carrot, peeled and cut into sticks

2 tablespoons Thai fish sauce

3 tablespoons oyster sauce

To garnish

handful of chopped cilantro leaves

handful of chopped mint leaves

chopped roasted peanuts

- Heat half the oil in a large wok or skillet until hot, add the chicken, and stir-fry over high heat for 3–4 minutes or until lightly browned and just cooked through. Remove with a slotted spoon and keep warm.

- Heat the remaining oil in the wok or skillet until hot, add the scallions, and stir-fry for 1–2 minutes, until softened. Add the garlic, red chile, star anise, lemon grass, cardamom, cinnamon stick, snow peas, and carrot and stir-fry for an additional 3–4 minutes or until the vegetables are softened.

- Return the chicken to the wok or skillet with the fish sauce and oyster sauce and continue to stir-fry for 3–4 minutes or until the chicken is cooked all the way through and piping hot.

- Spoon into warm bowls, sprinkle with chopped herbs and peanuts, and serve immediately.

 Vietnamese Chicken Soup

Put 3½ cups store-bought fresh chicken stock, 1 tablespoon lemon grass paste, 1 teaspoon chili paste, 1 teaspoon garlic paste, and 1 teaspoon ground cinnamon in a pan and bring to a boil. Stir in 1 lb store-bought, cooked chicken breasts, shredded, and cook for 1–2 minutes or until piping hot.

 Vietnamese Broiled Chicken

Chop 1¾ lb boneless, skinless chicken thighs into large pieces and put in a large bowl. Mix together the juice of 2 limes, a ¾ inch length of trimmed lemon grass stalk, chopped, 2 tablespoons Thai fish sauce, 1 tablespoon garlic paste, 2 seeded and diced red chiles, 2 tablespoons sugar, and 2 tablespoons sunflower oil in a bowl. Pour the mixture over the chicken, toss to coat evenly, then cover and let marinate for 5 minutes. Put the chicken on an oiled broiler rack in a single layer, brushing over any remaining marinade, and cook under a preheated medium-hot broiler for 6–8 minutes on each side or until cooked through. Serve with steamed rice.

30 Thai Green Chicken Curry

Serves 4

1 (14 fl oz) can coconut milk

2½ cups chopped cilantro

1 tablespoon sunflower oil

3 tablespoons Thai green
  curry paste

2 green chiles, seeded and finely
  chopped

1¾ lb boneless, skinless chicken
  thighs, cut into bite-size pieces

1 cup hot chicken stock

6 kaffir lime leaves

2 tablespoons Thai fish sauce

1 tablespoon grated jaggery or
  granulated sugar

7 oz Thai baby eggplants, halved
  if large, or cut into ¾ inch cubes
  (about 1⅔ cups)

1 cup trimmed green beans

juice of 1 lime

red chile slivers, to garnish

steamed jasmine rice, to serve

- Put the coconut milk and cilantro in a food processor or blender and blend until well mixed. Strain the mixture into a bowl using a fine-mesh strainer and discard the cilantro.

- Heat the oil in a large wok or heavy saucepan until hot, add the curry paste and green chiles, and stir-fry over high heat for 2–3 minutes. Add the chicken and stir-fry for an additional 5–6 minutes or until lightly browned.

- Stir in the coconut milk mixture, stock, lime leaves, fish sauce, sugar, and eggplants, then reduce the heat and simmer, uncovered, for 10–15 minutes, stirring occasionally, until the chicken is cooked all the way through. Add the green beans and simmer for an additional 2–3 minutes or until tender.

- Remove from the heat and stir in the lime juice. Ladle into warm bowls, sprinkle with red chile slivers, and serve with steamed jasmine rice.

---

10 Thai Green Chicken Stir-Fry

Heat 2 tablespoons sunflower oil in a large wok until hot, add 2 tablespoons Thai green curry paste, and stir-fry over medium heat for 1 minute. Increase the heat to high, add 1¼ lb boneless, skinless chicken breasts, sliced, and 1 cup canned coconut milk and stir-fry for 5–6 minutes, until the chicken is cooked all the way through. Serve with steamed rice.

20 Broiled Thai Green Chicken

Mix together 1 tablespoon Thai green curry paste, ½ cup canned coconut milk, and the juice of 1 lime in a bowl. Make 3–4 slashes on 4 large, boneless, skinless chicken breasts, then spread the mixture all over the chicken and into the slashes and season with salt. Cook under a preheated medium-hot broiler for 6–8 minutes on each side or until the chicken is cooked through. Serve with steamed rice, salad or noodles.

30 Thai Red Duck Curry

Serves 4

2 tablespoons sunflower oil
2 garlic cloves, crushed
1 teaspoon peeled and finely
   grated fresh ginger root
2 tablespoons Thai red curry
   paste
1 lb skinless duck breasts, thinly
   sliced
1 (14 fl oz) can coconut milk
3 cups diagonally halved
   snow peas
1 cup hot chicken stock
4 kaffir lime leaves
2 teaspoons grated jaggery or
   granulated sugar
2 lemon grass stalks, bruised
salt and pepper
chopped cilantro leaves,
   to garnish
steamed jasmine rice, to serve

- Heat the oil in a large wok or skillet until hot, add the garlic and ginger, and stir-fry over high heat for 20–30 seconds. Stir in the curry paste and stir-fry for 30 seconds, then add the duck and stir-fry for an additional 4–5 minutes.

- Stir in the coconut milk, snow peas, stock, lime leaves, sugar, and lemon grass and bring to a boil, then reduce the heat to medium and cook, uncovered, for 15–20 minutes, stirring occasionally, until the duck is cooked through. Season to taste.

- Ladle into warm bowls, sprinkle with chopped cilantro, and serve with steamed jasmine rice.

 Thai-Style Red Duck Salad

Thinly slice 4 cooked, smoked duck breasts and put in a large salad bowl with a large handful of mixed salad greens. Mix together 1 teaspoon Thai red curry paste, ⅓ cup light olive oil, 2 teaspoons honey, and 3 tablespoons red wine vinegar in a bowl, then season. Pour the dressing over the salad, toss to mix well, and serve with warm crusty bread.

 Broiled Thai Red Duck

Mix together 1 tablespoon Thai red curry paste and ½ cup coconut milk in a bowl. Using a sharp knife, score the skin side of 4 large duck breasts, then spread the red curry mixture all over the breasts and season. Place the duck in a single layer, skin-side up, on an oiled broiler rack and cook under a preheated medium broiler for 4–5 minutes on each side or until cooked to your liking. Serve with steamed rice and Chinese greens.

30 Thai Green Coconut-Stuffed Chicken

Serves 4

4 large, boneless chicken breasts, with the skin
1 teaspoon Thai green curry paste
¼ cup coconut milk
2 tablespoons fresh white bread crumbs
finely grated rind of 1 lime
1 teaspoon lemon grass paste
sunflower oil, for drizzling
salt and pepper

To serve

steamed jasmine rice
steamed Chinese greens

- Using a small, sharp knife, cut a slit down the side of each chicken breast to form a deep pocket. Mix together the remaining ingredients in a bowl, then season well. Divide the mixture evenly among the 4 chicken pockets.

- Drizzle with a little oil, then transfer to a nonstick baking sheet. Place in a preheated oven, at 350°F, for 18–20 minutes or until the chicken is cooked through.

- Serve with steamed jasmine rice and Chinese greens.

 Quick Thai Green Chicken Curry

Heat 2 tablespoons sunflower oil in a large wok or skillet until hot, add 2 tablespoons Thai green curry paste, and stir-fry over medium heat for 1–2 minutes. Stir in 4 store-bought, cooked chicken breasts, skin removed and diced, and 1 (14 fl oz) can coconut milk and bring to a boil. Cook for 3–4 minutes or until piping hot, then remove from the heat, season, and stir in ¼ cup each of chopped cilantro and Thai basil leaves. Serve with steamed rice or noodles.

 Thai Green Chicken Fried Rice

Heat 2 tablespoons sunflower oil in a large wok or skillet until hot, add 6 sliced scallions, 1 chopped garlic clove, 1 teaspoon peeled and grated fresh ginger root, a ¾ inch length of trimmed lemon grass stalk, finely chopped, and 1 tablespoon Thai green curry paste, and stir-fry over high heat for 1–2 minutes. Stir in ½ cup coconut milk, 3½ cups cooked long-grain rice, and 4 store-bought, cooked chicken breasts, skin removed and thinly sliced, then reduce the heat to medium and stir-fry for 7–8 minutes or until piping hot. Season, then serve immediately.

 # Sweet and Spicy Chicken Noodles

Serves 4

10 oz dried medium egg noodles
2 tablespoons sunflower oil
1 lb boneless, skinless chicken
  breasts, cut into cubes
1 (12 oz) package stir-fry
  vegetables, thawed, if frozen
2 red chiles, seeded and sliced
1 garlic clove, crushed
1 tablespoon cornstarch
⅓ cup light soy sauce
⅓ cup sweet chili sauce
1 tablespoon rice wine vinegar
¼ cup tomato puree
1 tablespoon light brown sugar
½ teaspoon ground ginger
¼ cup water
1 (8 oz) can pineapple slices,
  drained cut into small pieces
4 scallions, thinly sliced

- Cook the noodles according to the package directions, then drain and keep warm.

- Meanwhile, heat the oil in a large wok or skillet until hot, add the chicken, and stir-fry over medium-high heat for 6–8 minutes or until lightly browned and just cooked through. Add the stir-fry vegetables and stir-fry for an additional 3–4 minutes.

- Mix together the red chiles, garlic, cornstarch, soy sauce, chili sauce, vinegar, tomato puree, sugar, and ground ginger in a small bowl. Add this mixture to the wok with the measured water, pineapple, and scallions and stir-fry for 2–3 minutes or until all the ingredients are well coated.

- Add the reserved noodles to the wok, toss to mix well, and heat until piping hot. Divide into warm bowls and serve immediately.

 ### Sweet and Spicy Chicken and Pea Rice

Heat 2 tablespoons sunflower oil in a large wok until hot, add 3½ cups cooked rice, 2 cups frozen peas, 1 tablespoon sweet chili sauce, ¼ cup light soy sauce, 1 tablespoon garlic paste, and 1 tablespoon ginger paste, and stir-fry over high heat for 4–5 minutes. Add 1 lb store-bought cooked chicken breasts, diced, and stir-fry for 2–3 minutes or until piping hot.

 ### Sweet and Spicy Chicken Drumsticks

Make 3–4 deep slashes in 12 large chicken drumsticks and put in an ovenproof casserole dish. Mix together 3 seeded and sliced red chiles, 2 crushed garlic cloves, ½ cup light soy sauce, ⅓ cup sweet chili sauce, 2 tablespoons rice wine vinegar, 1 tablespoon light brown sugar, ¼ cup sunflower oil, and 1 teaspoon ground ginger in a bowl. Pour the mixture over the chicken and toss to coat evenly.

Place in a preheated oven, at 425°F, for 20–25 minutes or until the chicken is cooked all the way through. Serve with noodles or steamed rice.

30 Rose Harissa and Chicken Meatball Moroccan Stew

Serves 4

2 teaspoons finely peeled and
grated fresh ginger root
4 teaspoons finely grated garlic
1 teaspoon ground cinnamon
1 cup finely chopped cilantro
leaves, plus extra to garnish
1¾ lb ground chicken
3 tablespoons sunflower oil
1 onion, finely chopped
2 tablespoons rose harissa paste
1 (14½ oz) can diced tomatoes
1 cup hot chicken stock
salt and pepper
couscous, to serve

- Put the ginger, garlic, cinnamon, cilantro, and chicken in a mixing bowl, then season well. Using your hands, mix well to combine, then roll and shape tablespoons of the mixture into bite-size balls.

- Heat 2 tablespoons of the oil in a large skillet until hot, add the chicken balls, and cook in batches until lightly browned. Remove with a slotted spoon and set aside.

- Add the remaining oil to the skillet, add the onion, and cook, stirring, over medium heat for 1–2 minutes, then stir in the harissa paste and cook for an additional 1–2 minutes. Stir in the tomatoes and stock and bring to a boil, then reduce the heat to medium and cook, uncovered, for 10 minutes.

- Return the chicken balls to the skillet and stir gently to coat with the sauce. Simmer gently for 5–6 minutes or until piping hot and cooked all the way through.

- Spoon into warm bowls, sprinkle with chopped cilantro, and serve with couscous.

---

10 Quick Rose Harissa and Chicken Sauté

Heat 1 tablespoon sunflower oil in a large skillet, add 1¼ lb ground chicken, and sauté over high heat for 4–5 minutes or until sealed and browned. Stir in 3 tablespoons rose harissa paste and 1⅓ cups frozen peas and cook for another 2–3 minutes or until cooked all the way through and piping hot, then remove from the heat. Stir in ¼ cup chopped cilantro leaves and serve with rice or crusty bread.

20 Broiled Rose Harissa Chicken

Mix together 2 tablespoons rose harissa paste, the juice of 1 lemon, and ¼ cup plain yogurt in a small bowl, then season with salt. Using a small, sharp knife, make 3–4 deep slashes in 4 boneless, skinless chicken breasts and spread the mixture all over the chicken and into the cuts. Transfer the chicken to a lightly oiled broiler rack and cook under a medium-hot broiler for 6–8 minutes on each side or until cooked all the way through.

Serve immediately with a green salad, rice, or crusty bread.

Spicy Mango and Duck Salad

Serves 4

2½ cups fresh mango chunks

4 store-bought, cooked, smoked
duck breasts, skin removed and
coarsely shredded

½ cup store-bought mayonnaise

¼ cup sweet chili sauce

juice of 1 lime

salt and pepper

· Put the mango and shredded duck in a large salad bowl and
season well.

· Mix together the mayonnaise, sweet chili sauce, and lime
juice in a bowl. Pour the dressing over the salad, toss to mix
well, and serve.

 **Mango and Duck
Curry**

Heat 2 tablespoons sunflower
oil in a large wok until hot, add
1 chopped onion, 1 seeded and
chopped red chile, 1 chopped
garlic clove, and 1 teaspoon
peeled and grated fresh ginger
root, and stir-fry for 1–2 minutes.
Add 1¼ lb boneless, skinless
duck breasts, cut into bite-size
pieces, and stir-fry over high
heat for 3–4 minutes, until lightly
golden. Stir in 1 (14 fl oz) can
coconut milk, ½ cup water, and
2 tablespoons medium curry
paste and bring to a boil. Mix
well and cook, uncovered, for
10–12 minutes or until the duck is
cooked through. Stir in 2½ cups
fresh mango chunks and heat
until warmed through. Remove
from the heat and serve with
steamed rice.

 **Spicy Mango and
Duck Noodles**

Prepare 1½ lb medium egg
noodles according to the
package directions. Meanwhile,
put 2 large, skinless duck
breasts, cut into thin strips,
into a large bowl. Mix together
2 tablespoons sunflower oil,
2 tablespoons hot chili sauce,
¼ cup sweet chili sauce, and
¼ cup soy sauce in a small bowl,
then pour the mixture over the
duck, season, and toss to coat
evenly. Cover and let marinate
for 15 minutes. Heat a nonstick
wok or skillet until hot. Using a
slotted spoon, add the duck to
the wok, reserving the marinade,
and stir-fry over high heat for
5 minutes or until lightly golden
and just cooked through. Add
1¼ cups fresh mango chunks,
1 (12 oz) package stir-fry

vegetables, thawed, if frozen,
the noodles, and the reserved
marinade and stir-fry for an
additional few minutes, until
piping hot. Stir in ½ cup dry-
roasted peanuts, chopped.
Divide into warm bowls and
serve immediately.

Spicy Chicken, Mushroom, and Spinach Crepes

Serves 4

2 tablespoons butter, plus extra for greasing

5 cups sliced cremini mushrooms

6 scallions, finely sliced

2 garlic cloves, crushed

1 tablespoon hot curry powder

1 red chile, seeded and sliced

2 cups prepared cheese sauce

1 (12 oz) package baby spinach leaves

2 store-bought, cooked chicken breasts, skin removed and shredded

¼ cup chopped cilantro

8 crepes (make ahead with a pancake mix; see package directions), thawed, if frozen

½ cup grated Parmesan cheese

salt and pepper

mixed salad, to serve

• Heat the butter in a large skillet, add the mushrooms, scallions, garlic, curry powder, and red chile, and cook over high heat for 4–5 minutes, stirring frequently, until the mushrooms are softened. Stir in half of the cheese sauce and heat until just bubbling. Add the spinach and cook for 1 minute or until just wilted. Remove from the heat, stir in the chicken and cilantro, and season.

• Place 1 crepe on a clean work surface and spoon one-eighth of the mushroom and spinach mixture down the center. Carefully roll up the crepe and put into a shallow greased gratin dish. Repeat with the remaining crepes.

• Drizzle the remaining cheese sauce over the crepes, sprinkle with the Parmesan, and season. Cook under a preheated medium-hot broiler for 3–4 minutes or until piping hot and golden. Serve with a mixed salad.

Chicken, Mushroom, and Spinach Salad with Spicy Yogurt Dressing

Put 4 store-bought, cooked chicken breasts, skin removed and shredded, 1 (6 oz) package baby spinach leaves, and 3 cups thinly sliced button mushrooms in a salad bowl. Mix together 1¼ cups plain yogurt with 1 tablespoon mild curry powder, 2 tablespoons chopped cilantro, and the juice of 1 lemon in a bowl, then season. Drizzle the dressing over the salad, toss to mix well, and serve.

Spiced Chicken, Mushroom and Spinach Pilaf

Heat 2 tablespoons sunflower oil in a heavy saucepan, add 1 chopped onion, 1 seeded and finely chopped red chile, 2 teaspoons cumin seeds, 1 cinnamon stick, 1 bay leaf, 1 tablespoon medium or hot curry powder, and 1 lb boneless, skinless chicken breasts, diced, and cook, stirring, for 1–2 minutes, until the chicken is lightly browned. Add 2 cups long-grain rice, 4 cups chopped spinach leaves, and 3 cups sliced button mushrooms and season, then stir to mix well. Pour in 3½ cups hot vegetable stock and bring to a boil. Cover tightly, reduce the heat to low, and cook, undisturbed, for 15–20 minutes or until the liquid is absorbed, the rice is tender, and the chicken is cooked all the way through. Remove from the heat and let stand for a few minutes before serving.

Chicken, Chile, and Rosemary Soup

Serves 4

2 garlic cloves, crushed

1 red chile, seeded and finely chopped, plus extra to garnish

2 tablespoons finely chopped fresh rosemary

2 (14 oz) cans cream of chicken soup

crusty bread rolls, to serve

To garnish

chili oil

finely chopped chives

- Pour the soup into a saucepan, stir in the garlic and chile, and bring to a boil. Reduce the heat to medium and cook for a few minutes or until piping hot.

- Remove from the heat. Ladle into bowls, sprinkle with the chives and the remaining chopped chile, to garnish, and drizzle with chile oil. Serve immediately with crusty bread rolls.

 Creamy Chicken, Chile, and Rosemary Pasta

Cook 12 oz dried penne in a large saucepan of salted boiling water according to the package directions until al dente. Meanwhile, heat 2 tablespoons olive oil in a large skillet, add 2 chopped garlic cloves, 2 seeded and finely chopped red chiles, and 12 oz boneless, skinless chicken thighs, chopped, and cook over medium heat, stirring occasionally, for 8–10 minutes or until the chicken is sealed and cooked through. Add 1 teaspoon dried rosemary and 1 cup crème fraîche or Greek yogurt. Drain the pasta, add to the skillet, and season. Toss to mix well, then serve immediately with an arugula salad.

 Rosemary and Chile-Stuffed

Chicken Process ½ cup finely chopped flat-leaf parsley, 2 tablespoons finely chopped rosemary, 2 seeded and finely chopped red chiles, 2 tablespoons grated Pecorino cheese, 2 crushed garlic cloves, 1½ tablespoons softened unsalted butter, and the finely grated rind and juice of 1 lemon to a paste in a food processor or blender, then season well. Take 4 large, boneless chicken breasts and carefully lift the skin away from the breast meat, but leaving it still attached at one end. Spoon the herb mixture onto the chicken breasts, then smooth the skin back down to cover the herb mixture. Heat 2 tablespoons olive oil and

1½ tablespoons butter in an ovenproof skillet, add the chicken breasts, skin-side down, and carefully sauté for 1–2 minutes or until the skin is crisp and golden brown. Turn the chicken over and cook for an additional 1 minute. Transfer the skillet to a preheated oven, at 350°F, and cook for 12–15 minutes or until the chicken is cooked all the way through. Cover with aluminum foil and let rest for 5 minutes before serving with a salad.

30 Curried Chicken and Peas

Serves 4

3 tablespoons vegetable oil

2 teaspoons cumin seeds

2 onions, finely chopped

1 tablespoon peeled and grated
fresh ginger root

1 tablespoon grated garlic

1 lb ground chicken

2 tablespoons ground coriander

1 teaspoon hot chili powder

1 tablespoon ground cumin

1 tablespoon garam masala

1 red bell pepper, cored, seeded,
and finely chopped

⅔ cup frozen peas

2 ripe tomatoes, finely chopped

juice of ½ lime

chopped cilantro leaves,
to garnish

To serve

warm chapatis or parathas

plain yogurt

- Heat the oil in a large wok or skillet until hot, add the cumin seeds, and stir-fry over medium heat for 1 minute. Add the onions and stir-fry for an additional 3–4 minutes, until softened, then add the ginger and garlic and continue to stir-fry for 1 minute.

- Add the ground chicken and the ground spices and stir-fry for 5–7 minutes or until sealed and lightly browned. Stir in the red bell pepper, peas, and tomatoes and stir-fry for an additional 3–4 minutes or until cooked all the way through and piping hot.

- Remove from the heat and stir in the lime juice. Spoon into warm bowls, sprinkle with chopped cilantro, and serve with warm chapatis or parathas and a spoonful of yogurt.

1 Quick Chicken and Pea Curry

Heat 2 tablespoons olive oil in a large wok until hot, add 1¼ lb ground chicken and 2 tablespoons green curry paste, and stir-fry over high heat for 3–4 minutes or until the chicken is cooked all the way through. Stir in 1 (14 fl oz) can coconut milk and ⅔ cup frozen peas and cook for an additional 3–4 minutes. Season well, then serve with jasmine rice or crusty bread.

2 Spicy Chicken and Pea Sauce with Pasta

Heat 1 tablespoon olive oil in a saucepan, add 4 chopped shallots, 2 teaspoons cumin seeds, 4 crushed garlic cloves, ⅔ cup frozen peas, 1 teaspoon peeled and grated fresh ginger root, 1 teaspoon ground cumin, 1 teaspoon ground coriander, and 1 teaspoon hot chili powder, and stir-fry over high heat for 1–2 minutes. Add 1 lb ground chicken and stir-fry for an additional 2–3 minutes, until lightly browned, then add 1 (14½ oz) can diced tomatoes, ½ cup tomato puree, and 1 teaspoon sugar. Season, bring to a boil, then reduce the heat to medium and cook for 20 minutes. Meanwhile, cook 1 lb dried spaghetti in a large saucepan of boiling, salted water according to the package directions. Serve the sauce spooned over the spaghetti.

30 Chicken, Shrimp, and Lemon Grass Cakes

Serves 4

12 oz ground chicken

12 oz peeled jumbo shrimp

1½ inch length of trimmed lemon grass stalk, finely chopped

1 cup chopped cilantro

⅓ cup chopped mint

1 tablespoon peeled and grated fresh ginger root

2 large garlic cloves, crushed

1 red chile, seeded and finely chopped

1 tablespoon medium curry powder

8 oz dried rice noodles

2 tablespoons sunflower oil, for brushing

salt and pepper

To serve

lime wedges

sweet chili dipping sauce

- Put the chicken, shrimp, lemon grass, chopped herbs, ginger, garlic, red chile, and curry powder in a food processor or blender and process until smooth. Using wet hands, divide the mixture into 12 portions and shape each portion into a cake. Transfer to a nonstick baking sheet, cover, and chill for 8–10 minutes.

- Meanwhile, cook the rice noodles according to the package directions, then drain and keep warm.

- Brush the cakes with oil and season. Cook under a preheated medium-hot broiler, turning once or twice, for about 10 minutes or until browned and just cooked through.

- Transfer the cakes to 4 serving plates and serve with the rice noodles, lime wedges, and a sweet chili dipping sauce.

 Chicken, Shrimp, and Lemon Grass Stir-Fry Heat 2 tablespoons sunflower oil in a large wok or skillet until hot, add 1 lb ground chicken, 1 tablespoon green curry paste, and 1 tablespoon lemon grass paste, and stir-fry over high heat for 3–4 minutes or until sealed and browned. Stir in 10 oz cooked, peeled shrimp, 1 tablespoon light soy sauce, and 1 tablespoon Thai fish sauce and heat for 3–4 minutes, until piping hot. Serve with noodles.

 Chicken, Shrimp, and Lemon Grass Skewers Place 12 oz ground chicken, 12 oz peeled jumbo shrimp, 1 tablespoon lemon grass paste, 1 teaspoon each ginger paste and garlic paste, 1 teaspoon sweet chili sauce, and 2 cups fresh white bread crumbs in a food processor or blender and process until smooth, then season. Divide into 12 portions, then shape each portion around a metal skewer into a long sausage shape and cook under a preheated medium-hot broiler for 3–4 minutes on each side or until cooked all the way through. Serve with a mixed salad.

Curried Chicken and Grape Salad

Serves 4

4 large store-bought, cooked chicken breasts, with skin, cut into bite-size pieces

large handful Boston lettuce leaves

12 cherry tomatoes, halved

1⅓ cups halved seedless green grapes

6 scallions, thinly sliced

For the curry mayonnaise

1 cup mayonnaise

2 teaspoons medium or hot curry powder

finely grated rind and juice of 1 lemon

½ cup finely chopped cilantro leaves

- To make the curry mayonnaise, put all the ingredients in a bowl and stir to mix well. Set aside.

- Put the chicken breasts, lettuce leaves, tomatoes, grapes, and scallions in a large salad bowl and mix well.

- Spoon the mayonnaise over the salad, toss to mix well, and serve with crusty bread, if desired.

2 Curried Chicken Pasta Salad

Cook 8 oz dried penne in a large saucepan of salted boiling water according to the package directions until al dente. Meanwhile, put 4 store-bought, cooked chicken breasts, skin removed and cut into bite-size pieces, 1 diced cucumber, 12 halved cherry tomatoes, 1 finely diced red onion, and 1 diced apple in a large salad bowl. Mix together 1¼ cups mayonnaise, 2 teaspoons medium-hot curry powder, the juice of 2 limes, 1 teaspoon honey, 2 teaspoons toasted cumin seeds, and a small handful of finely chopped cilantro leaves in a bowl, then season and stir to mix well. Drain the pasta, then add to the chicken mixture. Pour the dressing over the salad, toss to mix well, and serve warm or at room temperature.

3 Broiled Chicken with Curry Mayonnaise

Make the curry mayonnaise as above. Put 4 large, boneless, skinless chicken breasts in a bowl. Mix ⅓ cup olive oil, 1 teaspoon dried red pepper flakes, 2 teaspoons paprika, 2 crushed garlic cloves, and the grated rind and juice of 1 lemon in a bowl, then season. Pour the mixture over the chicken and toss. Cook under a preheated medium-hot broiler for 6–8 minutes on each side or until cooked through. Cover and let rest for 2–3 minutes. Serve with the curry mayonnaise and salad.

30 Duck Tikka Kebabs

Serves 4

4 large, skinless duck breasts, cut
 into bite-size pieces
1 cup plain yogurt
3 tablespoons tikka paste
1 tablespoon finely grated garlic
1 tablespoon peeled and finely
 grated fresh ginger root
juice of 2 limes
2 red bell peppers, cored, seeded,
 and cut into bite-size pieces
salt and pepper
chopped cilantro leaves,
 to garnish

To serve

steamed rice
chopped cucumber salad

- Put the duck in a large nonmetallic bowl. Mix together the yogurt, tikka paste, garlic, ginger, and lime juice in a small bowl, then season. Pour the mixture over the duck and toss to coat evenly, then cover and let marinate for 10 minutes.

- Thread the duck onto 8 metal skewers, alternating with the red bell peppers. Cook under a preheated medium-hot broiler for 5–6 minutes on each side or until the edges are lightly charred in places and the duck is just cooked through (it should still be a little pink in the center).

- Transfer the kebabs to 4 serving plates and serve with steamed rice and a chopped cucumber salad.

 Duck and Vegetable Tikka Stir-Fry

Heat 1 tablespoon sunflower oil in a large wok or skillet until hot, add 1 tablespoon tikka paste, 8 sliced scallions, and 1 (12 oz) package stir-fry vegetables, thawed, if frozen, and stir-fry over high heat for 3–4 minutes, until softened. Add 2 store-bought smoked duck breasts, sliced, 3 tablespoons sweet chili sauce, and 2 tablespoons soy sauce and stir-fry for an additional 4–5 minutes or until piping hot. Serve immediately with steamed rice.

 Tikka-Spiced Duck Omelet

Heat 2 tablespoons sunflower oil in medium ovenproof skillet, add 6 sliced scallions, 2 chopped garlic cloves, and 1 seeded and finely chopped red chile, and cook over high heat, stirring, for 1–2 minutes, until softened. Add 1 tablespoon tikka paste and 2 finely diced smoked duck breasts and cook for an additional 1–2 minutes. Meanwhile, beat together 6 eggs and ¼ cup chopped cilantro leaves in a bowl, then season and pour into the skillet.

Cook over medium heat for 10–12 minutes or until the bottom is set, then place the skillet under a preheated medium-hot broiler and cook for 4–5 minutes or until the top is golden and set. Serve warm or at room temperature.

30 Chinese Turkey Chow Mein

Serves 4

3 turkey cutlets, thinly sliced
¼ cup light soy sauce
1 tablespoon hot chili sauce
2 teaspoons white wine vinegar
4 garlic cloves, crushed
2 teaspoons peeled and finely
  grated fresh ginger root
1 teaspoon 5-spice powder
8 oz dried egg noodles
2 tablespoons vegetable oil
3 cups halved snow peas
1 (8 oz) can water chestnuts,
  drained
⅔ cup drained, canned bamboo
  shoots
1 red bell pepper, cored, seeded,
  and thinly sliced
8 scallions, sliced diagonally
3 tablespoons oyster sauce
2 tablespoons sweet chili sauce
2 tablespoons dark soy sauce
½ teaspoon toasted sesame oil

- Put the turkey in a shallow nonmetallic bowl. Mix together the light soy sauce, hot chili sauce, vinegar, garlic, ginger, and 5-spice powder in a bowl. Pour the marinade over the turkey and toss to coat evenly, then cover and let marinate for 10 minutes.

- Meanwhile, cook the noodles according to the package directions, then drain.

- Heat the vegetable oil in a large wok or skillet until hot, add the turkey mixture. and stir-fry over high heat for 4–5 minutes, until lightly browned. Add all the vegetables and stir-fry for an additional 4–5 minutes, then add the drained noodles, oyster sauce, sweet chili sauce, dark soy sauce, and sesame oil and toss together for 4 minutes or until piping hot and the turkey is cooked all the way through.

- Divide into warm bowls and serve immediately.

 Chinese Turkey and Noodle Salad

Cook 10 oz dried medium egg noodles according to the package directions, drain, and refresh under cold running water, then drain again. Put the noodles, 12 oz store-bought cooked, sliced turkey breast, ½ cucumber, thinly shredded, and ½ carrot, peeled and thinly shredded, in a large salad bowl, then add 2 sliced scallions. Mix together 2 tablespoons sweet chili sauce, 2 tablespoons light soy sauce, 1 teaspoon hot chili sauce, and 3 tablespoons rice wine vinegar in a bowl. Drizzle the dressing over the salad, toss to mix well, and serve.

 Glazed Chinese-Style Turkey Cutlets

Put 4 turkey cutlets in a dish. Mix 1 tablespoon hot chili sauce, 2 tablespoons sweet chili sauce, 2 tablespoons light soy sauce, and 1 tablespoon oyster sauce in a bowl. Spread over the turkey, cover, and let marinate for 5–10 minutes. Cook under a preheated medium-hot broiler for 3–4 minutes on each side or until the turkey is cooked through. Serve with rice.

QuickCook
Meat

Recipes listed by cooking time

30

African Curried Beef and Mango Chutney Casserole 76

Chinese Beef with Tofu and Vegetables 78

Burmese Lemon Grass and Chile Pork 80

Curried Calves' Liver with Caramelized Onions 82

Tandoori Roast Rack of Lamb 84

Spicy Spaghetti with Meat Sauce 86

Spicy Lamb, Spinach, and Chickpea Rice 88

Pork, Red Pepper, and Pea Curry 90

Chorizo Sausage, Paprika, and Bean Stew 92

Beef and Mixed Peppercorn Pilaf 94

Spicy Beef Meatballs with Mint Relish 96

Spicy Chili Sausages in Rolls 98

Spiced Lamb Pilaf 100

Merguez Sausage and Tomato Tortilla 102

Spicy Beef Enchiladas 104

Spicy Chorizo and Spinach Frittata 106

Spicy Ham and Pea Risotto 108

Spicy Sausage and Tomato Casserole 110

Spicy Lamb and Vegetable Stew 112

Sticky Spicy Pork with Vegetable Noodles 114

Veal and Scallion Kebabs with Sweet Chili Dip 116

Thai Pork Noodle Salad 118

Jamaican Curried Beef and Black Bean Stew 120

Spicy Pork and Vegetable Broth 122

20

Curried Beef and Mango Chutney Wraps 76

Chinese Beef, Tofu, and Vegetable Noodles 78

Pork Chops with Lemon Grass and Chile 80

Curried Calves' Liver with Herbed Salad 82

Broiled Tandoori Lamb Chops 84

Spicy Steak, Potato, and Arugula Salad 86

Lamb Chops with Spicy Chickpeas and Spinach 88

Curried Pork Chops 90

Pan-Fried Chorizo, Paprika, and Beans 92

Quick Spiced Beef and Mushroom Pie 94

Beef Meatball Curry 96

Spicy Sausage and Bean Stew 98

Spicy Lamb and Herb Kebabs 100

Spicy Eggs with Merguez Sausages and Tomato 102

Spicy Enchilada Beef Rice 104

10

Chorizo, Spinach, and Egg Salad with Paprika Croutons 106

Spicy Ham and Pea Tortilla 108

Spicy Sausage and Tomato Pasta 110

Spicy Lamb and Vegetable Curry 112

Spicy Pork, Vegetable, and Noodle Stir-Fry 114

Veal and Scallion Kebabs with Sweet Chili Dip 116

Thai Pork Larb Salad 118

Curried Beef and Black Bean Pilaf 120

Five-Spice Pork Chops with Green Beans 122

Curried Beef and Mango Chutney Rolls 76

Chinese Beef, Tofu, and Vegetable Salad 78

Pork, Lemon Grass, and Chile Stir-Fry 80

Warm Curried Calves' Liver Salad 82

Tandoori Lamb Wraps 84

Hot and Spicy Steak and Arugula Ciabattas 86

Spicy Lamb, Spinach, and Chickpea Salad 88

Vietnamese-Style Pork Baguettes 90

Quick Chorizo, Paprika, and Bean Soup 92

Beef and Mixed Peppercorn Stroganoff 94

Spicy Meatball Heroes 96

Spicy Sausage Salad 98

Spicy Lamb Stir-Fry 100

Spicy Scrambled Eggs with Merguez Sausages 102

Spicy Beef Enchilada Wraps 104

Spicy Chorizo and Spinach Egg-Fried Rice 106

Spicy Ham and Pea Noodles 108

Spicy Sausage and Tomato Salad 110

Broiled Spicy Lamb Cutlets 112

Broiled Spicy Pork 114

Sweet Chile Veal and Scallion Rice 116

Spicy Thai Scrambled Eggs with Pork 118

Curried Beef and Black Bean Stir-Fry 120

Spicy Pork and Vegetable Stir-Fry 122

3⃝ African Curried Beef and Mango Chutney Casserole

Serves 4

2 tablespoons sunflower oil
1 lb ground beef
1 large onion, finely chopped
2 garlic cloves, crushed
2 tablespoons medium
  curry powder
¼ cup mango chutney
2 cups fresh white bread crumbs
1 cup Greek yogurt
3 extra-large eggs
salt and pepper
chopped cilantro leaves,
  to garnish
leafy green salad, to serve

- Heat the oil in a large wok or skillet until hot, add the beef, and stir-fry over high heat for 2–3 minutes, until browned. Add the onion, garlic, and curry powder and stir-fry for an additional 1–2 minutes, until beginning to soften.

- Remove from the heat, stir in the mango chutney and bread crumbs, and toss to mix well. Spoon the mixture into a shallow ovenproof dish.

- Beat together the yogurt and eggs in a bowl and season well, then pour over the beef mixture. Cook in a preheated oven, at 400°F, for 20–25 minutes or until piping hot and the top is set and golden brown.

- Sprinkle with chopped cilantro and serve with a leafy green salad.

 Curried Beef and Mango Chutney Rolls Halve 4 warm bread rolls, then spread each half with 1 tablespoon mayonnaise and lightly sprinkle with a little medium curry powder. Top each bottom with 1 tablespoon mango chutney and 3–4 thin slices of store-bought cooked roast beef. Sandwich with the lids and serve.

 Curried Beef and Mango Chutney Wraps Heat 2 tablespoons sunflower oil in a large skillet, add 10 oz ground beef, 1 teaspoon ginger paste, 1 teaspoon garlic paste, and 1 tablespoon medium curry paste, and cook, stirring, over medium heat for 5–6 minutes or until browned and cooked through. Add 2 chopped tomatoes and 4 sliced scallions and cook for an additional 2–3 minutes. Season, remove from the heat, and stir in 3 tablespoons mango chutney. Warm 8 large flatbreads in a flat griddle pan or dry skillet according to the package directions, then spread each with 1 tablespoon plain yogurt. Divide the beef mixture among the flatbreads, roll up to form wraps, and serve immediately.

Chinese Beef with Tofu and Vegetables

Serves 4

2 tablespoons sunflower oil

2½ cups ¾ inch firm tofu cubes

2 teaspoons grated fresh
  ginger root

6 scallions, chopped, plus extra,
  to garnish

1 red chile, seeded and finely
  chopped, plus extra, to garnish

½ red bell pepper, cored, seeded
  and cut into thick strips

½ yellow bell pepper, cored,
  seeded, and cut into thick strips

7 oz sliced shiitake mushrooms

1 tablespoon cornstarch

2 tablespoons dark soy sauce

2 tablespoons oyster sauce

¼ cup mirin

1 cup hot vegetable stock

12 oz cooked roast beef slices,
  cut into strips

steamed rice, to serve

· Heat the oil in a wok until hot, add the tofu in batches, and stir-fry over high heat for 3–4 minutes or until golden. Remove with a slotted spoon and drain on paper towels.

· Add the ginger, scallions, red chile, red and yellow bell peppers, and mushrooms to the wok and stir-fry over high heat for 3–4 minutes, until softened.

· Mix the cornstarch with 2 tablespoons of water in a small bowl. Add the soy sauce, oyster sauce, mirin, and stock and mix well. Add the liquid to the wok and bring to a boil. Reduce the heat to medium-low, return the tofu to the wok with the beef strips, toss to mix well, and simmer gently for 2–3 minutes, until heated through.

· Ladle into warm bowls, sprinkle with sliced scallion and red chile, and serve with steamed rice.

---

1 **Chinese Beef, Tofu, and Vegetable Salad**
Core, seed, and slice 1 red bell pepper and 1 yellow bell pepper, then put in a large salad bowl with 12 oz cooked roast beef slices, 6 sliced scallions, and 1¼ cups firm tofu cubes. Mix 1 teaspoon ginger paste, 1 teaspoon chili oil, 1 teaspoon sesame oil, ¼ cup sunflower oil, and ⅓ cup light soy sauce in a bowl. Stir to mix well, pour the dressing over the salad, and serve.

2 **Chinese Beef, Tofu, and Vegetable**
Noodles Prepare 10 oz rice noodles according to the package directions. Meanwhile, heat 2 tablespoons sunflower oil in a large wok or skillet until hot, add 12 oz tenderloin steak, cut into thin strips, and stir-fry over high heat for 3–4 minutes, until browned. Add 8 sliced scallions, 1 cored, seeded, and thinly sliced red bell pepper, 1 cored, seeded, and thinly sliced yellow bell

pepper, and 7 oz thinly sliced shiitake mushrooms and stir-fry for an additional 4–5 minutes. Add ½ cup prepared Chinese stir-fry sauce, the prepared rice noodles, and 1¼ cups firm tofu cubes and continue to stir-fry for 2–3 minutes or until piping hot. Serve immediately.

30 Burmese Lemon Grass and Chile Pork

Serves 4

1 tablespoon sesame oil
2 tablespoons vegetable oil
1 lb pork tenderloin, cut into
   bite-size pieces
3 inch length of trimmed lemon
   grass stalk, finely chopped
2 tablespoons tamarind paste
1 tablespoon Thai fish sauce
1 cup hot water
chopped cilantro leaves,
   to garnish
steamed rice, to serve

For the spice paste

1 large onion, coarsely chopped
2 garlic cloves, chopped
1 teaspoon peeled and finely
   grated fresh ginger root
1 teaspoon ground turmeric
1 red chile, seeded and
   finely chopped
1 teaspoon chili powder

- To make the spice paste, put all the ingredients in a food processor or blender and blend to a paste, adding a little water, if needed.

- Heat the oils in a wok or skillet until hot, add the spice paste, and stir-fry over medium-high heat for 1–2 minutes. Add the pork and stir to mix well, then increase the heat to high and stir-fry for an additional 8–10 minutes.

- Add the lemon grass, tamarind paste, fish sauce, and measured water and stir well. Cook for 3–4 minutes or until the pork is cooked through.

- Sprinkle with chopped cilantro leaves and serve with steamed rice.

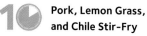 **Pork, Lemon Grass, and Chile Stir-Fry**

Heat 2 tablespoons sunflower oil in a large wok or skillet until hot, add 8 sliced scallions, 10 oz pork tenderloin, cut into thin strips, and 1 seeded and sliced red chile, and stir-fry over high heat for 3–4 minutes, until the pork is browned. Add 1 tablespoon lemon grass paste and ¼ cup light soy sauce and stir-fry for an additional 1–2 minutes or until the pork is cooked through. Serve immediately with noodles or steamed rice.

 Pork Chops with Lemon Grass and Chile Mix together 1 tablespoon lemon grass paste, 1 teaspoon ginger paste, 1 teaspoon garlic paste, 1 teaspoon chili paste, and 1 teaspoon tamarind paste in a bowl. Stir in 2 teaspoons honey, then spread the mixture all over 4 pork chops, about 7 oz each, and season. Cook under a preheated hot broiler for 5–6 minutes on each side or until just cooked through. Serve with a green salad.

Curried Calves' Liver with Herby Salad

Serves 4

2 heads Boston lettuce
4 plum tomatoes
large handful of cilantro leaves
large handful of mint leaves
1 lb calves' liver, trimmed
1 tablespoon medium curry powder
1 teaspoon ground cumin
1 teaspoon ground coriander
1 teaspoon crushed fennel seeds
½ teaspoon chili powder
1 teaspoon ground garlic
1 teaspoon peeled and finely
  grated fresh ginger root
2 tablespoons white wine vinegar
¼ cup vegetable oil
salt and pepper
pinch of paprika, to garnish
lemon wedges, to serve

- Coarsely shred the lettuce leaves and chop the tomatoes. Place in a bowl with the cilantro and mint, lightly toss together, then set aside.

- Put the liver in a separate bowl. Mix together the curry powder, cumin, ground coriander, fennel seeds, chili powder, garlic, ginger, and vinegar to make a smooth paste. Season well, then spread the mixture all over the liver.

- Heat the oil in a large skillet over high heat. Add the liver and cook, in batches, if necessary, stirring, for 3–4 minutes, until the liver is lightly browned but still slightly pink on the inside, then thickly slice.

- Divide the salad among 4 plates, top with the curried liver slices, and sprinkle with the paprika. Serve with lemon wedges for squeezing over.

 Warm Curried Calves' Liver Salad

Heat 2 tablespoons sunflower oil in a skillet, add 10 oz sliced calves liver, and cook for 2–3 minutes or until just sealed. Put in a salad bowl with 1 teaspoon ground cumin, ½ teaspoon chili powder, 1 teaspoon crushed fennel seeds, 1 teaspoon finely chopped garlic, a handful each of chopped mint and cilantro leaves. and the torn leaves of 2 heads Boston lettuce. Drizzle with 2 tablespoons olive oil and the juice of 1 lemon. Toss to mix well, season with salt, and serve with crusty bread.

 Curried Calves' Liver with Caramelized Onions

Heat 2 tablespoons sunflower oil in large skillet, add 3 thinly sliced onions, and cook over low heat for 15–20 minutes or until lightly caramelized and golden. Season, then set aside. Meanwhile, cut 1 lb trimmed calves liver into bite-size pieces and sprinkle with 2 tablespoons mild curry powder. Season with salt and toss to mix well. Wipe out the skillet, add 4 tablespoons butter, and heat until foaming. Add the seasoned liver and cook, stirring, for 40–50 seconds. Return the onions to the skillet, then cook for an additional 1–2 minutes, until the liver is just cooked through. Remove from the heat, then stir in the juice of 1 lemon and a small handful of chopped cilantro. Serve with warm crusty rolls or naan.

 Broiled Tandoori Lamb Chops

Serves 4

8 lamb chops or cutlets
3 garlic cloves, finely grated
1 teaspoon peeled and finely
   grated fresh ginger root
juice of 2 large lemons
1 tablespoon ground cumin
3 tablespoons tandoori
   curry paste
1 cup plain yogurt
salt and pepper
chopped mint leaves, to garnish

To serve
cucumber salad
mini naans (optional)

· Put the lamb in a single layer in a shallow nonmetallic dish. Mix together the remaining ingredients in a bowl, then season well. Pour the mixture over the lamb, toss to coat evenly, then cover and let marinate for 10 minutes.

· Place the lamb on a lightly oiled broiler rack and cook under a preheated hot broiler for 2–3 minutes on each side or until cooked to your liking.

· Transfer to 4 warm serving plates, sprinkle with chopped mint, and serve with cucumber salad and mini naans, if using.

 Tandoori Lamb Wraps

Prepare and cook the lamb chops as above, omitting the marinating time. Meanwhile, warm 4 flatbreads in a flat griddle pan or dry skillet according to the package directions, then spread with mayonnaise. Divide 2 sliced tomatoes, ½ sliced red onion, and ¼ sliced cucumber among the flatbreads, then top with the finely sliced cooked lamb chops. Roll up the flatbreads to form wraps and serve immediately.

 Tandoori Roast Rack of Lamb

Mix together 3 tablespoons tandoori paste and ½ cup Greek yogurt in a bowl. Using a small, sharp knife, make deep slashes in the meat of 2 French-trimmed racks of lamb (with 7–8 ribs each). Season well, then spread the tandoori paste all over the lamb. Put the racks, rib-side up, on a nonstick baking sheet and place in a preheated oven, at 350°F, for 15–20 minutes or until cooked to your liking. Cover with aluminum foil and let rest for a few minutes before serving.

10 Hot and Spicy Steak and Arugula Ciabattas

Serves 4

2 large tenderloin steaks
olive oil, for brushing
2 large ciabatta loaves
2 tablespoons chili sauce
½ cup prepared garlic mayonnaise
small handful of arugula leaves
salt and pepper

- Season the steaks and brush with a little oil. Place on a preheated, smoking-hot, ridged grill pan and cook for 2–3 minutes on each side or until cooked to your liking.

- Meanwhile, put the ciabatta loaves on a baking sheet and place in a preheated oven, at 400°F, for 4–5 minutes or until warmed through.

- Mix together the chili sauce and garlic mayonnaise in a bowl. Slice the ciabatta loaves in half horizontally, spread the halves with the spicy mayonnaise, and top the bottoms with some arugula leaves.

- Thinly slice the steaks, divide between the bottoms and top with the ciabatta lids. Cut each ciabatta into 2 and serve.

20 Spicy Steak, Potato, and Arugula Salad

Cook 8 baby new potatoes in a large saucepan of boiling water for 12–15 minutes or until just tender. Meanwhile, mix together ½ cup prepared garlic mayonnaise, 2 tablespoons hot chili sauce, the juice of 1 lemon, 1 cup plain yogurt, ⅓ cup finely chopped chives, and ⅓ cup finely chopped dill in a bowl. Season and set aside. Place 2 large tenderloin steaks on a preheated, smoking-hot ridged grill pan and cook for 2–3 minutes on each side or until cooked to your liking, then cut into thin strips. Drain the potatoes, then halve and put in a large salad bowl with 5 cups arugula leaves and the steak strips. Pour the spicy dressing over the salad, toss to mix well, and serve.

30 Spicy Spaghetti with Meat Sauce

Heat 1 tablespoon olive oil in a skillet. Add 1 chopped onion, 3 chopped garlic cloves, 2 chopped red chiles, and 1 lb ground beef. Cook over high heat for 1-2 minutes, then stir in 1 (14½ oz) can diced tomatoes and 1 cup beef stock. Season and bring to a boil. Cook, uncovered, over medium heat for 20 minutes, stirring occasionally. Meanwhile, cook 12 oz spaghetti in a large saucepan of salted water according to the package directions. Drain and divide among 4 warm pasta bowls. Spoon the meat sauce over the pasta and serve with a salad.

HOT-MEAT-ZYG

Lamb Chops with Spicy Chickpeas and Spinach

Serves 4

2 tablespoons olive oil

8 lamb chops, about 5 oz each

2 (15 oz) cans chickpeas (garbanzo beans), drained and rinsed

2 red chiles, seeded and finely chopped

2 teaspoons cumin seeds

1 teaspoon crushed coriander seeds

½ cup sliced, drained roasted red peppers from a jar

finely grated rind and juice of 1 lemon

1 (12 oz) package baby spinach leaves

small handful of cilantro leaves, chopped, plus extra to garnish

salt and pepper

- Heat the oil in a large skillet, add the chops, in batches if necessary, and cook over medium heat for 2–3 minutes on each side or until cooked to your liking. Remove from the skillet, cover with aluminum foil, and keep warm.

- Add the remaining ingredients to the skillet, increase the heat to high, and cook, stirring, for 4–5 minutes or until piping hot and the spinach has wilted.

- Spoon the chickpea mixture into 4 warm bowls and season to taste. Top with the lamb chops, sprinkle with extra chopped cilantro, and serve immediately.

Spicy Lamb, Spinach, and Chickpea Salad

Brush 4 lamb cutlets, about 5 oz each, with 1 tablespoon olive oil, then cook under a preheated hot broiler for 2–3 minutes on each side or until cooked to your liking. Meanwhile, put 3½ cups baby spinach leaves, 2 chopped tomatoes, and 1 (15 oz) can chickpeas (garbanzo beans), rinsed and drained, in a large salad bowl. Cut the slightly cooled lamb into bite-size pieces and add to the bowl. Pour ⅔ cup store-bought fresh vinaigrette over the lamb, then sprinkle with 1 teaspoon hot curry powder and season. Toss to mix well and serve.

Spicy Lamb, Spinach, and Chickpea Rice

Cook the Lamb Chops with Spicy Chickpeas and Spinach as above. Using a sharp knife, cut the meat from the cooked chops and cut into strips. Heat 1 tablespoon olive oil in a large skillet until hot, add the cooked chickpea mixture and 2 cups cooked long-grain rice, and cok over high heat for 4–5 minutes. Stir in the lamb and ½ cup hot vegetable stock and cook for 2–3 minutes or until piping hot. Serve immediately.

HOT-MEAT-DEL

30 Pork, Red Pepper, and Pea Curry

Serves 4

3 tablespoons vegetable oil

2 teaspoons cumin seeds

2 onions, finely chopped

1 tablespoon peeled and grated
  fresh ginger root

1 tablespoon grated garlic

1 lb ground pork

2 tablespoons ground coriander

1 tablespoon ground cumin

1 tablespoon garam masala

1 red bell pepper, seeded and
  finely chopped

⅔ cup frozen peas

2 ripe tomatoes, finely chopped

juice of ½ lime

salt

chopped cilantro leaves,
  to garnish

To serve

plain yogurt

warm parathas or chapattis
  (optional)

- Heat the oil in a large wok or skillet until hot, add the cumin seeds, and cook over medium heat for 1 minute, then add the onions and sauté for an additional 3–4 minutes, until softened. Add the ginger and garlic and continue to sauté for 1 minute.

- Add the ground pork and all the ground spices, season with salt, and cook for 8–10 minutes or until the pork is browned and cooked through. Stir in the red bell pepper, peas, and tomatoes and cook for an additional 3–4 minutes or until the vegetables are tender. Remove from the heat and stir in the lime juice.

- Sprinkle with chopped cilantro and serve with a spoonful of yogurt and warm parathas or chapattis, if desired.

---

1 Vietnamese Style Pork Baguettes

Prepare the cooked pork mixture as above. Meanwhile, slice 2 warmed baguettes in half lengthwise. Divide the cooked pork between the cut sides of the 2 baguettes. Top with 2 sliced tomatoes and a small handful of fresh mint and cilantro leaves. Top with the baguette lids and serve.

2 Curried Pork Chops

Mix together 2 teaspoons ginger paste, 2 teaspoons garlic paste, 1 tablespoon ground coriander, 2 teaspoons ground cumin, the juice of 1 lime, and 2 tablespoons sunflower oil in a bowl, then spread the mixture all over 4 pork chops, about 7 oz each, and season. Cover and let marinate for 5 minutes. Cook under a preheated hot broiler for 5–6 minutes on each side or until cooked through. Serve with a crisp green salad.

30 Chorizo Sausage, Paprika, and Bean Stew

Serves 4

2 tablespoons olive oil
7 oz bacon, coarsely chopped
8 oz mini cooking Spanish chorizo
   sausages
1 onion, finely chopped
3 (14½ oz) cans diced tomatoes
   with herbs
1 teaspoon sugar
1 tablespoon sweet smoked paprika
2 garlic cloves, crushed
1 carrot, peeled and finely diced
1 celery stick, finely diced
1 bay leaf
1 chicken bouillon cube, crumbled
3 cups rinsed and drained mixed
   canned beans, such as black-
   eyed peas and red kidney beans
¼ cup finely chopped flat-leaf
   parsley, plus extra to garnish
salt and pepper
crusty bread, to serve (optional)

- Heat the oil in a large, heavy saucepan, add the bacon and chorizo sausages, and cook over high heat for 3–4 minutes, until golden brown.

- Stir in the onion, tomatoes, sugar, paprika, garlic, carrot, celery, bay leaf, and crumbled bouillon cube, then reduce the heat to medium and cook, uncovered, for 15–20 minutes.

- Stir in the mixed beans and bring back to a boil, then cook for 2–3 minutes or until piping hot. Season and stir in the parsley.

- Ladle into warm bowls, sprinkle with extra chopped parsley, and serve with crusty bread, if desired.

 1 **Quick Chorizo, Paprika, and Bean Soup** Heat 1 tablespoon olive oil in a large saucepan, add 7 oz diced chorizo, and cook over high heat for 2–3 minutes. Stir in 1 teaspoon sweet smoked paprika, then add 2½ cups prepared tomato soup and 3 cups rinsed and drained, mixed canned beans. Bring to a boil, reduce the heat to medium, and cook for 3–4 minutes or until piping hot. Serve with crusty bread.

 2 **Pan-Fried Chorizo, Paprika, and Beans** Heat 1 tablespoon olive oil in a large skillet, add 1 lb cooking chorizo, thinly sliced, and cook, stirring, over high heat for 4–5 minutes, until golden brown. Add 1 chopped onion, 2 chopped garlic cloves, and 2 teaspoons sweet smoked paprika and cook for an additional 4–5 minutes, until softened, then add 3 cups rinsed and drained, mixed canned beans, such as black- eyed peas and red kidney beans. Season, then heat through until piping hot and serve with warmed tortillas, sour cream, and guacamole.

10 Beef and Mixed Peppercorn Stroganoff

Serves 4

2 tablespoons butter

1 red onion, thinly sliced

3 cups halved white button mushrooms

3 tablespoons tomato paste

2 teaspoons Dijon mustard

1 tablespoon pink peppercorns in brine, drained

1 tablespoon green peppercorns in brine, drained

1 teaspoon smoked paprika

1¼ cups hot beef stock

1 lb tenderloin steak, cut into thin strips

1 cup sour cream

salt and pepper

2 tablespoons chopped flat-leaf parsley, to garnish

steamed rice, to serve

- Heat a skillet until hot, then add half the butter. When foaming, add the red onion and cook for 2–3 minutes or until just softened. Add the mushrooms, tomato paste, mustard, pink and green peppercorns, and paprika and cook, stirring, for an additional 1–2 minutes. Pour in the beef stock and bring to a boil, then reduce the heat to low and simmer for 1–2 minutes.

- Meanwhile, heat a separate skillet and add the remaining butter. Season the beef. When the butter is foaming, add the beef and cook, stirring, for 2–3 minutes or until browned all over.

- Add the sour cream and beef to the onion and mushroom mixture and mix well, then season.

- Spoon into warm bowls, sprinkle with the parsley, and serve with steamed rice.

 Quick Spiced Beef and Mushroom Pie

Use the cooked beef and mushroom mixture from the above recipe to fill 4 individual pie dishes. Top each with 1 cup cooked mashed potatoes and place under a hot broiler for 3-4 minutes or until golden. Serve with a salad.

 Beef and Mixed Peppercorn Pilaf

Heat 1 tablespoon butter and 1 tablespoon sunflower oil in a heavy saucepan, add 1 chopped onion and 12 oz ground beef, and cook, stirring, over high heat for 3–4 minutes, until the onion is softened and the beef is browned. Add 1 tablespoon drained pink peppercorns in brine, 1 tablespoon drained green peppercorns in brine, 2 crushed garlic cloves, ¼ cup tomato paste, 3 cups baby white button mushrooms, and 2 cups long-grain rice and stir until well coated, then pour in 3½ cups hot beef stock, season, and bring to a boil. Cover tightly, reduce the heat to medium-low, and cook gently, undisturbed, for 15–20 minutes or until the rice is tender. Remove from the heat and let stand for a few minutes before serving.

30 Spicy Beef Meatballs with Mint Relish

Serves 4

1¼ lb ground beef
1 red onion, finely chopped
2 garlic cloves, crushed
1 red chile, seeded and chopped
small handful of mint, chopped
small handful of cilantro, chopped
1 teaspoon ground ginger
1 teaspoon mild chili powder
1 teaspoon ground cumin
2 teaspoons crushed coriander seeds
1 egg, beaten
2 cups fresh white bread crumbs
2 tablespoons sunflower oil
salt and pepper
lime wedges, to serve

For the mint relish

1 onion, finely chopped
2 tomatoes, finely chopped
½ cucumber, finely chopped
⅔ cup plain yogurt
¼ cup chopped mint leaves
2 tablespoons mint jelly
juice of 1 lime

- To make the mint relish, mix together all the ingredients in a bowl, cover, and chill until needed.

- Put the beef, red onion, garlic, red chile, and herbs in a food processor or blender. Add the ground ginger, chili powder, cumin, coriander seeds, and egg. Season well, then process until smooth and well combined.

- Divide the mixture into 16 balls. Roll each ball in the bread crumbs, place on a baking sheet, and drizzle with the oil. Place in a preheated oven, at 400°F, for 15–20 minutes or until cooked through.

- Serve the beef meatballs on toothpicks, with the mint relish and lime wedges for squeezing over the meatballs.

 1 Spicy Meatball Heroes
Halve 4 ciabatta rolls and spread mayonnaise over the bottoms. Top each with a small handful of shredded iceberg lettuce, then divide 12 oz) store-bought cooked meatballs among the bottoms. Squeeze some chile ketchup over them, top with the ciabatta lids, and serve.

 2 Beef Meatball Curry Put 1¼ lb ground beef, 1 tablespoon ginger paste, 1 tablespoon garlic paste, 1 seeded and chopped red chile, and 1 tablespoon medium curry powder in a blender, then season and blend until well combined. Divide the mixture into bite-size balls. Heat 2 tablespoons sunflower oil in a large skillet, add the meatballs, and cook over medium heat for 2–3 minutes, until browned. Stir in 1¼ cups hot beef stock, 1 tablespoon medium curry paste, and 1 cup canned coconut milk. Bring to a boil, then cook, uncovered, for 8–10 minutes or until the meatballs are cooked through and piping hot. Serve with steamed rice.

Spicy Chili Sausages in Rolls

Serves 4

12 good-quality, small pork
   sausage links
¼ cup sweet chili sauce
½ cup ketchup
2 teaspoons hot chili sauce
¼ cup hoisin sauce
2 tablespoons honey
2 teaspoons Dijon mustard

To serve

12 bread rolls, sliced
12 Boston lettuce leaves

- Put the sausages in a roasting pan and insert a metal skewer through each lengthwise. Mix together the remaining ingredients in a bowl, pour over the sausages, and toss to mix well.

- Place in a preheated oven, at 400°F, for 20–25 minutes or until golden and cooked through.

- To serve, place 1 lettuce leaf in each of the rolls. Carefully remove the skewers from the sausages and serve in the rolls.

 ### Spicy Sausage Salad

Slice 1 (14 oz) package cooked, small pork sausage links lengthwise and put in a large salad bowl with 1 seeded and finely chopped red chile, 2 sliced tomatoes, 1 sliced cucumber, and 1 (4 oz) package mixed salad greens. Pour ⅔ cup store-bought salad dressing over the salad, season, and toss to mix well. Serve with warm rolls.

Spicy Sausage and Bean Stew

Heat 2 tablespoons sunflower oil in a heavy saucepan, add 12 coarsely chopped small pork sausage links, 1 chopped onion, 1 teaspoon ginger paste, 1 teaspoon garlic paste, and 1 teaspoon chili paste, and cook over high heat for 3–4 minutes, until the sausages are browned. Stir in 3 (15 oz) cans baked beans and 2 tablespoons tomato paste and bring to a boil, then reduce the heat to medium and cook, uncovered, for 8–10 minutes or until the sausages are cooked all the way through. Season, then stir in a small handful of flat-leaf parsley, chopped, and serve with baked potatoes.

20 Spicy Lamb and Herb Skewers

Serves 4

4 garlic cloves, crushed

3 red chiles, seeded and chopped

1 tablespoon ground coriander

2 tablespoons ground cumin

¼ red bell pepper, cored, seeded, and finely diced

¼ yellow bell pepper, cored, seeded, and finely diced

½ small onion, finely chopped

⅓ cup chopped mint leaves

¼ cup chopped flat-leaf parsley

1¼ lb ground lamb

¼ cup plain yogurt

olive oil, for brushing

sumac, for sprinkling

¼ iceberg lettuce, shredded

2 plum tomatoes, thinly sliced

¼ cucumber, halved and sliced

½ red onion, thinly sliced

juice of 2 limes, plus wedges, to serve

salt and pepper

- To make the kebabs, put the garlic, red chiles, ground spices, bell peppers, onion, mint, herbs, and lamb in a mixing bowl and season well. Using your hands, combine thoroughly until well mixed. Cover and let marinate for 10 minutes to let the flavors develop.

- Divide the lamb mixture into 12 portions, then shape each portion around a metal skewer into a long sausage shape. Place on a broiler rack, lightly brush with olive oil, and sprinkle the kebabs with a little sumac. Cook under a preheated medium-hot broiler for 4–5 minutes on each side or until cooked through.

- Meanwhile, make the salad by mixing the lettuce, tomatoes, cucumber, red onion, and lime juice in a bowl and season well.

- Serve the skewers with the salad and lime wedges to squeeze over the lamb.

10 Spicy Lamb Stir-Fry

Heat 2 tablespoons olive oil in a large wok until hot, add 1 chopped onion, 2 seeded and sliced red chiles, 2 teaspoons ground cumin, 1 teaspoon ground cinnamon, and 1¼ lb ground lamb, and stir-fry over high heat for 6–8 minutes or until the lamb is cooked through. Stir in ¼ cup each of chopped cilantro and mint leaves. Serve immediately with crusty bread.

30 Spiced Lamb Pilaf

Heat 2 tablespoons olive oil in a saucepan and add 1 chopped onion, 1 chopped garlic clove, 3 seeded and sliced red chiles, 1 tablespoon ground coriander, 2 teaspoons ground cumin, and 1 cinnamon stick. Gently cook for 2–3 minutes, until the onion has softened. Increase the heat to high, add 1 lb ground lamb, and cook, stirring, for 1–2 minutes, until browned. Add 2½ cups long-grain rice and stir to coat, then stir in 3½ cups hot vegetable stock and 1 cored, seeded, and diced red bell pepper and bring to a boil. Cover tightly, reduce the heat to low, and cook, undisturbed, for 15–20 minutes or until the liquid is absorbed and the rice is tender. Remove from the heat and stir in ¼ cup each of chopped cilantro and mint leaves. Season and serve with spoonfuls of yogurt.

Spicy Eggs with Merguez Sausages and Tomato

Serves 4

2 tablespoons olive oil

1 onion, finely sliced

1 red chile, seeded and
finely chopped

1 garlic clove, crushed

10 oz merguez sausages or
other spicy sausage links,
coarsely chopped

1 teaspoon dried oregano

3 cups cherry tomatoes

½ cup tomato puree with herbs

1 (7 oz) jar roasted peppers,
drained and coarsely chopped

4 eggs

salt and pepper

¼ cup finely chopped cilantro
leaves, to garnish

- Heat the oil in a large skillet, add the onion, red chile, garlic, merguez sausages, and oregano and cook gently for about 5 minutes or until the onion is softened. Add the tomatoes, tomato puree, and roasted peppers and cook for another 5 minutes. If the sauce looks dry, add a splash of water.

- Season well, then make 4 hollows in the mixture, break an egg into each, and cover the skillet. Cook for 5 minutes or until the eggs are set.

- Divide among 4 warm serving plates, sprinkle with chopped cilantro, and serve immediately.

Spicy Scrambled Eggs with Merguez Sausages Heat 2 tablespoons butter in a large skillet until foaming, add 7 oz thinly sliced merguez or other spicy sausages and cook over high heat for 3–4 minutes. Meanwhile, beat together 6 eggs, 1 teaspoon garlic salt, 1 seeded and chopped red chile, and 1 teaspoon dried oregano in a bowl, then add to the skillet. Scramble together with the sausages and cook until the eggs are cooked to your liking. Serve with warm tortillas.

Merguez Sausage and Tomato Tortilla Heat 2 tablespoons sunflower oil in medium ovenproof skillet, add 1 chopped onion, 7 oz coarsely chopped merguez or other spicy sausages, 1 seeded and chopped red chile, and 1 chopped garlic clove, and cook over medium heat for 3–4 minutes. Add 2 chopped tomatoes and cook for an additional 3–4 minutes. Lightly beat 6 eggs in a bowl, then season and pour into the skillet. Cook over medium heat for 10–12 minutes or until the bottom is set, then place the skillet under a preheated medium-hot broiler and cook for 4–5 minutes or until the top is golden and set. Cut the tortilla into wedges and serve.

1 Spicy Beef Enchilada Wraps

Serves 4

8 corn tortillas
½ cup hot chili sauce
½ cup store-bought guacamole,
  plus extra to serve
½ cup sour cream, plus extra
  to serve
¼ iceberg lettuce, shredded
12 oz cooked, roast beef slices,
  cut into thick strips
½ cup sliced green jalapeño chiles
  from a jar, drained
½ cup store-bought fresh salsa
salt and pepper

- Place 1 tortilla on a preheated, hot griddle pan or in a dry skillet and cook according to the package directions until heated through. Remove and keep warm, then repeat with the remaining tortillas.

- Lay the tortillas on a clean work surface and spread each one with 1 tablespoon each of the hot chili sauce, guacamole, and sour cream. Divide the lettuce among the tortillas, then top with the roast beef and 1 tablespoon each of the jalapeños and salsa. Season well.

- Roll up the filled tortillas to form wraps and serve immediately with extra guacamole and sour cream.

 Spicy Enchilada Beef Rice

Heat 2 tablespoons sunflower oil in a large skillet, add 1 chopped onion and 12 oz ground beef and cook, stirring, over high heat for 6–8 minutes, until browned. Stir in 1 (12 oz) jar enchilada sauce and cook for 2–3 minutes or until bubbling. Add 3½ cups cooked long-grain rice and continue to stir and cook for 3–4 minutes or until piping hot. Season and serve immediately.

 Spicy Beef Enchiladas

Heat 2 tablespoons sunflower oil in a large skillet, add 1 chopped onion, and 12 oz ground beef, and cook, stirring, over high heat for 4–5 minutes or until browned. Spread half of 1 (12 oz) jar enchilada sauce over the bottom of a shallow, medium-size baking dish. Divide the meat mixture among 8 corn tortillas and sprinkle over 2⅓ cups drained, sliced green jalapeño peppers from a jar. Roll up

tightly and place in a single layer in the prepared dish, seam-side down. Spoon over the remaining enchilada sauce and sprinkle over 3½ cups shredded cheddar cheese. Cook under a preheated medium broiler for 8–10 minutes or until the cheese is bubbling and golden. Serve with a green salad.

Chorizo, Spinach, and Egg Salad with Paprika Croutons

Serves 4

1 tablespoon sunflower oil
4 eggs
8 oz cooking chorizo, thickly
  sliced
4 handfuls of baby spinach leaves
salt and pepper

For the dressing

¼ cup extra-virgin olive oil
2 tablespoons red wine vinegar
2 teaspoons wholegrain mustard

For the croutons

½ ciabatta loaf, cut into
  bite-size pieces
2 tablespoons olive oil
1 tablespoon smoked paprika

- To make the dressing, beat together all the ingredients in a small bowl and set aside.

- To make the croutons, put the ciabatta in a bowl, toss in the olive oil, and sprinkle with the paprika, then transfer to a baking sheet. Place in a preheated oven, at 400°F, for 10 minutes or until golden.

- Meanwhile, heat the sunflower oil in a large skillet, add the eggs, and cook to your liking, then remove and keep warm. Put the chorizo in a separate skillet and dry-fry over medium heat for 3–4 minutes or until crisp and cooked through.

- Put the chorizo and spinach in a large bowl, drizzle a little of the dressing over the ingredients, and toss to mix well. Divide among 4 serving plates, then top each with one-quarter of the croutons and an egg. Drizzle with the remaining dressing. Season and serve immediately.

 Spicy Chorizo and Spinach Egg-Fried Rice Put 1 (7 oz) package fresh spinach leaves in a saucepan, pour over enough boiling water to cover, and let stand for 2 minutes or until wilted, then drain well and chop. Meanwhile, heat 2 tablespoons sunflower oil in a large wok or skillet until hot, add 12 oz diced chorizo, and cook for 2–3 minutes over high heat. Add 3½ cups cooked egg-fried rice and the spinach and stir-fry for an additional 2–3 minutes or until piping hot, then season. Serve immediately.

 Spicy Chorizo and Spinach Frittata Put 1 (7 oz) package spinach leaves in a saucepan, pour over enough boiling water to cover, and let stand for 2 minutes or until wilted, then drain well and chop. Meanwhile, heat 2 tablespoons sunflower oil in medium ovenproof skillet, add 2 finely chopped onions, and cook over medium-low heat for 8–10 minutes, stirring occasionally, until lightly browned and softened. Add 2 seeded and chopped red chiles and 8 oz coarsely chopped chorizo and cook for an additional 3–4 minutes, then add the spinach and stir to mix well. Lightly beat 6 eggs, then season and pour into the skillet. Cook over medium heat for 10–12 minutes or until the bottom is set, then place the skillet under a preheated hot broiler and cook for 4 minutes or until the top is golden and just set. Serve cut into wedges with a salad.

30 Spicy Ham and Pea Risotto

Serves 4

1 tablespoon olive oil
2 tablespoons butter
1 onion, chopped
1 teaspoon dried red pepper flakes
1 red chile, seeded and finely
   chopped
2 garlic cloves, crushed
1⅓ cups risotto rice
3¾ cups hot chicken stock
1⅓ cups frozen peas
1 cup grated Parmesan cheese
10 oz cooked ham, diced
1 bunch of flat-leaf parsley,
   finely chopped
salt and pepper

- Heat the oil and butter in a heavy saucepan, add the onion, red pepper flakes, red chile, and garlic, and cook over medium heat for 3–4 minutes, until softened and beginning to brown.

- Add the rice and stir for 1 minute or until the grains are well coated, then pour in 2 cups of the stock and cook until it has been absorbed, stirring frequently, then add the remaining stock and the peas and continue to cook, stirring continuously, until the liquid has been absorbed and the rice is tender but still firm (al dente).

- Stir in the Parmesan, ham, and parsley, season, and serve immediately.

 Spicy Ham and Pea Noodles

Heat 2 tablespoons sunflower oil in a wok or skillet until hot, add 12 oz cooked ham, cut into strips, 2¾ cups frozen peas, and ½ cup spicy Szechuan-style stir-fry sauce and stir-fry over high heat for 2–3 minutes. Stir in 12 oz fresh egg noodles and stir-fry for 3–4 minutes or until piping hot. Serve immediately.

 Spicy Ham and Pea Tortilla

Heat 2 tablespoons sunflower oil in medium ovenproof skillet, add 1 chopped onion, 2 seeded and finely chopped red chiles, 3 chopped garlic cloves, and 1 teaspoon smoked paprika, and cook over high heat for 2–3 minutes, until softened, then add 12 oz cooked ham, diced, and 2 cups frozen peas and cook for an additional 1–2 minutes. Lightly beat 6 eggs in a bowl, then season well and pour into the skillet. Cook over medium heat for 8–10 minutes or until the bottom is set, then place the skillet under a preheated medium-hot broiler and cook for 4–5 minutes or until the top is golden and set. Serve with a crisp green salad.

 # Spicy Sausage and Tomato Pasta

Serves 4

2 tablespoons olive oil

8 thick, spicy Italian sausage links, cut into ¾ inch pieces

1 red chile, seeded and finely chopped

4 garlic cloves, finely chopped

1 onion, finely chopped

1 teaspoon dried red pepper flakes

1 (14½ oz) can diced tomatoes with herbs

1 teaspoon sugar

2 teaspoons chopped rosemary

1 lb fresh penne

salt and pepper

¼ cup chopped flat-leaf parsley, to garnish

1 cup grated Parmesan cheese, to serve

- Heat the oil in a large skillet, add the sausages, and cook over high heat for 3–4 minutes, until browned. Add the red chile, garlic, onion, and red pepper flakes and cook for an additional 1–2 minutes.

- Stir in the tomatoes, sugar, and rosemary and bring to a boil, then reduce the heat to medium and cook for 8–10 minutes.

- Meanwhile, cook the pasta in a large saucepan of salted, boiling water according to the package directions until al dente. Drain well, then add to the sausage mixture. Season and toss to mix well.

- Spoon into warm bowls, sprinkle with chopped parsley, and serve with the grated Parmesan.

 ### Spicy Sausage and Tomato Salad

Put 1 (14 oz) package cooked, small sausage links, 1 (4 oz) package mixed salad greens, and 12 halved cherry tomatoes in a salad bowl. Mix together ½ cup store-bought fresh Caesar salad dressing and 1 tablespoon chili sauce in a small bowl. Pour the dressing over the salad, season, and toss to mix well. Serve with crusty bread rolls.

 ### Spicy Sausage and Tomato Casserole

Heat 2 tablespoons sunflower oil in a large skillet, add 8 thick, spicy Italian sausage links, and cook over high heat for 2–3 minutes or until lightly browned. Add 1 chopped onion, 3 chopped garlic cloves, and 2 seeded and chopped red chiles and cook for an additional 2–3 minutes. Transfer to a shallow ovenproof dish, add 1 (14½ oz) can diced tomatoes, 1 teaspoon sugar, and 1 teaspoon dried red pepper flakes, then season and toss to mix well. Place in a preheated oven, at 400°F, for 20–25 minutes or until the sausages are cooked all the way through. Sprinkle a small handful of chopped flat-leaf parsley over the casserole and serve with crusty bread.

30 Spicy Lamb and Vegetable Stew

Serves 4

1 tablespoon sunflower oil
1¼ lb lamb shoulder cutlets,
   cut into ¾ inch cubes
1 onion, chopped
1 garlic clove, crushed
1 teaspoon peeled and grated
   fresh ginger root
2 tablespoons medium curry paste
1 large Yukon gold or white round
   potato, peeled and cut into
   ¾ inch cubes
1 large carrot, peeled and cut
   into ¾ inch cubes
1⅔ cups hot lamb stock
1 cup canned coconut milk
1⅓ cups frozen peas
small handful of cilantro leaves,
   to garnish
steamed rice, to serve (optional)

- Heat the oil in a large, heavy saucepan, add the lamb, onion, garlic, and ginger, and cook over high heat for 3–4 minutes, stirring frequently, until the lamb is browned and the onion is softened. Reduce the heat to medium, add the curry paste, and cook, stirring, for an additional 1–2 minutes.

- Stir in the potato, carrot, stock, and coconut milk and bring to a boil. Cook, uncovered, for 15–20 minutes or until the lamb and vegetables are tender. Stir in the peas 3 minutes before the end of the cooking time.

- Ladle into warm bowls, sprinkle with the cilantro leaves, and serve with steamed rice, if desired.

 Broiled Spicy Lamb Cutlets

Mix together 2 tablespoons medium or hot curry paste and ⅓ cup plain yogurt in a bowl, then spread the mixture all over 12 lamb cutlets and season. Cook under a preheated hot broiler for 2–3 minutes on each side or until cooked to your liking. Serve with warm flatbreads and a salad.

 Spicy Lamb and Vegetable Curry

Heat 2 tablespoons sunflower oil in a large wok or skillet until hot, add 1 chopped onion, 2 chopped garlic cloves, and 1 teaspoon peeled and grated fresh ginger root, and cook over high heat for 1–2 minutes. Add 1¼ lb ground lamb, 3 tablespoons medium curry paste, 1 large, peeled Yukon gold or white round potato, cut into ½ inch cubes, and 3 large, peeled carrots, cut into ½ inch cubes, and cook for an additional 1–2 minutes, until the lamb is browned. Pour in 1 cup canned coconut milk and cook, uncovered, over medium heat for 10–12 minutes, stirring frequently, until the lamb and vegetables are tender. Season, then serve immediately with steamed rice or crusty bread.

30 Sticky Spicy Pork with Vegetable Noodles

Serves 4

2¼ lb pork belly, cut into
thick slices

2 tablespoons chili sauce

⅓ cup hoisin sauce

2 tablespoons oyster sauce

1 cup water

3 cups snow peas

2 carrots, peeled and cut into
matchsticks

2 red chiles, seeded and
finely chopped

2 teaspoons peeled and grated
fresh ginger root

2 tablespoons toasted sesame oil

10 oz medium egg noodles,
cooked

½ cup chopped mint leaves

- Bring a large saucepan of water to a boil, add the pork, bring back to a boil, and cook for 1 minute. Drain, pat dry with paper towels, and put on a baking sheet.

- Mix together the chili sauce, ¼ cup of the hoisin sauce, and the oyster sauce in a bowl, pour over the pork, and toss to mix well. Place in a preheated oven, at 475°F, for 20 minutes or until sticky and cooked all the way through.

- Meanwhile, bring the measured water to a boil in a large wok or skillet, add the snow peas, carrots, red chiles, and ginger, cover, and cook for 2 minutes. Add the oil, noodles, and remaining hoisin sauce and heat through for 2 minutes, then add the mint and toss to mix well.

- Divide the noodles among warm bowls and serve immediately topped with the pork rashers.

---

10 Broiled Spicy Pork

Mix together 2 tablespoons chili sauce, 2 tablespoons sweet chili sauce, and 1 tablespoon hoisin sauce in a bowl, then spread the mixture all over 4 thin pork cutlets. Cook under a preheated hot broiler for 3–4 minutes on each side or until cooked all the way through. Serve with steamed rice or noodles.

20 Spicy Pork, Vegetable, and Noodle Stir-Fry

Cook 2 pork chops, about 7 oz each, under a preheated hot broiler for 5–6 minutes on each side or until cooked all the way through. Cool slightly, then finely dice and set aside. Heat 2 tablespoons sunflower oil in a large wok or skillet until hot, add 8 finely sliced scallions, 4 chopped garlic cloves, 1 teaspoon peeled and grated fresh ginger root, and 1 seeded and finely chopped red chile, and stir-fry over high heat for 1 minute. Add 1 (12 oz) package stir-fry vegetables, thawed, if frozen, 10 oz fresh egg noodles, ½ cup hoisin sauce, and 1 tablespoon chili sauce and stir-fry for an additional 3–4 minutes. Add the diced pork and continue to stir-fry for 2–3 minutes, until piping hot, tossing to mix well. Serve immediately.

Veal and Scallion Kebabs with Sweet Chili Dip

Serves 4

12 oz veal cutlets, cut into
  bite-size pieces

8–10 scallions, cut into
  ¾ inch lengths

2 red bell peppers, cored, seeded,
  and cut into bite-size pieces

½ cup sweet chili sauce

1 tablespoon hot chili sauce

finely grated rind and juice of
  2 limes

¼ cup kecap manis (thick
  soy sauce)

- Thread the veal pieces onto 12 metal skewers, alternating with pieces of scallion and red bell pepper.

- Beat together the remaining ingredients a small bowl, then transfer half to a serving dish and set aside. Brush the remaining mixture over the skewers on both sides until evenly coated. Cover and let marinate for 10 minutes.

- Cook the kebabs on a preheated barbecue or under a preheated medium-hot broiler for 4–5 minutes on each side or until the meat is cooked through.

- Transfer the kebabs to 4 serving plates and serve with the reserved marinade for dipping.

 Sweet Chile Veal and Scallion Rice

Heat 2 tablespoons sunflower oil in a large wok or skillet until hot, add 1 lb ground veal and 6 sliced scallions, and stir-fry over high heat for 1–2 minutes, until lightly browned. Add 3½ cups cooked rice, ¼ cup sweet chili sauce, 1 teaspoon hot chili sauce, and 2 teaspoons light soy sauce and stir-fry for an additional 3–4 minutes or until piping hot and cooked through. Serve immediately.

 Sweet Chile Veal and Scallion

Noodles Prepare 1 lb medium egg noodles according to the package directions and set aside. Meanwhile, heat 2 tablespoons sunflower oil in a large wok or skillet until hot, add 1 lb ground veal, and stir-fry over high heat for 2–3 minutes, until lightly browned. Add 8 sliced scallions, 1 seeded and finely chopped red chile, 1 teaspoon ginger paste, 1 teaspoon garlic paste, and ⅓ cup sweet chili sauce and stir-fry for an additional 3–4 minutes. Add 2 cups hot vegetable stock and 1 lb pack ready-cooked medium egg noodles and place in a preheated oven, 400°F, for 15 minutes or until piping hot and the noodles are cooked through and the veal is tender. Season, toss to mix well, and serve immediately.

2 Thai Pork Noodle Salad

Serves 4

2 tablespoons vegetable oil

6 scallions, thinly sliced

2 garlic cloves, finely chopped

2 teaspoons peeled and grated
   fresh ginger root

1 red chile, seeded and
   finely chopped

¾ inch length of trimmed lemon
   grass stalk, finely chopped

12 oz ground pork

3 tablespoons Thai fish sauce

2 tablespoons Chinese rice wine

¼ cup sweet chili sauce

juice of 1 lime

2 tablespoons honey

4 oz cellophane noodles

small handful of cilantro, chopped

small handful of mint, chopped

8–12 large iceberg lettuce leaves

⅔ cup chopped chile-roasted
   peanuts, to serve

- Heat the oil in a large wok or skillet until hot, add the scallions, garlic, ginger, red chile, and lemon grass and stir-fry over high heat for 30 seconds, then add the pork and stir-fry for an additional 4–5 minutes or until browned and cooked through.

- Stir in the fish sauce, rice wine, chili sauce, lime juice, and honey, reduce the heat, and simmer for 2 minutes, then remove the wok or skillet from the heat.

- Meanwhile, prepare the noodles according to the package directions, then drain and cut into short strands with kitchen scissors.

- Add the noodles to the pork mixture and mix through. Return the wok or skillet to the heat and cook over high heat for 3–4 minutes or until piping hot. Remove from the heat and stir in the chopped herbs.

- Spoon the mixture into the lettuce leaves and transfer to 4 serving plates. Serve sprinkled with the chopped peanuts.

---

1 Spicy Thai Scrambled Eggs

with Pork Heat 2 tablespoons sunflower oil in a skillet. Add 8 oz ground pork and 1 tablespoon thai red curry paste and stir-fry over high heat for 1–2 minutes. Stir in 6 beaten eggs and continue to cook over high heat, stirring, for 2–3 minutes. Remove from the heat and serve on toasted bread.

3 Thai Green Pork Rice

Heat 2 tablespoons sunflower oil in a heavy saucepan, add 6 sliced scallions, 2 chopped garlic cloves, 1 teaspoon grated fresh ginger root, 1 seeded and chopped red chile, a ¾ inch length of trimmed lemon grass stalk, finely chopped, 12 oz ground pork, and 1 tablespoon green curry paste, and cook, stirring, over high heat for 1–2 minutes, until the pork is

browned. Add 2⅓ cups jasmine rice and stir until well coated, then pour in 2½ cups hot vegetable stock and 1 cup canned coconut milk and bring to a boil. Cover tightly, reduce the heat to low, and cook, undisturbed, for 15–20 minutes or until the liquid is absorbed and the rice is tender. Remove from the heat and let stand for a few minutes before serving.

30 Jamaican Curried Beef and Black Bean Stew

Serves 4

3 tablespoons sunflower oil

1¾ lb ground beef

6 whole cloves

1 onion, finely chopped

2 tablespoons medium curry powder

2 carrots, peeled and cut into ½ inch cubes

2 celery sticks, diced

1 tablespoon thyme leaves

2 garlic cloves, crushed

¼ cup tomato paste

2½ cups hot beef stock

1 large potato, peeled and cut into ½ inch cubes

1 cup rinsed and drained, canned black beans

1 CUP rinsed and drained, canned black-eyed peas

salt and pepper

lemon wedges, to serve

- Heat the oil in a large, heavy saucepan, add the beef, and cook, stirring. over medium-high heat for 5–6 minutes or until browned.

- Add the cloves, onion, and curry powder and cook for 2–3 minutes, until the onions are beginning to soften, then stir in the carrots, celery, thyme, garlic, and tomato paste.

- Pour in enough beef stock to just cover the meat and stir well, then add the potato and canned beans and bring to a boil. Reduce the heat slightly and simmer for 20 minutes, uncovered, or until the potatoes and beef are tender, then season to taste.

- Ladle into warm bowls and serve with lemon wedges.

 Curried Beef and Black Bean Stir-Fry

Heat 2 tablespoons sunflower oil in a large wok or skillet until hot, add 1 lb ground beef and 1 tablespoon medium curry paste, and stir-fry over high heat for 3–4 minutes, until browned. Add ½ cup canned coconut milk and 1 cup rinsed and drained, canned black beans and stir-fry for an additional 3–4 minutes or until piping hot and cooked through. Season and serve immediately with noodles.

 Curried Beef and Black Bean Pilaf

Heat 2 tablespoons sunflower oil in a large wok or skillet until hot, add 1 lb ground beef and 1 tablespoon medium curry paste, and stir-fry over high heat for 2–3 minutes, until browned. Add ½ cup canned coconut milk, reduce the heat to medium, and simmer gently for 6–8 minutes or until most of the liquid has been absorbed and the beef is cooked through. Stir in 3½ cups cooked long-grain rice and 1 cup rinsed and drained, canned black beans and heat through for 2–3 minutes or until piping hot. Season, then serve immediately.

Five-Spice Pork Chops with Green Beans

Serves 4

2 garlic cloves, minced

2 red chiles, seeded and finely chopped

2 teaspoons five-spice powder

¼ cup sweet chili sauce

2 tablespoons dark soy sauce

4 pork chops, about 7 oz each

3 cups trimmed green beans

2 tablespoons extra-virgin olive oil

1 tablespoon finely grated lemon rind

juice of ½ lemon

salt and pepper

- Mix together the garlic, red chiles, five-spice powder, sweet chili sauce, and soy sauce in a small bowl, then spread the mixture all over the pork chops and season. Cover and let marinate for 10 minutes.

- Put the pork chops on a baking sheet lined with aluminum foil, then cook under a preheated hot broiler for 5–6 minutes on each side or until cooked through.

- Meanwhile, cook the beans in a large saucepan of lightly salted, boiling water for 3–4 minutes, until just tender. Drain well, then put in a bowl with the olive oil, lemon rind, and juice and toss together. Cover and keep warm.

- Transfer the pork chops to warm serving plates and serve with the green beans.

Spicy Pork and Vegetable Stir-Fry

Heat 2 tablespoons sunflower oil in a large wok or skillet until hot, add 12 oz pork tenderloin, cut into thin strips, and stir-fry over high heat for 2–3 minutes, until browned. Add 1 (12 oz) package stir-fry vegetables, thawed, if frozen, and ½ cup sweet chili stir-fry sauce and stir-fry for an additional 3–4 minutes or until piping hot and the pork is cooked through. Serve immediately with rice or noodles.

Spicy Pork and Vegetable Broth

Heat 2 tablespoons sunflower oil in a large, heavy saucepan, add 1 chopped onion, 2 seeded and chopped red chiles, 2 teaspoons peeled and grated fresh ginger root, 2 teaspoons grated garlic, and 1 teaspoon five-spice powder, and cook over medium heat for 3–4 minutes, stirring occasionally, until the onion is softened. Add 1 lb pork tenderloin, cubed, and ½ cup long-grain rice and cook, stirring, for 2–3 minutes, until the pork is browned. Pour in 4 cups hot chicken stock and bring to a boil, then reduce the heat to medium and cook, uncovered, for 20 minutes, until the pork is cooked through and the rice is tender, adding 1 (14 oz) package thawed, frozen vegetables 4–5 minutes before the end of the cooking time. Season, then serve immediately.

QuickCook
Fish and Seafood

Recipes listed by cooking time

30

Spicy Herb and Coconut
Salmon Packages   128

Chile and Garlic-Braised
Clams   130

Creamy Curried
Mussel Pilaf   132

Chile and Cilantro
Crab Cakes   134

Tomato and Tamarind
Fish Curry   136

Mexican Fish and
Salsa Casserole   138

Grilled Piri Piri Squid with
Mint and Cilantro   140

Shrimp and Salmon
Laksa   142

Spicy Monkfish and Bell
Pepper Kebabs   144

Spicy Shrimp and
Tomato Gratin   146

Tandoori Shrimp Biryani   148

Thai Fish Ball Curry   150

Caribbean Crayfish and
Coconut Curry   152

Spicy Clam and
Coconut Chowder   154

Spicy Lobster Gratin   156

Goan Fish Curry   158

Hot, Sweet, and Sour
Salmon   160

Mustard and Curry
Leaf Halibut   162

Shrimp, Lemon Grass,
and Mango Curry   164

Scallop Molee   166

Chile, Tomato, and
Shrimp Gratin   168

Sumac and Lemon
Monkfish Stew   170

Yellow Fish, Potato, and
Tomato Curry   172

Turmeric Mackerel Skewers
with Chile Rice Noodles   174

20

Spicy Salmon and
Herb Rice   128

Chile Spaghetti with
Clams   130

Creamy Curried
Mussel Soup   132

Crab, Chile, and Cilantro
Pasta   134

Baked Tamarind Fish
with Cherry Tomatoes   136

Lemon Sole with
Spicy Salsa   138

Crispy Fried Piri Piri
Squid   140

Laksa Salmon and Shrimp
Omelet   142

Spicy Monkfish and Bell
Pepper Stew   144

Spicy Shrimp and
Tomato Curry   146

Tandoori Jumbo Shrimp
Skewers with Mint and
Yogurt Dip   148

Thai Fish Ball Noodles   150

Crayfish, Vegetable, and
Coconut Stir-Fry   152

Coconut Spiced Clams   154

Creamy Spiced Lobster
Tail   156

10

Goan Fish Cakes   158

Hot and Sour Fish Soup   160

Baked Mustard and
Curry Leaf Fish   162

Shrimp, Lemon Grass,
and Mango Curry   164

Scallop, Chile, and
Coconut Pasta   166

Garlicky Chile and
Tomato Shrimp   168

Sumac, Chile and Lemon-
Spiced Monkfish Kebabs   170

Spicy Yellow Fish and
Tomato Rice   172

Turmeric Mackerel Curry   174

Spicy Salmon and
Herb Salad   128

Clam and Chile Rice   130

Curried Smoked Mussel
Omelet   132

Warm Crab and Chile
Rice Salad   134

Broiled Tomato and
Tamarind Fish   136

Fish and Spicy Salsa
Salad   138

Piri Piri Squid and
Seafood Salad   140

Hot Salmon and Shrimp
Laksa Rice   142

Chinese Monkfish and
Bell Pepper Stir-Fry   144

Spicy Shrimp and
Tomato Salad   146

Tandoori Shrimp Stir-Fry   148

Quick Thai Fish Ball Soup   150

Spiced Crayfish and Arugula
Sandwiches   152

Spicy Clam Omelet   154

Spicy Lobster Bisque   156

Goan Fried Fish   158

Broiled Hot, Sweet, and
Sour Salmon   160

Pan-Fried Fish with Mustard
and Curry Leaves   162

Shrimp, Lemon Grass, and
Mango Stir-Fry   164

Pan-Fried Scallops with Chile,
Cilantro, and Coconut   166

Shrimp, Tomato, and
Chile Salad   168

Sumac and Chile Fish Rolls
with Lemon Mayo   170

Spicy Fish and Tomato
Soup   172

Mackerel and Rice Noodle
Stir-Fry   174

Spicy Herb and Coconut Salmon Packages

Serves 4

fresh banana leaves (optional)
4 thick, skinless salmon fillets,
   about 8 oz each
juice of 1 lime, for drizzling

For the spice paste

2 teaspoons ground cumin
2 teaspoons ground coriander
1½ teaspoons sugar
2 cups grated fresh coconut
2 red chiles, seeded and finely
   chopped, plus extra to garnish
1 cup chopped cilantro leaves
¼ cup chopped mint leaves
3 garlic cloves, crushed
1 teaspoon grated fresh ginger root
juice of 1 lime
3 tablespoons vegetable oil
salt

To serve

lime wedges
pilaf rice

· Cut the banana leaves, if using, into four 9½ inch squares, then soften by dipping into a saucepan of hot water for a few seconds. As they become pliant, remove the leaves from the pan and pat dry with paper towels.

· To make the spice paste, put all the ingredients in a mini food processor and blend to a paste, then season with salt.

· Place the banana leaf squares on a clean work surface. Spread the paste liberally on both sides of each piece of fish, then drizzle with the lime juice. Place a piece of fish on a banana leaf, wrap up like a package, and secure with bamboo skewers or kitchen string. Repeat with the remaining fish to make 4 packages. Alternatively, place the fish on 4 large squares of aluminum foil and seal well to form packages.

· Place the packages on a baking sheet and bake in a preheated oven, at 400°F, for 15–20 minutes or until cooked through.

· Transfer the packages to serving plates, unwrap, and sprinkle with extra chopped chile. Serve with lime wedges to squeeze over the fish and with pilaf rice.

 Spicy Salmon and Herb Salad

Arrange 2 (4 oz) packages herb salad greens in a large serving dish. Flake 1 lb cooked, smoked salmon fillets into the salad, removing any bones. Mix together the juice of 2 limes, 1 seeded and chopped red chile, 1 teaspoon honey, 1 teaspoon ground cumin, and ⅓ cup olive oil in a bowl, then season. Drizzle the dressing over the salad, toss to mix well, and serve.

 Spicy Salmon and Herb Rice

Heat 2 tablespoons sunflower oil in a large wok or skillet until hot, add 4 sliced shallots, and cook over medium-low heat, stirring occasionally, for 10–12 minutes or until softened and lightly golden. Increase the heat to high, add 2 teaspoons cumin seeds, 1 tablespoon mild curry powder, 1 seeded and chopped red chile, and 1 lb skinless salmon fillets, boned and cut into bite-size pieces, and stir-fry for 2–3 minutes or until the fish is almost cooked through. Add 3½ cups cooked long-grain rice and stir-fry for an additional 2–3 minutes or until piping hot, then season. Remove from the heat and stir in a small handful each of chopped mint and cilantro leaves. Serve immediately.

 # Chile Spaghetti with Clams

Serves 4

1 lb dried spaghetti

⅓ cup extra-virgin olive oil, plus extra to serve

2 garlic cloves, chopped

2 red chiles, seeded and finely chopped

4 anchovy fillets in oil, drained and chopped

small handful of flat-leaf parsley, finely chopped

2¼ lb fresh clams, scrubbed

½ cup dry white wine

salt and pepper

· Cook the pasta in a large saucepan of salted boiling water according to the package directions until al dente. Drain, then return to the pan.

· Meanwhile, heat the oil in a skillet, add the garlic, red chiles, anchovies, and half the parsley and cook gently for a couple of minutes. Add the clams to the skillet, discarding any that are cracked or don't shut when tapped. Pour in the wine, then increase the heat to high, cover tightly, and cook for 4–5 minutes or until the clams have opened. Discard any that remain closed.

· Add the clams and the juices to the spaghetti with the remaining parsley, then season and toss to mix well. Divide among warm bowls, drizzle with a little extra olive oil, and serve immediately.

 ### Clam and Chile Rice

Heat 2 tablespoons sunflower oil in a wok or skillet until hot, add 2 seeded and finely diced red chiles, 1 teaspoon garlic paste, 2 (10 oz) cans clams, rinsed and drained, and 3½ cups cooked long-grain rice, and stir-fry over high heat for 3–4 minutes or until piping hot, then season. Remove from the heat and stir in a small handful of chopped flat-leaf parsley. Serve immediately.

 ### Chile and Garlic–Braised Clams

Heat 2 tablespoons olive oil in a heavy saucepan, add 4 chopped shallots and cook over medium heat, stirring occasionally, for 6–8 minutes, until softened. Add 2 crushed garlic cloves and 2 seeded and finely chopped red chiles and cook, stirring, for 1–2 minutes. Stir in 2 tablespoons tomato paste and 4 finely chopped plum tomatoes and cook for another 8–10 minutes. Add 2 cups hot fish stock and 1¾ lb scrubbed fresh clams, discarding any that are cracked or don't shut when tapped, then bring to a boil, cover tightly, and cook for 4–5 minutes or until the clams have opened. Discard any clams that remain closed. Season, ladle into warm bowls, and serve.

Creamy Curried Mussel Soup

Serves 4

1 tablespoon butter

2 shallots, thinly sliced

2 garlic cloves, crushed

1 teaspoon peeled and finely
  grated fresh ginger root

2 large red chiles, seeded and
  finely diced

1 teaspoon medium curry powder

1 large pinch of saffron threads

½ cup dry white wine

1¾ cups hot vegetable stock

2¼ lb fresh mussels, scrubbed
  and debearded

1 cup heavy cream

⅓ cup finely chopped
  cilantro leaves

salt and pepper

- Heat the butter in a large wok or skillet, add the shallots, garlic, ginger, red chiles, and curry powder, and sauté over high heat for 1 minute. Add the saffron, white wine, and stock and bring to a boil, then reduce the heat to medium and cook for 1–2 minutes.

- Add the mussels to the wok, discarding any that are cracked or don't shut when tapped. Increase the heat to high, cover tightly, and cook for 2–3 minutes, shaking the wok occasionally, until the mussels have opened. Discard any that remain closed. Remove the mussels with a slotted spoon and set aside.

- Add the cream to the stock mixture and bring back to a boil, then reduce the heat and simmer gently, uncovered, for 5–6 minutes. Return the mussels to the wok, stir in the cilantro, and season.

- Ladle into warm soup bowls and serve with crusty bread.

 Curried Smoked Mussel Omelet

Beat together 4 eggs and 2 teaspoons hot curry powder in a bowl, then season with salt. Heat 2 tablespoons butter in a large skillet and add the egg mixture, swirling to coat evenly. Cook for 1–2 minutes, then add 1 (3 oz) can smoked mussels, drained, down the center. Fold the egg mixture over the mussels. Flip to seal and cook for 1–2 minutes. Keep warm while you make another omelet. Halve each omelet and serve one-half per person.

 Creamy Curried Mussel Pilaf

Heat 1 tablespoon butter and 1 tablespoon sunflower oil in a heavy saucepan, add 4 sliced shallots, and cook, stirring, for 2–3 minutes, until softened. Add a large pinch of saffron threads, 1 tablespoon medium curry powder, and 2½ cups long-grain rice and stir for 1–2 minutes, until the rice is well coated, then add 1 (1 lb) package frozen, cooked mussels. Pour in 2½ cups hot fish stock and ⅔ cup heavy cream, season, then bring to a boil. Cover tightly, reduce the heat to low, and cook, undisturbed, for 15–20 minutes or until the liquid is absorbed and the rice is tender. Remove from the heat and let stand for a few minutes before serving.

30 Chile and Cilantro Crab Cakes

Serves 4

12 oz fresh white crabmeat
8 oz raw peeled jumbo shrimp,
   coarsely chopped
1 tablespoon hot curry paste
2 garlic cloves, minced
1 red chile, seeded and
   finely chopped
1 red onion, finely chopped
¼ cup chopped cilantro leaves,
   plus extra to garnish
1 medium egg, beaten
2 cups fresh white bread crumbs
sunflower oil, for brushing
salt and pepper

To serve

lemon wedges
green salad

- Put the crabmeat, shrimp, curry paste, garlic, red chile, red onion, cilantro, egg, and bread crumbs in a food processor or blender. Season well, then blend for a few seconds until well mixed. Transfer to a bowl then, using your fingers, combine to make a thick mixture.

- Line a baking sheet with nonstick parchment paper and brush with a little oil. Using wet hands, divide the crab mixture into 12 equal portions and shape each one into a round cake. Transfer the crab cakes to the prepared baking sheet, brush with a little oil, and bake in a preheated oven, at 400°F, for 15–20 minutes or until lightly browned and cooked through.

- Transfer to 4 serving plates and serve with lemon wedges to squeeze over and a crisp green salad.

 Warm Crab and Chile Rice Salad

Heat a large nonstick wok or skillet until hot, add 2¾ cups cooked rice, and stir-fry over high heat for 3–4 minutes or until piping hot. Remove from the heat and stir in 12 oz cooked white crabmeat, a handful of chopped cilantro, and a small handful of chopped mint. Transfer to a large serving dish. Mix together 1 seeded and diced red chile, ⅓ cup olive oil, and the juice of 2 limes, then season. Pour the dressing over the salad, toss to mix, and serve.

Crab, Chile, and Cilantro Pasta

Cook 12 oz linguine in a large saucepan of salted, boiling water according to the package directions until al dente. Meanwhile, heat 3 tablespoons olive oil in a large skillet, add 4 finely chopped garlic cloves and 1 seeded and finely chopped red chile, and cook over medium-low heat, stirring occasionally, for 4–5 minutes, until softened. Add 12 oz fresh white crabmeat and cook for an additional 2–3 minutes or until piping hot. Drain the pasta and add to the crab mixture with a large handful of chopped cilantro leaves. Season, toss to mix well, and serve immediately.

30 Tomato and Tamarind Fish Curry

Serves 4

1¾ lb skinless halibut, cod, or
   flounder fillets, boned and cut
   into chunks
1 tablespoon tamarind paste
¼ cup rice wine vinegar
2 tablespoons cumin seeds
1 teaspoon ground turmeric
2 teaspoons hot curry powder
1 teaspoon salt
¼ cup sunflower oil
1 onion, finely chopped
3 garlic cloves, finely grated
2 teaspoons grated fresh ginger root
2 teaspoons black mustard seeds or
   nigella seeds (black onion seeds)
2½ cups canned diced tomatoes
1 teaspoon sugar
12 cherry tomatoes
chopped cilantro, to garnish

To serve

poppadums
steamed long-grain rice (optional)

- Put the fish in a shallow nonmetallic bowl. Mix together the tamarind, vinegar, cumin seeds, turmeric, curry powder, and salt in a small bowl. Spoon over the fish and toss to coat evenly, then cover and let marinate.

- Meanwhile, heat the oil in a large wok or skillet over high heat until hot, add the onion, garlic, ginger, and mustard or nigella seeds, then reduce the heat to medium and stir-fry for 1–2 minutes.

- Add the diced tomatoes and sugar, stir through, and bring to a boil. Reduce the heat again, cover, and cook gently, stirring occasionally, for 15–20 minutes.

- Add the cherry tomatoes and the fish with its marinade and stir gently to mix. Cover and simmer gently for 5–6 minutes or until the fish is cooked through and flakes easily.

- Ladle into warm bowls, sprinkle with chopped cilantro, and serve with poppadums and steamed basmati rice, if desired.

 Broiled Tomato and Tamarind Fish

Mix together 1 teaspoon tamarind paste, 1 teaspoontomato paste, 1 tablespoon hot curry powder, and 2 tablespoons sunflower oil in a bowl, then spread the mixture over 4 skinless halibut, cod, or flounder fillets, about 5–5½ oz each, and season with salt. Cook under a preheated hot broiler for 6–8 minutes or until just cooked through. Serve with steamed rice.

Baked Tamarind Fish with Cherry Tomatoes Mix together 1 teaspoon tamarind paste, 1 tablespoon hot curry powder, 2 tablespoons sunflower oil, 2 crushed garlic cloves, and 1 teaspoon peeled and grated fresh ginger root in a bowl, then spread the mixture over 4 skinless halibut, cod, or flounder fillets, about 5–5½ oz each, and season with salt. Place

in an ovenproof dish and sprinkle with 3 cups cherry tomatoes. Place in a preheated oven, at 425°F, for 12–15 minutes or until the fish is cooked through. Serve with steamed rice and salad.

HOT-FISH-DUS

Lemon Sole with Spicy Salsa

Serves 4

4 lemon sole fillets, 7½ oz each, skinned

salt and pepper

For the salsa

1 ripe mango, peeled, pitted, and finely diced

1 red bell pepper, cored, seeded, and finely chopped

6 cherry tomatoes, quartered

1 red onion, finely chopped

½ teaspoon sugar

1 red chile, seeded and finely chopped

¼ cup chopped cilantro leaves, plus extra to garnish

2 tablespoons rice vinegar

finely grated rind and juice of 1 lime

1 teaspoon chile oil

2 tablespoons olive oil

To serve

lime wedges

steamed long-grain rice

- To make the salsa, mix together all the ingredients in a large bowl and season well.

- Place the fish fillets on a clean work surface, skinned-side up, and cut into half lengthwise. Spoon some of the salsa onto the tail ends of the fish, roll up tightly, then season and place in a large nonstick skillet. Cover and cook over low heat for 8–10 minutes. Remove the lid and cook, uncovered, for an additional 3 minutes or until cooked through.

- Transfer the fish to serving plates and sprinkle with chopped cilantro. Serve with the remaining salsa, lime wedges to squeeze over the fish, and steamed basmati rice.

Fish and Spicy Salsa Salad

Make the salsa in a large salad bowl as above and add the torn leaves of 1 romaine lettuce. Flake 12 oz cooked, smoked salmon or trout fillets into large pieces, removing any bones, and add to the salad. Drizzle ½ cup thousand island dressing over the salad and toss to mix well.

Mexican Fish and Salsa Casserole

Place 4 thick, skinless white fish fillets, such as red snapper, tilapia, or halibut, about 6 oz each, in a single layer in a shallow ovenproof dish and season well. Finely dice 3 plum tomatoes, 1 small red onion, 2 seeded red chiles, 2 garlic cloves, and ⅔ cup mango flesh and mix together in a bowl. Stir in the finely grated rind and juice of 1 lime, 2 tablespoons sunflower oil, and 1 teaspoon cumin seeds. Season, then spoon the mixture over the prepared fish fillets. Place in a preheated oven, at 400°F, for 20 minutes or until cooked through. Serve immediately.

Grilled Piri Piri Squid with Mint and Cilantro

Serves 4

1¾ lb squid, cleaned and tentacles removed

finely grated rind and juice of 1 lime

1 teaspoon ground cumin

2 teaspoons piri piri seasoning

1 red chile, seeded and finely diced

1 teaspoon sea salt

1 garlic clove, crushed

¼ cup olive oil, plus extra to serve

½ cucumber

small handful of mint leaves, coarsely chopped

small handful of cilantro leaves, coarsely chopped

lime wedges, to serve (optional)

- Cut down the side of the squid so that it can be laid flat on a cutting board. Using a sharp knife, lightly score the inside flesh in a crisscross pattern, which will help to tenderize it, and cut into bite-size pieces.

- Put the squid pieces in a shallow nonmetallic bowl. Mix together the lime rind, cumin, piri piri seasoning, red chile, sea salt, garlic, and oil in a small bowl, then rub into the squid. Cover and let marinate for 10–15 minutes.

- Meanwhile, using a mandolin, finely shred the cucumber and set aside.

- Heat a nonstick, ridged grill pan until smoking hot. Remove the squid from the marinade, add to the grill pan, and cook for no more than 2 minutes on each side, pushing the squid down with the back of a spatula, until it is just cooked through. Transfer to a large shallow bowl.

- Add the cucumber and chopped herbs to the bowl and toss to mix well. Serve immediately, with a drizzle of extra olive oil and lime wedges, if desired.

 Piri Piri Squid and Seafood Salad

Put 14 oz mixed, cooked seafood with squid and 1 (8 oz) package mixed salad greens in a salad bowl. Mix together 2 teaspoons piri piri seasoning and ⅔ cup thousand island dressing in a small bowl, then season. Pour the dressing over the salad, toss to mix well, and serve immediately.

 Crispy Fried Piri Piri Squid

Fill a large saucepan one-quarter full with sunflower oil and heat to 350–370°F, or until a cube of bread browns in 30 seconds. Meanwhile, mix together 2 cups chickpea (besan) flour, 2 tablespoons piri piri seasoning, and 1 teaspoon sea salt in a large bowl. Add a little cold water to the flour mixture to make a thick batter (resembling thick heavy cream). Cut 1¼ lb cleaned squid, tentacles discarded, into thick rings and dip into the batter. Remove the squid rings from the batter and deep-fry in batches for 1–2 minutes or until they turn golden and crispy. Remove with a slotted spoon and drain on paper towels. Serve immediately.

30 Shrimp and Salmon Laksa

Serves 4

1 tablespoon sunflower oil

8 scallions, thickly sliced, plus extra, shredded, to garnish

3 garlic cloves, finely chopped

1 red chile, seeded and finely chopped, plus extra to garnish

3 teaspoons grated fresh ginger root

2 tablespoons lemon grass paste

2 tablespoons laksa curry paste

1¾ cups can coconut milk

1¾ cups hot chicken stock

1 lb skinless salmon fillets, boned and cut into cubes

12 cooked jumbo shrimp, peeled and deveined, with tails left on

small handful of fresh bean sprouts

2 tablespoons chopped cilantro leaves, plus extra to garnish

1 teaspoon Thai fish sauce

1 tablespoon light soy sauce

8 oz dried rice noodles

¼ cucumber, cut into matchsticks

salt and pepper

- Heat the oil in a large wok or skillet until hot, add the scallions, garlic, red chile, ginger, lemon grass paste, and curry paste, and stir-fry over high heat for 2–3 minutes. Pour in the coconut milk and stock and bring to a boil, then simmer gently for 4–5 minutes.

- Add the salmon and bring to a boil, then reduce the heat to low and simmer, uncovered, for 5–7 minutes or until the fish is just cooked through. Add the shrimp, bean sprouts, cilantro, fish sauce, and soy sauce and heat through for a few minutes, until piping hot, then season. Keep warm.

- Cook the noodles according to the package directions, then drain and divide among warm bowls. Top with the salmon and shrimp, then ladle over the laksa broth. Sprinkle with the cucumber, extra scallions, red chile, and cilantro leaves and serve immediately.

 Hot Salmon and Shrimp Laksa Rice

Heat 2 tablespoons sunflower oil in a large wok until hot, add 3½ cups cooked rice and 1 tablespoon laksa curry paste, and stir-fry over high heat for 3–4 minutes. Stir in 12 oz flaked cooked, smoked salmon fillets, bones removed, and 12 oz cooked, peeled shrimp and toss to mix well. Heat through and serve.

 Laksa Salmon and Shrimp Omelet

Heat 2 tablespoons sunflower oil in medium ovenproof skillet, add 6 finely sliced scallions and 1 seeded and chopped red chile, and cook, stirring, for 1–2 minutes. Meanwhile, beat together 6 eggs, 1 tablespoon laksa curry paste, and a small handful of finely chopped cilantro leaves in a bowl. Add to the skillet with 10 oz flaked cooked, smoked salmon fillets, bones removed, and 12 oz cooked, peeled jumbo shrimp. Cook over medium heat for 10–12 minutes or until the bottom is set, then place the skillet under a preheated medium-hot broiler and cook for 3–4 minutes or until the top is lightly golden and just set. Serve immediately with a crisp salad.

Spicy Monkfish and Bell Pepper Stew

Serves 4

2 tablespoons vegetable oil

2 onions, finely chopped

2 tablespoons curry powder

1 teaspoon ground turmeric

2 lb monkfish tail, cut into
  bite-size pieces

2 garlic cloves, chopped

1 teaspoon peeled and finely
  grated fresh ginger root

½ teaspoon tamarind paste

1 tablespoon thyme leaves

1 star anise

2 cups hot fish stock

1 red bell pepper, cored, seeded,
  and cut into 1 inch pieces

1 yellow bell pepper, cored,
  seeded, and cut into
  1 inch pieces

steamed rice, to serve (optional)

- Heat the oil in a heavy saucepan, add the onions, and cook over medium heat, stirring occasionally, for 2–3 minutes, until softened. Stir in the curry powder and turmeric and cook for an additional 1 minute, until fragrant.

- Add the remaining ingredients and stir together well. Bring to a simmer, then reduce the heat to low and cook, uncovered, for 8–10 minutes or until the fish is cooked through and the bell peppers are tender.

- Ladle into warm bowls and serve with steamed rice, if desired.

 Chinese Monkfish and Bell Pepper Stir-Fry Core, seed, and finely slice 1 red bell pepper and 1 yellow bell pepper. Heat 2 tablespoons sunflower oil in a large wok or skillet until hot, add the bell peppers and 1¼ lb monkfish tail, cubed, and stir-fry over high heat for 2–3 minutes. Add ½ cup oyster and scallion stir-fry sauce and cook for an additional 2–3 minutes or until the fish is cooked through and piping hot. Serve immediately with steamed rice.

 Spicy Monkfish and Bell Pepper Kebabs Cut 1½ lb monkfish fillets into bite-size pieces and put in a nonmetallic bowl. Stir in 1 tablespoon medium curry paste, ⅓ cup coconut milk, and the juice of 1 lime and season well. Cover and let marinate for 10–15 minutes. Meanwhile, core, seed, and cut 2 red bell peppers and 1 yellow bell pepper into bite-size pieces. Thread the monkfish onto 8 metal skewers, alternating with the bell peppers. Cook under a preheated medium-hot broiler for 4–5 minutes on each side or until the fish is cooked through. Serve with a green salad.

HOT-FISH-BEU

 # Spicy Shrimp and Tomato Curry

Serves 4

2 tablespoons hot curry powder
1 teaspoon ground turmeric
4 garlic cloves, crushed
2 teaspoons peeled and finely
   grated fresh ginger root
2 tablespoons ground cumin
⅓ cup tomato paste
1 teaspoon grated jaggery or
   granulated sugar
1¾ cups water
2 teaspoons tamarind paste
1¼ cups canned coconut milk
1¾ lb raw jumbo shrimp, peeled
   and deveined, with tails left on
12 cherry tomatoes
salt and pepper
chopped cilantro leaves,
   to garnish
warm naan (optional), to serve

- Put the curry powder, turmeric, garlic, ginger, cumin, tomato paste, sugar, and measured water in a heavy saucepan and mix together. Place over high heat and bring to a boil. Cover, reduce the heat to low, and simmer gently for 8–10 minutes.

- Increase the heat to high, stir in the tamarind paste and coconut milk, and bring back to a boil. Add the shrimp and cherry tomatoes and cook, uncovered, for 4–5 minutes or until the shrimp turn pink and are completely cooked through. Season well.

- Ladle into warm bowls, sprinkle with chopped cilantro leaves, and serve with warm naan, if desired.

 ### Spicy Shrimp and Tomato Salad

Arrange 1 lb cooked, peeled shrimp, 4 sliced tomatoes, and the leaves of 2 heads Boston lettuce in a large salad bowl. Mix together 1 tablespoon medium curry powder, ⅓ cup mayonnaise, the juice of 1 lemon, and ⅓ cup plain yogurt in a bowl, then season. Drizzle the dressing over the salad, toss to mix well, and serve with crusty bread or warm naan, if desired.

Spicy Shrimp and Tomato Gratin

Heat 2 tablespoons sunflower oil in a large skillet, add 2 finely chopped onions, and cook over medium-low heat, stirring occasionally, for 10 minutes, until softened and lightly browned. Add 2 chopped garlic cloves, 1 seeded and chopped green chile, 1 tablespoon curry powder, and 1 teaspoon grated fresh ginger root and cook, stirring, for 1–2 minutes. Add 3 cups halved cherry tomatoes and cook, stirring occasionally, for 4–5 minutes, until the tomatoes have softened. Remove from the heat and stir in 1 lb raw, peeled jumbo shrimp. Transfer to a shallow gratin dish, season, and cook under medium-hot broiler for 5–6 minutes or until the shrimp turn pink and are cooked through. Sprinkle with a small handful of chopped cilantro leaves and serve with lemon wedges to squeeze over the shrimp.

Tandoori Jumbo Shrimp Skewers with Mint and Yogurt Dip

Serves 4

1¾ lb raw, unpeeled jumbo shrimp
3 tablespoons tandoori paste
⅓ cup plain yogurt
juice of 2 limes
salt and pepper
lime wedges, to serve

For the dip

1 tablespoon mint jelly
2 tablespoons finely chopped
  mint leaves
1 tablespoon lime juice
1 cup plain yogurt

- Put the shrimp in a large, nonmetallic bowl. Mix together the tandoori paste, yogurt, and lime juice in a bowl, then season well. Pour over the shrimp and toss to coat evenly, then cover and let marinate for 8–10 minutes.

- Meanwhile, make the mint and yogurt dip. Mix together all the ingredients in a bowl until smooth, then season. Cover and chill until ready to serve.

- Thread each shrimp onto a small metal skewer, then cook under a preheated medium-hot broiler for 6–8 minutes, turning once, or until the shrimp turn pink and are cooked through.

- Transfer the skewers to 4 serving plates and serve with the dip and lime wedges to squeeze over the shrimp.

 ### Tandoori Shrimp Stir-Fry

Heat 2 tablespoons sunflower oil in a large wok or skillet until hot, add 2 tablespoons tandoori paste and 1¾ lb raw, peeled jumbo shrimp, season with salt, and stir-fry over high heat for 3–4 minutes or until the shrimp turn pink and are cooked all the way through. Remove from the heat, stir in the juice of 1 lemon, and serve immediately with steamed rice or warm naan.

 ### Tandoori Shrimp Biryani

Mix together ⅓ cup plain yogurt and 2 tablespoons tandoori paste in a large bowl, add 1¼ lb raw, peeled jumbo shrimp, then season and stir to mix well and set aside. Meanwhile, heat 2 tablespoons sunflower oil in a heavy saucepan, add ⅓ cup chopped onions, and sauté for a few minutes until softened and golden brown. Add 2½ cups long-grain rice, 1 cinnamon stick, 6 cardamom pods, 2 cloves, and 1 tablespoon cumin seeds and stir to mix well, then add the shrimp mixture and stir to coat evenly. Pour over 3½ cups hot vegetable stock or fish stock, season with salt, and bring to a boil. Cover tightly, reduce the heat to low, and cook, undisturbed, for 15–20 minutes or until all the liquid is absorbed, the rice is tender, and the shrimp are cooked through. Remove from the heat and let stand for a few minutes before serving.

Thai Fish Ball Curry

Serves 4

1 tablespoon sunflower oil
1 tablespoon Thai red curry paste
2½ cups canned coconut milk
2 teaspoons sugar
4 kaffir lime leaves, finely shredded
¾ inch length of trimmed lemon
   grass stalk, finely chopped
2 teaspoons Thai fish sauce
1 carrot, cut into thin matchsticks
2 cups halved snow peas
steamed jasmine rice, to serve

For the fish balls

1¾ lb firm white fish fillets, such as
   halibut or red snapper, skinned
   and boned
2 garlic cloves, crushed
2 tablespoons cornstarch
2 tablespoons dark soy sauce
2 tablespoons chopped cilantro
1 teaspoon grated fresh ginger root

To garnish

sliced red chile
cilantro leaves

- To make the fish balls, put all the ingredients in a food processor or blender and blend until fairly smooth. Roll the mixture into bite-size balls.

- Heat the oil in a large wok or heavy saucepan until hot, add the curry paste, and stir-fry over medium heat for 1–2 minutes, then add the coconut milk. Bring to a boil, then reduce the heat to low and simmer gently, uncovered, for 6–8 minutes.

- Add the fish balls, sugar, lime leaves, lemon grass, fish sauce, carrot, and snow peas and bring back to a boil. Reduce the heat to low and simmer, uncovered, for 10–12 minutes or until the fish balls are cooked through.

- Ladle into warm bowls, sprinkle with sliced red chile and cilantro leaves, and serve with steamed jasmine rice.

Quick Thai Fish Ball Soup

Put 2 (15 oz) cans vegetable soup, 2 teaspoons Thai red curry paste. and 12 oz cooked fish balls (available from Thai or other Asian food stores) in a saucepan and bring to a boil, then reduce the heat to medium and cook for 3–4 minutes or until piping hot. Serve immediately.

Thai Fish Ball Noodles

Prepare 10 oz rice noodles according to the package directions and set aside. Meanwhile, heat 2 tablespoons sunflower oil in a large wok or skillet until hot, add 12 oz cooked fish balls (available from Thai or other Asian food stores), and stir-fry over high heat for 4–5 minutes, until browned. Add 1 tablespoon Thai red curry paste and 1 cup canned coconut milk and stir-fry for an additional 2–3 minutes, then add a 1 (12 oz) package stir-fry vegetables, thawed, if frozen, and the rice noodles. Toss to mix well, bring to a boil, and cook for 2–3 minutes or until piping hot. Season, then serve immediately.

HOT-FISH-RAT

# 10 Spiced Crayfish and Arugula Sandwiches

Serves 4

1 cup mayonnaise
1 tablespoon mild curry powder
8 thick slices wheat bread
small handful of arugula leaves
1 lb cooked crayfish meat

To serve

potato chips
salad (optional)

- Mix together the mayonnaise and curry powder in a bowl, then spread onto 8 thick slices of wheat bread.

- Top 4 of the slices with a small handful of arugula leaves and add one-quarter of the crayfish meat each.

- Sandwich the remaining slices over the crayfish and press lightly to secure. Serve with potato chips and a salad, if desired.

20 Crayfish, Vegetable, and Coconut

Stir-Fry Heat 2 tablespoons sunflower oil in a large wok until hot, add 6 sliced scallions, 2 chopped garlic cloves, 1 teaspoon peeled and grated fresh ginger root, 1 teaspoon curry powder, 1 seeded and sliced red chile, and stir-fry for 2–3 minutes over high heat. Add 1 (12 oz) package stir-fry vegetables, thawed, if frozen, and stir-fry for an additional 5–6 minutes. Add 1 cup coconut milk and 12 oz cooked crayfish meat and continue to stir-fry for 4–5 minutes or until piping hot. Season and serve with noodles or rice.

30 Caribbean Crayfish and Coconut Curry

Heat 2 tablespoons sunflower oil in a large skillet, add 1 finely chopped onion, 2 crushed garlic cloves, 1 seeded and finely chopped Scotch bonnet chile, and 1 tablespoon thyme, and cook over medium heat for about 5 minutes, until the onion is softened. Stir in 1 tablespoon mild curry powder and cook for 1 minute until fragrant, then add 1 cored, seeded, and diced red bell pepper, 6 finely sliced scallions, and ¾ cup canned diced tomatoes and cook for an additional 2 minutes. Pour in 1 (14½ oz) can coconut milk and bring to a boil. Reduce the heat slightly, then simmer for 6–8 minutes. Add 1 lb cooked fresh crayfish meat and cook for 4–5 minutes, until heated through, then season. Ladle into bowls and serve with bread or steamed rice.

HOT-FISH-MUF

Coconut Spiced Clams

Serves 4

¼ cup vegetable oil
2 shallots, very finely chopped
1 red chile, slit lengthwise and
  seeded
1 inch piece of fresh ginger root,
  peeled and shredded
2 garlic cloves, finely chopped
2 plum tomatoes, finely chopped
1 tablespoon medium or hot
  curry powder
1 cup canned coconut milk
1¾ lb fresh clams, scrubbed
1 large handful of chopped
  cilantro leaves
3 tablespoons grated fresh coconut

To serve (optional)

salad
crusty bread

- Heat the oil in a large wok or saucepan until hot, add the shallots, red chile, ginger, and garlic, and stir-fry over medium heat for 3–4 minutes. Increase the heat to high, stir in the tomatoes, curry powder, and coconut milk, and cook for an additional 4–5 minutes.

- Add the clams to the wok, discarding any that have cracked or don't shut when tapped, stir to mix, and cover tightly, then continue to cook over high heat for 6–8 minutes, until the clams have opened. Discard any that remain closed.

- Stir in the chopped cilantro and sprinkle with the grated coconut. Ladle into bowls and serve immediately with a fresh salad and crusty bread to mop up the juices.

10 Spicy Clam Omelet

Beat together 4 eggs, 2 teaspoons hot curry powder, and a handful of chopped cilantro in a bowl. Heat 2 tablespoons olive oil in a skillet, add the egg mixture, and swirl to coat evenly. Cook for 1–2 minutes, then add 1 (10 oz) can clams, rinsed and drained, and fold over the sides of the omelet to enclose the filling. Flip to seal and cook for 1–2 minutes. Keep warm while you repeat the recipe to make another omelet. Divide each omelet in two and serve each half with a crisp green salad.

30 Spicy Clam and Coconut Chowder

Heat 2 tablespoons sunflower oil in a heavy saucepan, add 1 chopped onion, 1 seeded and chopped red chile, 1 tablespoon medium or hot curry powder, and 2 chopped garlic cloves and cook, stirring, for 2–3 minutes. Add 2⅔ cups peeled and finely diced potatoes, 1 cup canned coconut milk, and 2½ cups hot fish stock and bring to a boil, then reduce the heat to medium and cook, uncovered, for 12–15 minutes or until the potatoes are tender. Increase the heat to high, stir in 12 oz fresh scrubbed clams, discarding any that are cracked or don't shut when tapped, cover tightly, and bring to a boil, then cook for 4–5 minutes or until the clams have opened. Discard any that remain closed. Season, stir in a small handful of chopped cilantro, and serve immediately.

Creamy Spiced Lobster Tail

Serves 4

2 egg yolks, beaten

½ cup heavy cream

2 tablespoons butter

2 tablespoons dry sherry

½ teaspoon salt

1 tablespoon medium curry powder

¼ cup finely chopped cilantro leaves, plus extra leaves to garnish

1 lb cooked lobster tail meat, cut into bite-size pieces

To serve

lemon wedges

steamed rice

- Beat together the egg yolks and heavy cream in a small bowl until well blended. Melt the butter in a saucepan over low heat, then stir in the egg mixture and sherry. Cook, stirring, for about 10–12 minutes or until the mixture thickens, but do not let boil.

- Remove from the heat, then stir in the salt, curry powder, and cilantro. Stir in the lobster, then return the pan to low heat and cook gently until heated through.

- Spoon into warm bowls, sprinkle with cilantro leaves, and serve with lemon wedges to squeeze over the lobster and with steamed rice.

 Spicy Lobster Bisque

Heat 1 tablespoon butter in a saucepan, add 1 seeded and finely chopped red chile, 1 teaspoon garlic paste, and 1 teaspoon ginger paste and cook, stirring, for 30 seconds. Add 2 (15 oz) cans lobster bisque soup and bring to a boil, then reduce the heat to medium and cook for a few minutes or until piping hot. Stir in ¼ cup finely chopped cilantro leaves and serve with warm ciabatta bread.

 Spicy Lobster Gratin

Melt 4 tablespoons butter in a saucepan over low heat, add 2 tablespoons all-purpose flour and 2 tablespoons medium or hot curry powder, and cook, stirring, for 1–2 minutes. Gradually beat in 1 cup heavy cream and ½ cup milk and cook, stirring continuously, for about 5 minutes or until thickened. Cut 1 lb cooked lobster tail meat into large pieces and add to the pan. Toss to mix well, season, and pour into a shallow casserole dish. Sprinkle over 4 cups fresh white bread crumbs and place in a preheated oven, at 425°F, for 15–20 minutes or until bubbling. Serve warm with a crisp green salad.

Goan Fried Fish

Serves 4

1 teaspoon ground turmeric
1 teaspoon ginger paste
1 teaspoon garlic paste
1 teaspoon chili powder
1 teaspoon ground cumin
1 teaspoon ground coriander
juice of 2 lemons
4 skinless halibut fillets,
    about 7 oz each
¼ cup sunflower oil
green salad, to serve (optional)

- Mix together the ground spices and pastes in a bowl. Add the juice of 2 lemons and stir to mix well. Spread the mixture all over the fish and season well.

- Heat the sunflower oil in a large skillet, add the fish, and cook over medium-high heat for 2–3 minutes on each side or until just cooked through. Serve with a green salad, if desired.

Goan Fish Cakes

Place 12 oz skinless halibut fillets, boned, and 12 oz raw, peeled shrimp in a food processor or blender. Add 1 tablespoon Goan curry paste and process until smooth. Using wet hands, shape the mixture into 12 cakes. Heat 2 tablespoons sunflower oil in a large skillet, add the fish cakes, and cook over medium-high heat for 3–4 minutes on each side or until cooked through. Serve with steamed rice and a salad.

Goan Fish Curry

Heat 2 tablespoons sunflower oil in a large, heavy saucepan, add 2 finely chopped onions, and cook over medium heat, stirring occasionally, for 1–2 minutes, until beginning to soften. Add 1 tablespoon grated fresh ginger root, 4 crushed garlic cloves, and 2 seeded and finely sliced red chiles and cook, stirring, for 1–2 minutes. Add ¼ teaspoon ground turmeric, 2 teaspoons each ground coriander and cumin, and 1 teaspoon chili powder and cook, stirring, for an additional 1–2 minutes, until fragrant, then stir in 1 tablespoon tamarind paste, 1 cup canned coconut milk and 1¼ cups water and bring to a boil. Add 1 teaspoon brown sugar, then reduce the heat to low and simmer gently, uncovered, for 12–15 minutes. Stir in 1¾ lb skinless halibut fillets, boned and cut into bite-size pieces, increase the heat to high, and cook for 4–5 minutes or until just cooked through, then season. Ladle into warm bowls and serve with steamed rice, poppadums, and pickles.

30 Hot, Sweet, and Sour Salmon

Serves 4

1 tablespoon Thai fish sauce

1 teaspoon grated jaggery or
granulated sugar

2 lemon grass stalks, bruised

2½ cups water

2 tablespoons lemon juice

1 tablespoon tamarind paste

1 cup pineapple chunks

8 salmon fillets, about 3 oz each

steamed rice, to serve

For the spice paste

2 garlic cloves

4 dried red chiles

1 teaspoon sea salt

1 teaspoon ground turmeric

1½ inch length of trimmed lemon
grass stalk, finely chopped

3 tablespoons shrimp paste

- To make the spice paste, put all the ingredients in a food processor or blender and combine, adding a little water, if needed.

- Transfer the paste to a large saucepan and stir in the fish sauce, sugar, lemon grass stalks, and 1¾ cups of the measured water. Bring to a boil, then reduce the heat slightly and simmer, uncovered, for 8–10 minutes.

- Mix together the lemon juice, tamarind paste, and remaining water in a small bowl, then add to the pan with the pineapple and stir to mix well. Add the salmon and simmer gently for 8–10 minutes or until the fish is cooked through.

- Spoon into warm bowls and serve with steamed rice.

 Broiled Hot, Sweet, and Sour Salmon

Mix together 1 teaspoon lemon grass paste, 1 teaspoon hot chili sauce, 1 teaspoon tamarind paste, and 2 teaspoons sweet chili sauce in a bowl, then spread the mixture over 4 large salmon fillets. Cook under a preheated hot broiler for 5–6 minutes or until just cooked through. Serve immediately with salad.

 Hot and Sour Fish Soup

Heat 1 tablespoon sunflower oil in a heavy saucepan, add 8 finely sliced scallions and 1 chopped garlic clove, then cook, stirring, for 1–2 minutes. Stir in 1 teaspoon medium curry powder, 1 teaspoon red chili paste, 1 teaspoon lemon grass paste, and 1 teaspoon tamarind paste and cook for an additional 30 seconds. Pour in 2½ cups hot fish stock and 1 (14 fl oz) can coconut milk and bring to a boil, then cook, stirring, for 4–5 minutes. Add 12 oz skinless salmon fillets, boned and cubed, and cook gently for 5–6 minutes or until the fish is just cooked through. Serve immediately.

30 Mustard and Curry Leaf Halibut

Serves 4

1 teaspoon ground turmeric
1 tablespoon chili powder
2 tablespoons grated fresh coconut
¼ cup vegetable oil
1 teaspoon black mustard seeds
20 fresh curry leaves
2 onions, thinly sliced
4 green chiles, seeded and sliced
1 inch piece of fresh ginger root,
   peeled and cut into matchsticks
6 garlic cloves, finely chopped
2¼ lb skinless halibut fillets, boned
   and cut into bite-size pieces
1¾ cups can coconut milk
1¼ cups water
1 tablespoon tamarind paste
salt
steamed long-grain rice, to serve

- Mix together the turmeric, chili powder, and coconut in a small bowl and set aside.

- Heat the oil in a large wok or heavy saucepan until hot, then add the mustard seeds and cook over medium-high heat for a few minutes, until the seeds begin to pop, then add the curry leaves, onions, green chiles, ginger, and garlic and stir-fry for about 5 minutes, until fragrant.

- Stir in the turmeric mixture and stir-fry for an additional 1 minute. Add the fish, then stir in the coconut milk and measured water. Finally, add the tamarind paste. Bring to a boil, then reduce the heat to low and simmer gently, uncovered, for 15 minutes or until the fish is cooked through. Season well with salt.

- Ladle into warm bowls and serve with steamed long-grain rice, if desired.

 Pan-Fried Fish with Mustard and Curry Leaves Mix together 2 tablespoons whole-grain mustard, 6 crushed dried curry leaves, 1 teaspoon chili powder, and 1 teaspoon curry powder in a bowl. Season with salt, then spread the mixture all over 4 skinless flounder fillets. Heat 2 tablespoons sunflower oil in a large skillet and cook the fish fillets for 2–3 minutes on each side or until cooked through. Serve with a green salad.

 Baked Mustard and Curry Leaf Fish Mix together 1 tablespoon curry paste, ¼ cup coconut milk, 2 tablespoons whole-grain mustard, and the juice of 1 lemon in a bowl, then spread the mixture all over 4 thick, skinless halibut fillets. Arrange in a shallow, ovenproof dish in a single layer, sprinkle with 10–12 fresh curry leaves, and season. Place in a preheated oven, at 425°F, for 12–15 minutes or until the fish is cooked through. Serve with steamed vegetables and rice.

20 Shrimp, Lemon Grass, and Mango Curry

Serves 4

2 tablespoons vegetable oil
2 garlic cloves, finely chopped
2 shallots, thinly sliced
1 carrot, peeled and cut into thin matchsticks
3 inch length of trimmed lemon grass stalk, finely chopped
1 red chile, seeded and chopped
1 tablespoon hot curry powder
1¼ cups canned coconut milk
1 cup water
1 tablespoon Thai fish sauce
2¼ lb raw jumbo shrimp, peeled and deveined, with tails left on
2 cups ¾ inch mango cubes
Thai basil leaves, to garnish
steamed jasmine rice, to serve

- Heat the oil in a heavy saucepan, add the garlic, shallots, and carrot, and cook over medium heat, stirring occasionally, for 1–2 minutes, until softened. Add the lemon grass, red chile, and curry powder and cook for an additional 3 minutes or until fragrant.

- Pour in the coconut milk, measured water, and fish sauce and bring to a simmer. Cook for 5 minutes, then reduce the heat to medium-low, stir in the shrimp and mango, and simmer gently, partly covered, for 5 minutes or until the shrimp turn pink and are cooked through.

- Ladle into warm bowls, sprinkle with Thai basil leaves, and serve with steamed jasmine rice.

---

1 Shrimp, Lemon Grass, and Mango Stir-Fry Heat 2 tablespoons sunflower oil in a large wok until hot, add 2 chopped shallots, 2 seeded and chopped red chiles, 2 chopped garlic cloves, and a 3 inch length of trimmed lemon grass stalk, finely chopped, and stir-fry over high heat for 1 minute. Add 1 tablespoon hot curry powder, 1¼ lb cooked, peeled shrimp, and the diced flesh of 1 ripe mango and stir-fry for another 3–4 minutes or until piping hot. Serve with noodles.

3 Shrimp, Lemon Grass, and Mango Rice Heat 2 tablespoons sunflower oil in a heavy saucepan, add 2 teaspoons cumin seeds, 2 cloves, 1 cinnamon stick, 2 chopped shallots, 2 seeded and chopped red chiles, and 2 chopped garlic cloves, and cook, stirring, for 2–3 minutes. Add 1 tablespoon hot curry powder, 2½ cups long-grain rice, and 1 tablespoon lemon grass paste and stir until the rice is well coated, then pour in 3½ cups hot vegetable stock and bring to a boil. Add 1 lb raw, peeled jumbo shrimp and the diced flesh of 1 ripe mango. Cover tightly, reduce the heat to low, and cook, undisturbed, for 15–20 minutes or until the liquid is absorbed, the rice is tender and the shrimp are cooked through. Remove from the heat and let stand in the pan for a few minutes before serving.

3⊙ Scallop Molee

Serves 4

1 onion, coarsely grated
4 garlic cloves, crushed
2 green chiles, seeded and
  finely chopped
1 tablespoon ground cumin
1 teaspoon ground coriander
1 teaspoon ground turmeric
¾ cup cilantro leaves, finely
  chopped, plus extra to garnish
1 cup water
2 tablespoons sunflower oil
6 fresh curry leaves, plus extra
  to garnish
1¾ cups can coconut milk
1½ lb large scallops, cleaned
salt and pepper
steamed long-grain rice, to serve

- Put the onion, garlic, green chiles, ground spices, chopped cilantro, and measured water in a food processor or blender and blend until smooth.

- Heat the oil in a large, heavy skillet, add the curry leaves, and cook, stirring, for 20–30 seconds, then add the blended mixture, stir, and cook over high heat for 3–4 minutes. Reduce the heat to low, pour in the coconut milk, and simmer gently, uncovered, for 12–15 minutes.

- Add the scallops to the skillet, bring back to a boil, then reduce the heat to low and simmer gently for 2–3 minutes or until the scallops are just cooked through. Season well.

- Spoon into warm bowls, sprinkle with a few curry and cilantro leaves, and serve with steamed long-grain rice.

1⊙ Pan-Fried Scallops with Chile, Cilantro, and Coconut

Heat 2 tablespoons sunflower oil in a large skillet, add 1½ lb cleaned, large scallops, and cook over high heat for 1 minute on each side. Transfer to warm serving plates, season, and sprinkle with 1 seeded and finely chopped red chile and a large handful of chopped cilantro. Drizzle ¼ cup coconut milk over the scallops and serve.

2⊙ Scallop, Chile, and Coconut Pasta

Cook 12 oz dried linguine in a large saucepan of salted, boiling water according to the package directions until al dente. Meanwhile, heat 2 tablespoons sunflower oil in a large skillet, add 1 lb cleaned, large scallops in a single layer, and cook for 1 minute on each side. Transfer to a large dish and keep warm. Wipe out the skillet and add 1 tablespoon sunflower oil.

Stir in 1 seeded and chopped red chile and 2 chopped garlic cloves and cook, stirring, for 1–2 minutes. Remove the skillet from the heat and return the scallops to the skillet with ½ cup coconut milk and a handful of chopped cilantro leaves. Drain the pasta, then add to the scallop mixture. Toss to mix well, season, and serve.

Garlicky Chile and Tomato Shrimp

Serves 4

1¾ lb raw jumbo shrimp, peeled
and deveined, with tails left on

juice of 1 lime

1 teaspoon salt

2 tablespoons sunflower oil

1 onion, finely chopped

1 red chile, seeded and
finely chopped

4 garlic cloves, finely chopped

2 teaspoons sweet smoked
paprika

4 plum tomatoes, coarsely
chopped

2 teaspoons tomato paste

1 teaspoon sugar

chopped flat-leaf parsley,
to garnish

- Put the shrimp in a nonmetallic bowl and add the lime juice and salt. Set aside.

- Heat the oil in a large wok or skillet until hot, add the onion, red chile, and garlic, and stir-fry over high heat for 1–2 minutes. Add the paprika and tomatoes and stir-fry for an additional 1–2 minutes.

- Add the shrimp and their reserved juices to the wok and continue to stir-fry for 3–4 minutes or until the shrimp turn pink and are cooked through. Stir in the tomato paste and sugar and cook, stirring, for 1–2 minutes.

- Remove from the heat, sprinkle with chopped parsley, and serve.

Shrimp, Tomato, and Chile Salad

Put 1 lb cooked, peeled shrimp, the leaves from 2 heads Boston lettuce, and 3 cups halved cherry tomatoes in a large salad bowl. Mix together 1 seeded and finely chopped red chile, ⅓ cup extra-virgin olive oil, the juice of 1 lemon, 1 teaspoon honey, and 1 teaspoon Dijon mustard in a bowl, then season. Pour the dressing over the salad, toss to mix well, and serve.

Chile, Tomato, and Shrimp Gratin

Heat 1 tablespoon sunflower oil in a skillet, add 1 chopped onion, 4 chopped garlic cloves, and 1 seeded and sliced red chile, and cook over medium heat for 3–4 minutes, until softened. Add 1 (14½ oz) can diced tomatoes and cook over medium heat for 6–8 minutes or until thickened. Season, then spoon into a shallow, ovenproof dish. Spoon 1¾ lb raw, peeled jumbo shrimp over the tomato mixture, toss to mix well, and cook under a preheated medium-hot broiler for 5–6 minutes or until the shrimp turn pink and are cooked through. Sprinkle with chopped flat-leaf parsley and serve with crusty bread.

Sumac, Chile, and Lemon-Spiced Monkfish Kebabs

Serves 4

1¾ lb monkfish tail, cut into bite-size pieces

3 lemons

2 tablespoons extra-virgin olive oil

2 teaspoons sumac

3 teaspoons dried red pepper flakes

4 garlic cloves, finely chopped

1 red chile, seeded and finely chopped

½ cup finely chopped flat-leaf parsley

salt and pepper

arugula salad, to serve

- Put the fish in a large nonmetallic bowl. Finely grate 2 of the lemons and set aside the grated rind. Halve the grated lemons and squeeze the juice over the fish.

- Add the oil, sumac, and red pepper flakes to the fish mixture, season well with salt, and toss to coat evenly. Cover and let marinate until ready to cook.

- Mix together the reserved lemon rind, garlic, chopped red chile, and parsley in a bowl. Season well and set aside.

- Cut the remaining lemon into thin slices. Thread the monkfish onto 8 long, metal skewers, alternating with the lemon slices. Cook under a preheated hot broiler for 4–5 minutes on each side or until the fish is cooked through.

- Transfer the kebabs to 4 serving plates, sprinkle with the lemon rind mixture, and serve with an arugula salad.

 Sumac and Chile Fish Rolls with Lemon Mayo Poach 1 lb skinless cod fillets in a saucepan of simmering water for about 4–5 minutes or until cooked through. Meanwhile, halve 4 warm rolls and thickly spread each half with store-bought lemon mayonnaise. Lightly sprinkle each half with a little sumac and chili powder. Flake the poached fish with a fork, removing any bones, then divide among the roll bottoms. Spoon 1 tablespoon sweet chili sauce over each and top with the roll lids. Serve with fries and a salad.

 Sumac and Lemon Monkfish Stew Heat 2 tablespoons sunflower oil in a heavy saucepan, add 1 chopped onion, 2 chopped garlic cloves, 1 tablespoon mild curry powder, and 1 cinnamon stick, and cook over medium heat, stirring occasionally, for 3–4 minutes, until the onion is softened. Add 1¼ lb monkfish tail, thickly sliced, and cook for an additional 1–2 minutes. Stir in 2 cups hot fish stock and bring to a boil, then reduce the heat to low and simmer gently, uncovered, for 12–15 minutes. Add 2 tablespoons chopped preserved lemon, remove from the heat, and sprinkle 1 teaspoon sumac and a small handful of chopped flat-leaf parsley over the stew. Serve with couscous or steamed rice.

30 Yellow Fish, Potato, and Tomato Curry

Serves 4

2 tablespoons sunflower oil
1 onion, finely chopped
1 tablespoon ground turmeric
1 (14 fl oz) can coconut milk
1 cup water
2 Yukon gold or white round
   potatoes, peeled and cubed
1¾ lb thick skinless salmon fillets,
   boned and cut into chunks
2 tomatoes, coarsely chopped
salt
chopped cilantro, to garnish

For the spice paste

3 teaspoons garlic paste
1 teaspoon ginger paste
2 green chiles, seeded and chopped
2 teaspoons grated fresh ginger root

To serve

steamed rice
lime wedges
chopped red chile

- To make the spice paste, pound together all the ingredients using a small mortar and pestle until you have a smooth paste. Alternatively, process in a mini food processor.

- Heat the oil in a large wok or heavy saucepan until hot, add the spice paste, and stir-fry over medium heat for 30–40 seconds, then add the onion and turmeric and stir-fry for an additional 2–3 minutes, until fragrant.

- Pour in the coconut milk and measured water, then stir in the potatoes. Bring to a boil, then reduce the heat to low and simmer gently, uncovered, for 10–12 minutes, stirring occasionally.

- Season the fish with salt, then add to the wok with the tomatoes and bring back to a boil. Reduce the heat to medium-low and simmer gently for 6–8 minutes, until the fish is cooked through.

- Ladle into warm bowls, sprinkle with chopped cilantro, and serve with steamed rice, lime wedges, and chopped red chile.

---

10 Spicy Fish and Tomato Soup

Heat 1 tablespoon sunflower oil in a saucepan, add 1 tablespoon mild curry paste, and cook, stirring, for 20–30 seconds. Add 2 (15 oz) cans cream of tomato soup and bring to a boil, then reduce the heat to medium, stir in 12 oz flaked, cooked, smoked salmon fillets, bones removed, and cook for a few minutes or until piping hot. Serve with crusty bread.

20 Spicy Yellow Fish and Tomato Rice

Poach 3 skinless salmon fillets in a saucepan of simmering water for 4–5 minutes, until cooked through, then flake into large pieces, removing any bones. Meanwhile, heat 1 tablespoon sunflower oil in a large skillet until hot, add 1 chopped onion, and stir-fry over high heat, stirring occasionally, for 3–4 minutes, until softened. Add 1 teaspoon cumin seeds, ½ teaspoon ground turmeric, 2 teaspoons hot curry powder, 1 teaspoon ginger paste, and 1 teaspoon garlic paste and stir-fry for another 2–3 minutes, then add 3½ cups cooked long-grain rice and ½ cup canned coconut milk. Stir, then cook for 6–8 minutes or until piping hot and the liquid is almost absorbed. Add the poached salmon with 2 diced plum tomatoes, toss to mix well, season, and serve.

30 Turmeric Mackerel Skewers with Chile Rice Noodles

Serves 4

4 large boned mackerel fillets, about 7 oz each, trimmed and cleaned
½ teaspoon ground turmeric
1 tablespoon mild curry paste
juice of 2 lemons
1 tablespoon sunflower oil
salt and pepper

For the noodles

8 oz dried rice noodles
1 tablespoon vegetable oil
1 red chile, seeded and finely sliced
6 scallions, finely shredded
¼ cup coarsely chopped mint, plus extra to garnish
¼ cup coarsely chopped cilantro leaves
3 tablespoons chile-roasted peanuts, coarsely chopped

- Put the fish fillets in a large, nonmetallic shallow dish. Mix together the turmeric, curry paste, lemon juice, and sunflower oil and pour over the fish. Season, then toss to mix well and set aside.

- Put the rice noodles in a heatproof bowl and pour over enough boiling water to cover. Let soak for 3–4 minutes, then drain and refresh under cold running water. Drain again and set aside.

- Thread 2 metal skewers through each fish fillet to keep them flattened while they cook, then place under a preheated medium-high broiler for 6–8 minutes or until just cooked through.

- Meanwhile, heat the vegetable oil in a large wok or skillet until hot, add the chile, scallions, and drained noodles, and stir-fry over high heat for 2–3 minutes or until piping hot, then stir in the mint and cilantro and season.

- Divide the noodles among warm serving plates or shallow bowls. Top each with the broiled fish and sprinkle with the chopped chile-roasted peanuts. Sprinkle with extra chopped mint and serve immediately.

 Mackerel and Rice Noodle Stir-Fry

Prepare 1¼ lb rice noodles according to package directions. Heat 2 tablespoons sunflower oil in a wok or skillet, add the noodles and ½ cup sweet chile stir-fry sauce. Stir-fry for 3-4 minutes or until piping hot. Remove from the heat and flake in 4 smoked mackerel fillets and 6 sliced scallions. Toss to mix well and serve immediately.

 Turmeric Mackerel Curry

Heat 1 tablespoon sunflower oil in a large saucepan, add 1 chopped onion, 1 teaspoon turmeric, and 1 tablespoon mild curry powder, and cook, stirring, for 3–4 minutes, until softened. Add 1 teaspoon ginger paste and 1 teaspoon garlic paste and cook for an additional 30–40 seconds, then pour in 1 (14 fl oz) can coconut milk and ½ cup hot fish stock. Bring to a boil, then add 4 large, boned mackerel fillets, about 7 oz each, trimmed and cleaned, and cook over medium heat for 8–10 minutes or until the fish is cooked through. Season, then serve with long-grain rice.

QuickCook
Vegetarian

Recipes listed by cooking time

30

Eggplant, Tomato, and Chile Curry 180

Chile, Cherry Tomato, and Goat Cheese Tart 182

Creamy Beet, Green Bean, and Tomato Curry 184

Mango and Coconut Curry 186

Island-Spiced Corn with Avocado and Tomato 188

Sweet Potato and Litchi Curry 190

Moroccan Vegetable Stew with Couscous 192

Roasted Cumin Potato Wedges 194

Spicy Cabbage and Carrot Casserole 196

Spiced Carrot and Green Bean Stew 198

Spicy Mushroom, Cauliflower, and Chickpea Stew 200

Spinach, Tomato, and Paneer Curry 202

Carrot, Pea, and Potato Curry 204

Spiced Green bean and Chile Pilaf 206

Spicy Mushroom and Tomato Rice 208

Spiced Coconut and Okra Rice 210

Butternut Squash and Red Pepper Curry 212

Middle Eastern Zucchini, Tomato, and Mint Curry 214

Spiced Baby Eggplants with Chile and Herbs 216

Tomato, Coconut, and Okra Curry 218

Spicy Tofu and Scallion Stir-Fry 220

Spicy Cabbage and Red Pepper Stew 222

Spanish Potatoes with Spicy Tomatoes 224

Spicy Roast Thai Massaman Vegetables 226

20

Chile, Eggplant, and Tomato Sauté 180

Chile, Cherry Tomato, and Goat Cheese Pasta 182

Curried Beet, Green Bean, and Tomato Rice 184

Spicy Mango and Coconut Rice 186

Spicy Corn, Avocado, and Tomato Pasta 188

Spicy Sweet Potato and Litchi Noodles 190

Moroccan Kebabs 192

Cumin Potato Curry 194

Spicy Cabbage and Carrot Stir-Fry 196

Spicy Carrot and Green Bean Soup 198

Spicy Mushroom, Cauliflower, and Chickpea Rice 200

Spicy Spinach and Tomato Soup with Crème Fraîche 202

Spicy Pea, Carrot, and Potato Frittata 204

Chinese-Style Green Beans with Chile 206

Curried Mushrooms and Tomatoes 208

Indonesian Okra with Coconut   210

Curried Roasted Butternut Squash and Red Beppers   212

Grilled Spicy Zucchini with Tomato and Mint   214

Spiced Baby Aubergine Pilaff   216

Spiced Okra, Tomato, and Coconut   218

Spicy Tofu with Bok Choy and Scallions   220

Malaysian Red Pepper and Cabbage Stir-Fry   222

Spicy Warm Potato and Tomato Salad   224

Thai Massaman Butternut Squash Curry   226

Eggplant, Tomato, and Chile Salad   180

Chile, Cherry Tomato, and Goat Cheese Salad   182

Curried Beet, Green Bean, and Tomato Broth   184

Spiced Mango and Coconut Salad   186

Spicy Corn, Avocado, and Tomato Salad   188

Spicy Sweet Potato and Litchi Salad   190

Moroccan Couscous Salad   192

Cumin Potatoes with Pomegranate Seeds   194

Spiced Red Cabbage and Carrot Salad   196

Spiced Carrot and Green Bean Slaw   198

Spicy Mushroom and Chickpea Soup   200

Spicy Spinach, Tomato, and Cottage Cheese Salad   202

Spicy Pea, Carrot and Potato Stir-Fry   204

Green Bean, Chile, and Egg-Fried Rice   206

Spicy Mushroom and Tomato Stir-Fry   208

Spicy Coconut Soup with Deep-Fried Okra   210

Curried Butternut Squash and Red Pepper Soup   212

Spicy Zucchini, Tomato, and Mint Salad   214

Deep-Fried Spiced Baby Eggplant   216

Spicy Fried Okra with Coconut   218

Japanese-Style Tofu with Scallions   220

Spicy Cabbage and Red Pepper Salad   222

Spicy Potato and Tomato Stir-Fry   224

Thai Massaman Vegetable Stir-Fry   226

30 Eggplant, Tomato, and Chile Curry

Serves 4

2 large eggplants
½ cup vegetable oil
2 onions, thinly sliced
6 garlic cloves, finely chopped
3 teaspoons peeled and grated, finely chopped fresh ginger root
2 red chiles, seeded and thinly sliced
1¼ cups canned diced tomatoes
6 kaffir lime leaves
1 tablespoon kecap manis (thick soy sauce)
2 tablespoons dark soy sauce
1 teaspoon light brown sugar
juice of 1 lime
small handful of chopped cilantro leaves
2 tablespoons chopped roasted peanuts
steamed rice or rice noodles, to serve

- Cut the eggplants into finger-thick batons. Reserve 1 tablespoon of the oil, then heat the remaining oil in a large skillet, add the eggplants, and cook over medium heat, stirring occasionally, for 5–6 minutes or until lightly browned. Remove with a slotted spoon and drain on paper towels.

- Heat the reserved oil in the skillet, add the onions and garlic, and cook over medium heat, stirring occasionally, for 6–7 minutes, until softened and lightly browned. Add the ginger, red chiles, tomatoes, and lime leaves and cook for 2–3 minutes, stirring frequently. Return the eggplants to the skillet with a splash of water and simmer gently for 2–3 minutes.

- Remove from the heat and stir in the kecap manis, soy sauce, sugar, lime juice, and chopped cilantro.

- Spoon into warm bowls, sprinkle with the chopped peanuts, and serve with steamed rice or rice noodles.

---

1 Eggplant, Tomatom and Chile Salad

Drain 1 (10 oz) jar roasted eggplants in olive oil, reserving the oil, and put the eggplants in a salad bowl with 8 sliced plum tomatoes and a handful of arugula leaves. Mix ⅓ cup of the reserved oil, the juice of 2 lemons, and 1 teaspoon chili paste in a bowl, then season. Pour the dressing over the salad, toss to mix well, and serve with crusty bread.

2 Chile, Eggplant, and Tomato Sauté

Cut 2 eggplants into ¾ inch cubes. Heat 2 tablespoons sunflower oil in a large skillet, add the eggplants, and cook over medium heat, stirring occasionally, for 6–8 minutes or until lightly browned on all sides. Stir in 1 finely chopped onion, 2 chopped garlic cloves, 2 seeded and sliced red chiles, and 2 teaspoons cumin seeds and cook for an additional for 4–5 minutes. Add 4 chopped plum tomatoes, season, and heat through until piping hot. Serve with steamed rice or bread.

30 Chile, Cherry Tomato, and Goat Cheese Tart

Serves 4

1 sheet ready-to-bake
  puff pastry
flour, for dusting
½ cup red chile jelly
3 cups halved mixed red and
  yellow cherry tomatoes
8 oz soft goat cheese
¼ cup finely chopped mint leaves,
  to garnish
arugula salad, to serve (optional)

- Unroll the puff pastry onto a lightly floured surface and cut into a 12 x 8 inch rectangle. Using a sharp knife, score a border ¾ inch from the edge of the pastry. Put the pastry on a baking sheet and place in a preheated oven, at 425°F, for 10–12 minutes or until the pastry has risen and is cooked through and lightly golden. Cool for 5 minutes.

- Spoon the chile jelly evenly over the bottom of the puff pastry shell, then top with the tomatoes. Crumble the goat cheese over the filling, then return the filled tart to the oven for 6–8 minutes or until the cheese has melted and the tart has heated through.

- Sprinkle with the chopped mint and serve with an arugula salad, if desired.

---

10 Chile, Cherry Tomato, and Goat Cheese Salad

Halve 3½ cups mixed red and yellow cherry tomatoes and put in a large serving dish, then crumble 8 oz soft goat cheese over the tomatoes. Mix together ⅓ cup extra-virgin olive oil, 1 seeded and finely chopped red chile, 3 tablespoons red wine vinegar, 1 teaspoon honey, and 1 teaspoon Dijon mustard in a bowl, then season. Drizzle the dressing over the tomato and goat cheese. Sprinkle with a small handful of mint leaves and serve.

20 Chile, Cherry Tomato, and Goat Cheese Pasta

Cook 12 oz dried penne in a saucepan of salted, boiling water according to the package directions until al dente. Meanwhile, heat ¼ cup olive oil in a large skillet, add 2 finely chopped shallots, and cook over medium heat, stirring occasionally, for 6–8 minutes, until softened. Add 3 chopped garlic cloves, 1 seeded and finely chopped red chile, and 2 cups halved, mixed red and yellow cherry tomatoes and cook, stirring, for an additional 2–3 minutes. Drain the pasta, then add to the skillet with 8 oz crumbled, soft goat cheese and season. Serve immediately.

30 Creamy Beet, Green Bean, and Tomato Curry

Serves 4

2 tablespoons sunflower oil

1 teaspoon black mustard seeds

1 onion, chopped

2 garlic cloves, chopped

2 red chiles, seeded and
  finely chopped

10–12 fresh curry leaves

1 teaspoon ground turmeric

1 teaspoon cumin seeds

1 cinnamon stick

5 raw beets, peeled and
  cut into matchsticks

2 cups trimmed green beans

6 plum tomatoes, chopped

1 cup water

½ cup canned coconut milk

juice of 1 lime

salt and pepper

chopped cilantro, to garnish

- Heat the oil in a large, heavy saucepan until hot, then add the mustard seeds and cook over medium heat for a few minutes, until the seeds begin to pop, then add the onion, garlic, and red chiles and cook, stirring occasionally, for 5 minutes, until the onion is soft and translucent.

- Add the remaining spices, the beets, and green beans and cook for an additional 1–2 minutes. Stir in the tomatoes and measured water and simmer, uncovered, stirring occasionally, for 15–20 minutes or until the beets are tender.

- Pour in the coconut milk and simmer for an additional 1–2 minutes, then stir in the lime juice and season. Ladle into warm bowls, sprinkle with chopped cilantro, and serve.

---

10 Curried Beet, Green Bean, and Tomato Broth

Put 1 (14½ oz) can sliced beets in a blender and process until fairly chunky. Transfer to a saucepan and stir in 1¼ cups canned coconut milk, 3 cups tomato soup, 2 cups finely chopped green beans, and 2 teaspoons mild curry paste. Bring to a boil, then reduce the heat to medium and cook for 3–4 minutes or until piping hot. Sprinkle with 3 cups croutons and serve.

20 Curried Beet, Green Bean, and Tomato Rice

Heat 1 tablespoon butter and 1 tablespoon olive oil in a large skillet, add 1 chopped red onion, 1 (14½ oz) can sliced beets, 3 cups finely sliced, trimmed green beans, and 1 tablespoon medium or hot curry powder, and cook, stirring, for 2–3 minutes, until softened. Add 1 (14½ oz) can diced tomatoes and bring to a boil, then cook for 6–8 minutes or until slightly thickened. Stir in 3½ cups cooked long-grain rice and continue to cook for 5–6 minutes or until piping hot. Season, stir in ¼ cup crème fraîche or sour cream and serve at once.

30 Mango and Coconut Curry

Serves 4

4 firm ripe mangoes, peeled, pitted, and cut into bite-size pieces
1 teaspoon ground turmeric
1 teaspoon chili powder
1 cup water
1¼ cups plain yogurt, lightly whisked
¼ cup sunflower oil
2 teaspoons black mustard seeds
3–4 hot dried red chiles
10–12 fresh curry leaves
steamed rice, to serve (optional)

For the coconut paste

4½ cups grated fresh coconut
3–4 green chiles, seeded and coarsely chopped
1 tablespoon cumin seeds
1 cup water

- To make the coconut paste, put all the ingredients in a food processor or blender and blend to a fine paste.

- Put the mangoes in a heavy saucepan, add the turmeric, chili powder, and measured water, and bring to a boil, then remove from the heat.

- Add the coconut paste to the mango mixture. Stir to mix well, then cover, return to medium heat, and simmer for 10–12 minutes, stirring occasionally. Add the yogurt and heat gently, stirring continuously, until just warmed through (do not let the mixture boil or it will curdle). Remove from the heat and keep warm.

- Heat the oil in a small skillet until hot, then add the mustard seeds and cook over medium-high heat for a few minutes, until the seeds begin to pop, then add the dried chiles and curry leaves and stir-fry for a few seconds until the chiles darken. Pour the oil mixture into the mango curry and stir in gently.

- Ladle into warm bowls and serve with steamed rice, if desired.

 Spiced Mango and Coconut Salad

Slice 4 ripe, peeled, and pitted mangoes and arrange on a large serving plate. Sprinkle with 1 cup grated fresh coconut. Meanwhile, heat ⅓ cup sunflower oil in a small skillet until hot, add 2 teaspoons black mustard seeds, and cook over medium-high heat for a few minutes, until the seeds begin to pop, then add 1 teaspoon cumin seeds, 1 dried red chile, and 10 fresh curry leaves and stir-fry for a few seconds until the chile darkens. Remove from the heat and drizzle the oil over the mango and coconut. Toss to mix well and serve.

 Spicy Mango and Coconut Rice

Cook 2 cups long-grain rice in a large saucepan of lightly salted, boiling water for 10–12 minutes or until just tender. Drain well, then put in a large bowl. Peel, pit, and cut 2 mangoes into bite-size pieces, then stir into the rice with a large handful of chopped cilantro, 1 seeded and finely chopped red chile, and 1 cup grated fresh coconut. Season and serve warm or at room temperature.

30 Island-Spiced Corn with Avocado and Tomato

Serves 4

2 ears of corn

3 tablespoons sunflower oil

1 red bell pepper, halved lengthwise, cored and seeded

1 avocado

½ Scotch bonnet chile or hot red chile, seeded and finely chopped

6 plum tomatoes, coarsely chopped

1 small bunch of cilantro leaves, coarsely chopped

juice of 2 limes

½ cup extra-virgin olive oil

salt and pepper

warm flatbreads, to serve

- Blanch the ears of corn in a large saucepan of boiling water for 30–45 seconds. Drain, then brush with the sunflower oil and cook under a broiler preheated to its highest setting for 4–5 minutes, turning frequently, until beginning to char at the edges. Using a sharp knife, cut the kernels from the cobs and put in a large bowl.

- Meanwhile, cook the red bell pepper halves, skin-side up, under the preheated broiler for 6–8 minutes, until the skin begins to blister. Place in a plastic food bag, seal, and let stand for 5 minutes. When cool, peel away the blackened skin, then dice the flesh and add to the bowl of corn.

- Halve, peel, and pit the avocado, then dice the flesh. Stir into the corn mixture with the chile and tomatoes.

- In a separate bowl, mix together the cilantro, lime juice, and olive oil, then season and mix well. Pour the dressing over the corn mixture and toss through gently. Serve with warm flatbreads.

 Spicy Corn, Avocado, and Tomato Salad Put 1 (11 oz) can corn kernels, drained, into a large salad bowl, then add 1 seeded and finely chopped red chile, 4 chopped tomatoes, and 2 peeled, pitted, and diced avocados. Pour over ⅔ cup Thai ginger and chile salad dressing. Season, toss to mix well, and serve.

 Spicy Corn, Avocado, and Tomato Pasta Cook 12 oz dried penne in a large saucepan of salted, boiling water according to the package directions until al dente. Meanwhile, heat 2 tablespoons olive oil in a large saucepan, add 1 chopped garlic clove, 1 seeded and finely chopped red chile, and 6 sliced scallions, and cook over medium heat, stirring, for 2–3 minutes. Stir in 3 diced plum tomatoes and 1 (11 oz) can corn kernels, drained, and cook for an additional 6–8 minutes or until piping hot. Drain the pasta, then add to the corn with 2 peeled, pitted and diced avocados. Season, toss to mix well, and serve sprinkled with chopped cilantro.

HOT-VEGE-KUS

30 Sweet Potato and Litchi Curry

Serves 4

2 cups jasmine rice, rinsed

1 tablespoon sunflower oil

3 tablespoons Thai red curry paste

1 teaspoon peeled and finely
   grated fresh ginger root

finely grated rind of 1 lime

1¾ cups hot vegetable stock

1 cup coconut milk

2½ cups drained canned litchis,
   the syrup reserved

2 sweet potatoes, peeled and cut
   into bite-size pieces

2 tablespoons Thai fish sauce

To garnish

4 kaffir lime leaves, finely
   shredded

1 red chile, seeded and finely
   sliced lengthwise

- Cook the rice in a large, heavy saucepan of lightly salted, boiling water, covered tightly, for 15–20 minutes or until just tender. Drain well and set aside.

- Meanwhile, heat the oil in a large wok or skillet until hot, add the curry paste, ginger, and lime rind, and stir-fry over medium heat for 1 minute or until fragrant.

- Pour over the stock and coconut milk, stir until well blended, and bring to a boil. Add the litchis and sweet potatoes, reduce the heat to medium, and simmer for 10–15 minutes or until the sweet potatoes are tender. Add ⅓ cup of the reserved litchi syrup and the fish sauce and stir through.

- Ladle into warm bowls and sprinkle with the lime leaves and thin strips of chile. Serve with the steamed jasmine rice.

 Spicy Sweet Potato and Litchi Salad

Put 2 cups cooked sweet potato cubes, 2½ cups drained, canned litchis, and 1 (4 oz) package mixed salad greens in a large salad bowl. Mix together ¼ cup light olive oil, ½ teaspoon Thai red curry paste, ⅓ cup coconut milk, 1 teaspoon grated jaggery or granulated sugar, and the juice of 1 lime in a small bowl, then season. Pour the dressing over the salad, toss to mix well, and serve.

 Spicy Sweet Potato and Litchi Noodles

Prepare 12 oz egg noodles according to the package directions and set aside. Meanwhile, heat 2 tablespoons sunflower oil in a large wok or skillet until hot, add 2 tablespoons Thai red curry paste, 2 cups peeled and finely diced sweet potatoes, and 8 sliced scallions, and stir-fry over high heat for 1–2 minutes, then add 1¼ cups hot vegetable stock and bring to a boil. Reduce the heat to medium and cook for 8–10 minutes or until the sweet potatoes are tender. Stir in ½ cup coconut milk and the prepared egg noodles and bring back to a boil. Add 2½ cups drained, canned litchis and cook gently for 3–4 minutes or until piping hot. Season well, then serve.

30 Moroccan Vegetable Stew with Couscous

Serves 4

1 cup couscous
2½ cups boiling water
2 tablespoons sunflower oil
1 large onion, finely chopped
2 garlic cloves, minced
1 teaspoon grated fresh ginger root
2 teaspoons ground cumin
1 teaspoon ground coriander
2 teaspoon ground cinnamon
1 teaspoon ground turmeric
2 teaspoons dried red pepper flakes
1 tablespoon harissa paste
1 (14½ oz) can diced tomatoes
1 cup hot vegetable stock
2 red bell peppers, cored, seeded, and cut into bite-size pieces
1½ lb butternut squash, peeled, seeded, and cubed
⅔ cup golden raisins
salt and pepper
chopped cilantro, to garnish

- Put the couscous in a large heatproof bowl and season with salt. Pour over the measured water, cover with plastic wrap, and let stand for 10 minutes, or according to the package directions, until the water is absorbed. Gently fork to separate the grains, then set aside and keep warm.

- Meanwhile, heat the oil in a large skillet, add the onion, and cook over medium heat, stirring occasionally, for 2–3 minutes, until softened. Add the garlic, ginger, ground spices, red pepper flakes, harissa, tomatoes, and stock and bring to a boil, then reduce the heat to low, cover, and simmer gently for 10–12 minutes.

- Stir in the red bell peppers, squash, and raisins, replace the lid, and increase the heat to medium. Simmer for 10–15 minutes or until the vegetables are tender, then season to taste.

- Spoon the couscous into warm bowls, then ladle over the stew and serve sprinkled with chopped cilantro.

 **Moroccan Couscous Salad**
Put 1¼ cups couscous in a large, heatproof bowl and pour over enough boiling water to just cover, then cover with plastic wrap and let stand for 6–8 minutes or until the water is absorbed. Meanwhile, put 1 (12 oz) jar roasted peppers, drained and chopped, 1 finely chopped red onion, and a large handful each of chopped mint and cilantro leaves in a large salad bowl. Mix together 2 teaspoons harissa paste, ¼ cup extra-virgin olive oil, and the juice of 1 lemon in a small bowl, then season. Gently fork the couscous to separate the grains and add to the salad bowl. Stir the dressing into the couscous mixture, toss to mix, well and serve.

Moroccan Kebabs
Cut 2 zucchini, 2 cored and seeded red bell peppers, and 1 eggplant into chunks and put in a large bowl. Mix together ½ cup olive oil, 1 tablespoon harissa paste, the juice of 2 lemons, and a small handful of chopped cilantro, pour over the vegetables, and toss. Thread the vegetables onto 12 metal skewers and season, then cook under a preheated medium broiler for 10–12 minutes, turning once. Serve with couscous.

Cumin Potatoes with Pomegranate Seeds

Serves 4

½ large pomegranate
¼ cup sunflower oil
1–2 teaspoons black mustard seeds
1 teaspoon hot chili powder
4 teaspoons cumin seeds
2 teaspoons sesame seeds
8–10 fresh curry leaves (optional)
2 teaspoons ground cumin
2 teaspoons ground coriander
1 teaspoon ground turmeric
2½ cups 1 inch cooked
  potato cubes
⅓ cup chopped cilantro leaves
juice of 1 small lemon
salt and pepper

- To remove the pomegranate seeds, place the pomegranate over a bowl, cut-side down, and hit with the back of a spoon, catching the seeds in the bowl. Set aside.

- Heat the oil in a large wok or skillet until hot, add the mustard seeds, and cook over medium-high heat for a few minutes, until the seeds begin to pop, then add the chili powder, cumin seeds, sesame seeds, and curry leaves, if using, and stir-fry for 30 seconds until fragrant.

- Add the ground spices and potatoes and season well, then increase the heat to high and stir-fry briskly for 4–5 minutes.

- Remove from the heat and stir in the chopped cilantro and pomegranate seeds. Stir in the lemon juice, then spoon into a warm serving dish and serve hot.

 Cumin Potato Curry

Heat 1 tablespoon sunflower oil in a heavy saucepan, add 1 chopped onion, and cook over high heat, stirring, for 1–2 minutes. Add 2 teaspoons cumin seeds, 1 teaspoon black mustard seeds, 2 teaspoons ground coriander, 1 teaspoon ground cumin, 1 teaspoon ground turmeric, 1 teaspoon ginger paste, and 1 teaspoon garlic paste and cook for an additional 1–2 minutes. Add 5 cups ½ inch peeled potato cubes, 4 chopped, ripe tomatoes, and 1¼ cups hot vegetable stock and bring to a boil. Season, then reduce the heat to medium and simmer for 12–15 minutes or until the potatoes are tender. Remove from the heat and stir in a small handful of chopped cilantro leaves. Serve with steamed rice or crusty bread.

 Roasted Cumin Potato Wedges

Cut 2¼ lb large baking potatoes into wedges and cook in a saucepan of boiling water for 6–8 minutes. Drain well, then place in a large bowl. Mix together 3 teaspoons cumin seeds, 1 teaspoon black mustard seeds, 2 teaspoons crushed coriander seeds, 1 tablespoon hot curry powder, and ⅓ cup sunflower oil, season with sea salt, then drizzle over the potatoes. Toss to mix well. Spread the potatoes in a single layer on a nonstick baking sheet and place in a preheated oven, at 425°F, for 20–25 minutes.

1 Spiced Red Cabbage and Carrot Salad

Serves 4

3 large carrots, peeled
½ small red cabbage, about
   8–10 oz
juice of 2 lemons
1 tablespoon sugar
1 tablespoon light olive oil
1 teaspoon nigella seeds (black
   onion seeds)
1 teaspoon crushed coriander
   seeds
1 green chile, seeded and
   finely chopped
salt

- Coarsely grate the carrots, or thinly shred using a mandolin, and put in a large salad bowl. Finely slice the red cabbage into thin shreds, add to the carrots, and toss together.

- Beat together the remaining ingredients in a small bowl, then season with salt. Pour the dressing over the vegetables, toss to mix well, and serve at room temperature.

2 Spicy Cabbage and Carrot Stir-Fry

Heat 2 tablespoons sunflower oil in a large wok, add 2 sliced red onions, and cook over medium-low heat, stirring occasionally, for 6–8 minutes, until softened. Increase the heat to high, stir in 2 chopped garlic cloves, 1 seeded and sliced green chile, 1 teaspoon cumin seeds, and 1 teaspoon medium or hot curry powder, and stir-fry for 1–2 minutes, then add 3 cups finely shredded red cabbage and 2 peeled and coarsely shredded carrots and stir-fry for an additional 6–8 minutes or until tender. Season, then serve with poppadums and yogurt.

3 Spicy Cabbage and Carrot Casserole

Cut 1 large red cabbage into 8 wedges and place in a deep casserole dish with 4 peeled and coarsely chopped carrots. Mix together 2 tablespoons sunflower oil, 2 finely chopped garlic cloves, 1 teaspoon peeled and grated fresh ginger root, 1 seeded and finely diced green chile, 1 tablespoon medium or hot curry powder, and 3 tablespoons sherry vinegar in a small bowl, then season. Pour the mixture over the vegetables and toss to coat evenly. Cover the casserole dish with the lid and place in a preheated oven, at 400°F, for 20–25 minutes or until tender. Serve immediately with brown rice or crusty bread.

30 Spiced Carrot and Green Bean Stew

Serves 4

1 tablespoon sunflower oil
1 onion, sliced
1–2 hot green chiles, seeded and
  sliced
1 garlic clove, crushed
5–6 fresh curry leaves
1 tablespoon medium curry powder
¼ teaspoon ground turmeric
½ teaspoon fenugreek seeds
2 carrots, peeled and cut into
  thin matchsticks
4½ cups trimmed and halved
  green beans
1 (14 fl oz) can coconut milk
juice of 1 lime
salt and pepper
steamed rice or bread, to serve

- Heat the oil in a heavy saucepan, add the onion, chiles, garlic, and curry leaves, and cook over medium heat, stirring occasionally, for 6–8 minutes, until the onion is softened and golden brown. Sprinkle with the curry powder, turmeric, and fenugreek seeds and season well.

- Add the carrots and green beans and cook, stirring, for an additional 3–4 minutes. Reduce the heat to low, pour the coconut milk over the vegetables, and simmer for 10–12 minutes or until the vegetables are tender.

- Remove from the heat and stir in the lime juice. Ladle into warm bowls and serve with steamed rice or bread, if desired.

---

 1 Spiced Carrot and Green Bean Slaw

Cook 3 cups halved, trimmed green beans in a saucepan of salted, boiling water for 2–3 minutes, until just tender. Drain and put in a salad bowl with 3 shredded, peeled carrots. Heat ¼ cup olive oil in a skillet, add 2 teaspoons black mustard seeds, 2 teaspoons cumin seeds, 1 seeded and chopped red chile, 1 teaspoon coriander seeds, and 6–8 fresh curry leaves. Cook over medium heat until the mustard seeds start to pop, then pour the oil mixture over the vegetables. Season and toss to mix well.

 2 Spicy Carrot and Green Bean Soup

Heat 1 tablespoon butter and 1 tablespoon sunflower oil in a heavy saucepan, add 1 finely chopped onion, 1 chopped garlic clove, 1 teaspoon peeled and grated fresh ginger root, and 1 tablespoon mild curry powder, and cook, stirring, for 1–2 minutes. Stir in 3 peeled and finely chopped carrots, 2 cups finely chopped, trimmed green beans, and 3½ cups hot vegetable stock and bring to a boil, then reduce the heat to medium and cook for 12–15 minutes or until the vegetables are tender. Remove from the heat and, using an electric immersion blender, process the soup until smooth. Season, then stir in 1 cup light cream. Serve with crusty bread.

Spicy Mushroom, Cauliflower, and Chickpea Stew

Serves 4

2 tablespoons sunflower oil

8 scallions, cut into 2 inch lengths

2 teaspoons grated garlic

2 teaspoons ground ginger

2 tablespoons hot curry powder

3 cups baby white button
  mushrooms

2 cups cauliflower florets

2 red bell peppers, halved
  lengthwise, seeded, and
  cut into chunks

1 (14½ oz) can diced tomatoes

1 cup rinsed and drained canned
  chickpeas (garbanzo beans)

3–4 tablespoons plain yogurt

salt and pepper

large handful of chopped mint
  leaves, to garnish

warm naan or steamed rice,
  to serve

- Heat the oil in a large skillet, add the scallions, and cook over medium heat for 1–2 minutes. Add the garlic, ground ginger, and curry powder and cook, stirring, for 20–30 seconds, until fragrant, then stir in the mushrooms, cauliflower, and red bell peppers and cook for an additional 2–3 minutes.

- Stir in the tomatoes and bring to a boil. Cover, then reduce the heat to medium and simmer, uncovered, for 10–15 minutes, stirring occasionally. Add the chickpeas, season, and bring back to a boil.

- Spoon into warm bowls, drizzle with the yogurt, and sprinkle with chopped mint. Serve with warm naan or steamed rice.

Spicy Mushroom and Chickpea Soup
Heat 1 tablespoon butter in a saucepan, add 2 sliced scallions and 1 tablespoon mild curry powder, and cook, stirring, for 30 seconds. Add 2 (15 oz) cans cream of mushroom soup and 1 cup rinsed and drained canned chickpeas (garbanzo beans) and bring to a boil, then reduce the heat to medium and cook for a few minutes or until piping hot. Serve with warm crusty bread.

 Spicy Mushroom, Cauliflower, and Chickpea Rice Heat 2 tablespoons sunflower oil in a large wok or skillet until hot, add 1 chopped onion, 1 seeded and chopped red chile, 1½ cups white button mushrooms, 1 tablespoon curry powder, ¾ cup small cauliflower florets, ½ cup rinsed and drained canned chickpeas (garbanzo beans), 1 teaspoon ginger paste, and 1 teaspoon garlic paste, and stir-fry over high heat for 6–8 minutes. Add 3½ cups cooked long-grain rice and stir-fry for an additional 3–4 minutes or until piping hot. Season, then serve immediately.

30 Spinach, Tomato, and Paneer Curry

Serves 4

1 lb spinach leaves

3 tablespoons unsalted butter

2 teaspoons cumin seeds

1 red chile, seeded and finely chopped

1 onion, minced

2 plum tomatoes, finely chopped

2 teaspoons finely grated garlic

1 tablespoon peeled and finely grated fresh ginger root

1 teaspoon chili powder

1 teaspoon ground coriander

8 oz paneer (Indian cottage cheese), cut into bite-size pieces

2 tablespoons heavy cream

1 teaspoon lemon juice

2 tablespoons finely chopped cilantro leaves

salt and pepper

flatbreads, to serve (optional)

- Cook the spinach in a large saucepan of boiling water for 2–3 minutes, then drain well. Transfer to a food processor or blender and blend to a smooth puree.

- Heat the butter in a large wok or skillet, add the cumin seeds, red chile, and onion, and stir-fry over medium-low heat for 6–8 minutes, until the onions have softened. Add the tomatoes, garlic, ginger, chili powder, and ground coriander and season well. Stir through and cook for 2–3 minutes.

- Increase the heat to high, add the paneer, and stir-fry for 1–2 minutes, then add the spinach puree and stir-fry for an additional 4–5 minutes, until well mixed and heated through.

- Remove from the heat and stir in the cream, lemon juice, and chopped cilantro. Spoon into warm bowls and serve with warm flatbreads, if desired.

 Spicy Spinach, Tomato and Cottage Cheese Salad Put 3 cups baby spinach leaves and 3 cups halved cherry tomatoes in a salad bowl. Mix together 1¾ cups cottage cheese, 1 teaspoon ginger paste, 1 teaspoon garlic paste, 1 teaspoon chili paste, and 2 teaspoons toasted cumin seeds in a bowl, then season. Add to the spinach and tomatoes, toss gently to mix, and serve with crusty bread or warm baguettes.

 Spicy Spinach and Tomato Soup with Crème Fraîche Heat 1 tablespoon butter and 1 tablespoon olive oil in a large, heavy saucepan, add 1 chopped red onion, 3 chopped garlic cloves, 1 teaspoon peeled and grated fresh ginger root, 1 seeded and sliced red chile, 2 teaspoons cumin seeds, and 2 teaspoons mild curry powder, and cook, stirring, for 2–3 minutes. Stir in 6 chopped plum tomatoes and 3 cups hot vegetable stock and bring to a boil, then cook, uncovered, over high heat for 6–8 minutes. Add 2 cups chopped spinach leaves and bring back to a boil. Remove from the heat and, using an electric immersion blender, process until smooth. Season, ladle into bowls, and serve with spoonfuls of crème fraîche or sour cream.

30 Carrot, Pea, and Potato Curry

Serves 4

2 teaspoons vegetable oil
3 whole cloves
2 cinnamon sticks
2 teaspoons white poppy seeds
2 teaspoons black peppercorns
4 dried red chiles
1 cup unsweetened dry coconut, lightly toasted
4 garlic cloves, coarsely chopped
2 onions, coarsely chopped
4 teaspoons sunflower oil
2 white round potatoes, peeled and chopped into 1 inch cubes
2 large carrots, peeled and chopped into 1 inch cubes
1 (14½ oz) can diced tomatoes
1½ cups frozen peas
salt
mini naans, to serve

- To make the spice paste, heat the vegetable oil in a small skillet over medium heat, add the cloves, cinnamon sticks, poppy seeds, peppercorns, and dried chiles and cook for 1–2 minutes, until fragrant. Put in a food processor or blender with the coconut, garlic, and onions and process to a coarse paste.

- Heat the sunflower oil in a heavy saucepan, add the potatoes and carrots, then cover and cook over medium heat for 2 minutes. Stir in the spice paste and chopped tomatoes and season with salt.

- Stir, replace the lid, and simmer for 15–20 minutes or until the potatoes and carrots are tender, adding the peas 5 minutes before the end of the cooking time.

- Spoon into warm bowls and serve with mini naans.

10 Spicy Pea, Carrot, and Potato Stir-Fry

Heat 2 tablespoons olive oil in a hot wok, add 2 teaspoons black mustard seeds, and cook over high heat until the seeds pop. Add 2 teaspoons cumin seeds, 1 teaspoon ground cumin, 1 teaspoon ground coriander, 2 teaspoons hot chili powder, 1 (14½ oz) can new potatoes, drained and diced, 1 (15 oz) can baby carrots, drained and diced, and 2 cups frozen peas. Stir-fry over high heat for 4–5 minutes. Squeeze the juice of 1 lemon over the vegetables, and serve.

20 Spicy Pea, Carrot, and Potato Frittata

Heat 2 tablespoons sunflower oil in medium ovenproof skillet, add 1 chopped onion, 2 teaspoons cumin seeds, 1 tablespoon hot curry powder, 1 (14½ oz) can new potatoes, drained and diced, ½ (15 oz) can baby carrots, drained and diced, and 1½ cups fresh or frozen peas, and cook over high heat, stirring, for 3–4 minutes. Lightly beat 6 eggs in a bowl, then season and pour into the skillet. Cook for 8–10 minutes or until the bottom is set, then place the skillet under a preheated medium-hot broiler and cook for 3–4 minutes or until the top is golden and set. Serve immediately with a crisp green salad.

Chinese-Style Green Beans with Chile

Serves 4

6 cups trimmed ¾ inch green
  beans pieces (about 1¼ lb)
3 tablespoons sunflower oil
1 teaspoon ground turmeric
salt
egg-fried rice, to serve (optional)

For the chili paste

2 red chiles, seeded and
  coarsely chopped
4 shallots, coarsely chopped
2 garlic cloves, finely chopped
2 teaspoons peeled and grated
  fresh ginger root
¼ cup light soy sauce

- Cook the beans in a large saucepan of lightly salted, boiling water for 3–4 minutes or until tender. Drain well, then set aside.

- To make the chili paste, put all the ingredients in a food processor or blender and blend to a smooth paste, adding a little water to loosen the mixture, if needed.

- Heat the oil in a large wok or skillet until hot, stir in the chili paste, and stir-fry over medium heat for 2–3 minutes, until fragrant. Add the drained beans and the turmeric, season with salt, and stir-fry for an additional 2–3 minutes or until piping hot. Serve immediately with egg-fried rice, if desired.

 Green Bean, Chile, and Egg-Fried Rice

Heat 2 tablespoons sunflower oil in a large wok or skillet until hot, add 3 cups finely sliced green beans, and stir-fry over high heat for 1–2 minutes. Add 3½ cups cooked egg-fried rice, 1 tablespoon hot chili sauce, 2 tablespoons sweet chili sauce, and 2 tablespoons light soy sauce and stir-fry for an additional 3–4 minutes or until piping hot. Serve immediately.

 Spiced Green Bean and Chile Pilaf

Heat 2 tablespoons sunflower oil in a heavy saucepan, add 6 chopped shallots, and cook over medium heat for 3–4 minutes, stirring ccasionally, until softened. Stir in 2 teaspoons cumin seeds, 1 cinnamon stick, 1 bay leaf, 6 green cardamom pods, 10 peppercorns, 4 cloves, and 4 dried red chiles and cook, stirring, for an additional 1–2 minutes. Add 2 cups long-grain rice and 4 cups sliced green beans and stir until well coated, then pour in 3½ cups hot vegetable stock and bring to a boil. Cover tightly, reduce the heat to low, and cook, undisturbed, for 15–20 minutes or until the liquid is absorbed and the rice is tender. Remove from the heat and let stand for a few minutes before serving with pickles and poppadums.

Curried Mushrooms and Tomatoes

Serves 4

⅓ cup sunflower oil
8 cups thickly sliced cremini
  mushrooms (about 1 lb)
½ cup heavy cream
2 ripe plum tomatoes,
  finely chopped
⅓ cup finely chopped
  cilantro leaves
salt and pepper
steamed rice, to serve

For the spice paste

4 garlic cloves, finely chopped
2 teaspoons peeled and finely
  chopped fresh ginger root
1 onion, finely chopped
1 tablespoon medium or hot
  curry powder
3 tablespoons water

- To make the spice paste, put all the ingredients in a food processor or blender and blend until smooth.

- Heat 3 tablespoons of the oil in a large wok until hot, add the mushrooms, and stir-fry over high heat for 4–5 minutes. Transfer the contents of the wok to a bowl and wipe out the wok with paper towels.

- Heat the remaining oil in the wok until hot, add the curry paste, and stir-fry over medium heat for 3–4 minutes. Return the mushrooms and any juices to the wok, add the cream and tomato, and cook, stirring, for 3–4 minutes or until piping hot. Season well.

- Remove from the heat, stir in the chopped cilantro, and serve immediately with steamed rice.

 Spicy Mushroom and Tomato Stir-Fry

Heat 2 tablespoons sunflower oil in a large wok or skillet until hot, add 8 cups sliced cremini mushrooms (about 1 lb), 1 tablespoon medium or hot curry powder, 1 teaspoon ginger paste, and 1 teaspoon garlic paste, and stir-fry over high heat for 4–5 minutes. Stir in ½ cup heavy cream and 2 chopped tomatoes and cook for 2–3 minutes or until piping hot. Sprinkle with a small handful of chopped cilantro and serve with steamed rice or noodles.

 Spicy Mushroom and Tomato Rice

Heat 2 tablespoons sunflower oil in a heavy saucepan, add 1 chopped onion, 1 teaspoon garlic paste, 1 tablespoon medium or hot curry powder, 8 cups chopped mushrooms (about 1 lb), and 2 chopped tomatoes, and cook, stirring, for 1–2 minutes, until softened. Add 2 cups long-grain rice and stir until well coated, then pour in 3½ cups hot vegetable stock and bring to a boil. Season, then cover tightly, reduce the heat to low, and cook, undisturbed, for 15–20 minutes or until the liquid is absorbed and the rice is tender. Remove from the heat and let stand for a few minutes before serving.

HOT-VEGE-TAL

20 Indonesian Okra with Coconut

Serves 4

2 tablespoons sunflower oil
1 onion, finely chopped
1 tablespoon black mustard seeds
1 tablespoon cumin seeds
2–3 dried red chiles
10–12 fresh curry leaves
1¼ lb okra, cut diagonally into
 ¾ inch lengths
1 teaspoon ground turmeric
1 cup grated fresh coconut
salt and pepper
steamed rice, to serve (optional)

· Heat the oil in a large wok or skillet until hot, add the onion, and stir-fry over medium heat for 5–6 minutes until softened.

· Increase the heat to medium-high, add the mustard seeds, and stir-fry for a few minutes, until the seeds begin to pop, then add the cumin seeds, dried chiles, and curry leaves and stir-fry for an additional 2 minutes, until fragrant.

· Stir in the okra and turmeric and continue to stir-fry for 3–4 minutes, then season well.

· Spoon onto warm serving plates and sprinkle with the coconut. Serve immediately with steamed rice, if desired.

---

10 Spicy Coconut Soup with Deep-Fried Okra Put 2½ cups hot vegetable stock, 1 (14 fl oz) can coconut milk, and 1 tablespoon mild curry paste in a large saucepan and bring to a boil, then reduce the heat to medium, season, and cook for 4–5 minutes. Meanwhile, fill a wok or small, deep saucepan one-quarter full with sunflower oil and heat to 350°F–375°F, or until a cube of bread browns in 30 seconds. Deep-fry 8 finely sliced okra in the oil for 1 minute, until crispy. Remove with a slotted spoon and drain on paper towels. To serve, ladle the soup into warm bowls and sprinkle with the fried okra.

30 Spiced Coconut and Okra Rice Heat 2 tablespoons sunflower oil in a heavy saucepan, add 1 tablespoon black mustard seeds, and cook over medium-high heat for a few minutes, until the seeds begin to pop, then add 1 finely chopped onion, 2 teaspoons cumin seeds, 2 dried red chiles, and 10 fresh curry leaves, and cook, stirring, for 3–4 minutes, until the onion is softened. Add 2 cups long-grain rice and stir until the grains are well coated. Add 10 oz thickly sliced okra, then pour in 1 (14 fl oz) can coconut milk and 1¾ cups hot vegetable stock. Bring to a boil, then cover tightly, reduce the heat to low, and cook, undisturbed, for 15–20 minutes or until the liquid is absorbed and the rice is tender. Remove from the heat and let stand for a few minutes before serving.

30 Butternut Squash and Red Pepper Curry

Serves 4

2 tablespoons sunflower oil

1 red onion, thinly sliced

2 garlic cloves, minced

1 teaspoon peeled and finely grated fresh ginger root

3 tablespoons Thai red curry paste

1¾ lb butternut squash, peeled, seeded, and cut into bite-size cubes

2 red bell peppers, cored, seeded, and cut into bite-size pieces

1 (14 fl oz) can coconut milk

1 cup water

6 kaffir lime leaves

2 teaspoons grated jaggery or granulated sugar

3 lemon grass stalks, bruised

⅓ cup skinless raw peanuts

small handful of Thai basil leaves

salt and pepper

steamed jasmine rice, to serve

- Heat the oil in a large wok or skillet until hot, add the onion, garlic, and ginger, and stir-fry over medium heat for 1–2 minutes, until softened. Stir in the curry paste, butternut squash, and red bell peppers and stir-fry for an additional 2–3 minutes.

- Pour the coconut milk and measured water over the squash and add the lime leaves, jaggery, and lemon grass. Bring to a boil, then reduce the heat to low and simmer gently, uncovered, stirring occasionally, for 15–20 minutes or until the squash is tender. Season to taste.

- Meanwhile, heat a small, nonstick skillet until hot, add the peanuts, and dry-fry for 3–4 minutes or until toasted. Let cool, then coarsely chop.

- Ladle the curry into warm bowls, sprinkle with the Thai basil leaves and chopped peanuts, and serve with steamed jasmine rice.

---

10 Curried Butternut Squash and Red Pepper Soup

Heat 1 tablespoon sunflower oil in a saucepan, add 1 tablespoon mild curry paste and 1 teaspoon lemon grass paste, and stir for 30–40 seconds. Add 2 (15 oz) cans vegetable and butternut squash soup and 1 cored, seeded and finely diced red bell pepper and bring to a boil. Reduce the heat to medium and cook for 4–5 minutes or until piping hot. Serve with warm bread rolls.

20 Curried Roasted Butternut Squash and Red Peppers

Put 1¼ lb butternut squash, peeled, seeded, and cut into ¾ inch cubes, and 2 red bell peppers, cored, seeded, and cut into bite-size pieces, in a roasting pan. Mix together ⅓ cup sunflower oil, 1 tablespoon medium curry paste, 1 teaspoon lemon grass paste, and 1 cup coconut milk in a bowl. Pour the mixture over the vegetables, season, and toss to mix well. Place in a preheated oven, at 425°F, for 15 minutes or until tender. Serve with rice or warm flatbreads.

Middle Eastern Zucchini, Tomato, and Mint Curry

Serves 4

2 tablespoons olive oil

2 onions, finely sliced

4 zucchini, cut into ½ inch cubes

2 (14½ oz) cans peeled tomatoes

2 garlic cloves, crushed

1 teaspoon mild chili powder

¼ teaspoon ground turmeric

2 teaspoons dried mint

salt and pepper

small handful of finely chopped
  mint leaves, to garnish

- Heat the oil in a large, heavy saucepan, add the onion, and cook over medium-low heat, stirring occasionally, for 6–8 minutes, until softened. Add the zucchini and cook, stirring occasionally, for an additional 5–6 minutes, until tender.

- Increase the heat to medium, add the tomatoes and garlic, and cook for 10–12 minutes, until the sauce is thickened. Stir in the chili powder, turmeric, and mint and cook for an additional 2–3 minutes. Season well.

- Ladle into warm bowls and serve sprinkled with the chopped mint leaves.

Spicy Zucchini, Tomato, and Mint Salad Coarsely shred 2 large zucchini and put in a salad bowl with 6 finely chopped tomatoes and a large handful of mint leaves. Mix together ⅓ cup extra-virgin olive oil, 1 teaspoon mild chili powder, 1 teaspoon garlic paste, 2 teaspoons honey, and the juice of 2 lemons in a bowl, then season. Pour the dressing over the salad, toss to mix well, and serve.

Grilled Spicy Zucchini with Tomato and Mint Thinly slice 3 large zucchini lengthwise. Brush the slices with olive oil and sprinkle with 2 teaspoons mild curry powder. Toss to mix well, then cook in batches on a preheated hot, ridged grill pan for 2–3 minutes on each side. Transfer to a serving plate in a single layer. Sprinkle with 4 finely diced plum tomatoes and a large handful of torn mint leaves. Squeeze the juice of

2 lemons over the vegetables, drizzle with 3 tablespoons extra-virgin olive oil, season, and serve with warm pita.

Deep-Fried Spiced Baby Eggplant

Serves 4

1¼ lb baby eggplants
2 tablespoons curry powder
sunflower oil, for deep-frying
small handful of chopped mint
  leaves, to garnish
salt

To serve

lemon wedges
chili powder
sea salt

- Thinly slice the eggplants and place in a bowl with the curry powder. Season with salt and toss to mix well.

- Fill a wok or small, deep saucepan one-quarter full with sunflower oil and heat to 350°F–375°F, or until a cube of bread browns in 30 seconds. Deep-fry the eggplants, in 2 or 3 batches, for 1–2 minutes or until crisp and golden. Drain on paper towels.

- Transfer the eggplants to a large serving plate, sprinkle with a small handful of chopped mint, and serve immediately with lemon wedges and a sprinkling of chili powder and sea salt.

 Spicy Eggplant Pilaff

Heat 2 tablespoons sunflower oil in a heavy saucepan, add 1 finely chopped onion, and cook over medium heat for 4–5 minutes. Stir in 2 teaspoons cumin seeds and 1 teaspoon black mustard seeds and cook for 40–50 seconds. Add 1 ½ cups long-grain rice, stir until well coated, and season well. Add 2 ½ cups hot vegetable stock and bring to the boil. Cover, reduce the heat to low, and cook for 12–15 minutes or until the liquid is absorbed. Meanwhile, cut 1 ¼ pounds baby eggplants into ½ inch cubes. Heat 2 tablespoons oil in a large skillet, add the eggplants, and cook for 6–8 minutes or until tender and cooked through. Stir in 1 tablespoon medium or hot curry powder and cook for an additional 1–2 minutes, then season. Stir the eggplants into the cooked rice with a handful of chopped mint leaves. Serve with tablespoonfuls of yogurt.

 Spiced Baby Eggplants with Chile and Herbs Blend 2 red chiles, 1 tablespoon finely grated ginger root, 4 grated garlic cloves, and 14 oz diced tomatoes until smooth. Heat 1 cup sunflower oil in a skillet over medium heat. Add 1¾ lb eggplants, halved, and cook for 2–3 minutes on each side, until brown. Remove and drain on paper towels. In the same skillet stir-fry 2 teaspoons fennel seeds and nigella seeds for 1 minute. Stir in the tomato mixture, cook for 3 minutes, add 1 tablespoon ground coriander, 1 teaspoon paprika, and ¼ teaspoon ground turmeric, season and simmer for 5 minutes. Return the eggplants to the skillet, toss to coat, cover, and cook for 10–12 minutes. Stir in a handful each of chopped cilantro and mint, and serve.

Spiced Okra, Tomato, and Coconut

Serves 4

2 tablespoons sunflower oil

6–8 fresh curry leaves

2 teaspoons black mustard seeds

1 onion, finely chopped

2 teaspoons ground cumin

1 teaspoon ground coriander

2 teaspoons medium or hot
   curry powder

1 teaspoon ground turmeric

3 garlic cloves, finely chopped

1 lb okra, trimmed and cut
   diagonally into 1 inch pieces

2 ripe plum tomatoes, chopped

3 tablespoons grated fresh
   coconut, to garnish

salt and pepper

- Heat the oil in a large wok or skillet until hot, add the curry leaves, mustard seeds, and onion, and stir-fry over medium heat for 3–4 minutes, until fragrant and the onion is beginning to soften. Add the cumin, ground coriander, curry powder, and turmeric and stir-fry for an additional 30 seconds until fragrant.

- Add the garlic and okra, increase the heat to high, and stir-fry for 2–3 minutes, then add the tomatoes and season well. Cover, then reduce the heat to low and cook gently, stirring occasionally, for 10–12 minutes or until the okra is just tender.

- Remove from the heat and sprinkle with the coconut, then ladle into warm bowls and serve.

 Spicy Fried Okra with Coconut

Fill a wok one-quarter full with sunflower oil and heat to 350°F–375°F, or until a cube of bread browns in 30 seconds. Put 1 lb sliced okra in a bowl with 2 teaspoons cornstarch, 2 teaspoons each ground cumin and hot chili powder, and 1 teaspoon ground coriander and toss to mix. Deep-fry the okra in batches for 1–2 minutes, until crisp. Remove from the oil using a slotted spoon and drain on paper towels. Sprinkle with ¼ cup grated fresh coconut and season with salt. Serve with rice and plain yogurt.

 Tomato, Coconut and Okra Curry

Heat 2 tablespoons sunflower oil in a large saucepan, add 1 chopped onion, and cook over medium heat, stirring occasionally, for 4–5 minutes, until softened. Stir in 1 (14½ oz) can diced tomatoes and 2 tablespoons medium or hot curry powder, increase the heat to high, and cook for 4–5 minutes, then add 1 (14 fl oz) can coconut milk and bring back to a boil. Add 1 lb okra, trimmed and cut into ¾ inch pieces, then reduce the heat to medium, cover, and simmer gently for 10–12 minutes or until the okra is just tender. Season well. Serve with steamed rice and warm naan.

Spicy Tofu with Bok Choy and Scallions

Serves 4

2 tablespoons sunflower oil
2 teaspoons grated fresh ginger root
8 garlic cloves, coarsely chopped
4 shallots, finely chopped
2 red chiles, seeded and chopped
3 inch length of trimmed lemon
  grass stalk, finely chopped
1 teaspoon ground turmeric
1 (14 fl oz) can coconut milk
1 cup hot vegetable stock
12 oz baby bok choy, halved or
  quartered
3 cups snow peas
14 oz firm tofu, cubed
1 tablespoon dark soy sauce
1 tablespoon lime juice
6 scallions, thinly sliced
salt and pepper

To garnish

small handful of Thai basil leaves
sliced red chiles

- Put the oil, ginger, garlic, shallots, chopped red chiles, lemon grass, turmeric, and half the coconut milk in a food processor or blender and blend until fairly smooth.

- Heat a large nonstick wok or skillet until hot, add the coconut milk mixture, and stir-fry over high heat for 3–4 minutes. Add the remaining coconut milk and the stock and bring to a boil, then reduce the heat to low and simmer gently, uncovered, for 6–8 minutes.

- Add the bok choy, snow peas, and tofu and simmer for an additional 6–7 minutes. Stir in the soy sauce and lime juice, then season and simmer for an additional 1–2 minutes.

- Remove from the heat and stir in the scallions. Ladle into warm bowls and serve sprinkled with Thai basil leaves and sliced red chiles.

 Japanese-Style Tofu with Scallions

Cut 1¾ lb firm tofu into cubes and place in a dish. Mix together 1 tablespoon sesame oil, 2 tablespoons sunflower oil, 1 tablespoon mirin, ¼ cup light soy sauce, 1 seeded and diced red chile, and 1 teaspoon chili powder mixed with 1 teaspoon sesame seeds, and drizzle the dressing over the tofu. Sprinkle with 8 finely sliced scallions and serve.

 Spicy Tofu and Scallion Stir-Fry

Prepare 12 oz medium egg noodles according to the package directions and set aside. Meanwhile, heat 2 tablespoons sunflower oil in a wok or skillet until hot, add 3 crushed garlic cloves and 1 teaspoon peeled and grated fresh ginger root, and stir-fry over high heat for 10–20 seconds. Stir in 12 thickly sliced scallions, 1¼ lb cubed firm tofu, and 1 seeded and diced red chile and stir-fry for an additional 4–5 minutes or until the tofu is lightly browned. Add ½ cup hot vegetable stock and 2 tablespoons dark soy sauce, reduce the heat to medium, and cook for 6–8 minutes or until all the liquid is absorbed. Stir in the prepared egg noodles and cook for a few minutes to heat through. Serve immediately.

Malaysian Red Pepper and Cabbage Stir-Fry

Serves 4

1 tablespoon sunflower oil

2 garlic cloves, crushed

2 teaspoons medium curry powder

1 red bell pepper, cored, seeded, and finely diced

½ green cabbage, finely shredded

3 eggs, lightly beaten

salt and pepper

crusty bread, to serve (optional)

- Heat the oil in a large wok or skillet until hot, add the garlic, curry powder and red bell pepper, and stir-fry over medium-high heat for 3–4 minutes, until softened.

- Increase the heat to high, add the cabbage, season, and stir-fry for 5 minutes or until the cabbage is cooked but still retains a bite.

- Stir in the eggs and mix well with the vegetables, then continue stirring until the eggs are scrambled and just cooked through. Serve immediately with crusty bread, if desired.

 Spicy Cabbage and Red Pepper Salad

Put ½ green cabbage, finely shredded, and 1 (7 oz) jar roasted red bell peppers, sliced, in a large salad bowl. Mix together ⅔ cup store-bought French salad dressing, 1 teaspoon garlic paste, and ½ teaspoon mild curry powder in a small bowl, then season. Pour the dressing over the salad, toss to mix well, and serve.

 Spicy Cabbage and Red Pepper Stew

Heat 2 tablespoons sunflower oil in a large saucepan, add 2 finely sliced onions, and cook over medium heat, stirring occasionally, for 6–8 minutes or until soft and translucent. Stir in 3 chopped garlic cloves, 1 seeded and sliced red chile, and 1 tablespoon mild curry paste, then pour over 1¾ cup hot vegetable stock and 1 (14 fl oz) can coconut milk and bring to a boil. Stir in ½ green cabbage, shredded, and 3 cored, seeded, and thinly sliced red bell peppers and bring back to a boil, then reduce the heat to medium and cook for 12–15 minutes or until the vegetables are tender. Season well, then serve with rice or crusty bread.

3 Spanish Potatoes with Spicy Tomatoes

Serves 4

7 white round potatoes, peeled
  and cut into small cubes
2 tablespoons olive oil
1 (14½ oz) can diced tomatoes
1 small red onion, finely chopped
2 garlic cloves, finely chopped
1 teaspoon dried red pepper flakes
1 teaspoon cayenne pepper
3 teaspoons sweet
  smoked paprika
1 bay leaf
1 teaspoon sugar
salt and pepper
finely chopped flat leaf parsley,
  to garnish
crusty bread, to serve

- Cook the potatoes in a large saucepan of salted, boiling water for 10–12 minutes or until tender, then drain well.

- Line a baking sheet with nonstick parchment paper. Place the potatoes in a single layer on the sheet, drizzle with the oil, and season. Place in a preheated oven, at 425°F, for 10–12 minutes or until lightly browned.

- Meanwhile, put the tomatoes, red onion, garlic, red pepper flakes, and cayenne pepper in a saucepan and cook over medium heat for 10 minutes, stirring occasionally, then stir in the paprika, bay leaf, and sugar and cook for an additional 4–5 minutes, until thickened.

- Transfer the potatoes to a warm serving dish, then pour the spicy tomato sauce over the potatoes and toss to mix well. Sprinkle with chopped parsley and serve with crusty bread.

 Spicy Potato and Tomato Stir-Fry

Heat 2 tablespoons sunflower oil in a large wok or skillet until hot, add 1½ (14½ oz) cans new potatoes, drained and cubed, 1 coarsely chopped onion, 1 teaspoon dried red pepper flakes, 1 tablespoon sweet smoked paprika, and 2 diced plum tomatoes, and stir-fry over high heat for 5–6 minutes or until piping hot, then season. Serve with a green salad and warm bread.

 Spicy Warm Potato and Tomato Salad

Cook 1¾ lb halved baby new potatoes in a large saucepan of salted, boiling water for 10–12 minutes or until just tender. Meanwhile, heat ⅓ cup olive oil in a large skillet, add 2 chopped garlic cloves, 1 coarsely chopped onion, 1 teaspoon dried red chile flakes, and 1 teaspoon sweet smoked paprika, and cook over medium heat for 8–10 minutes, stirring occasionally, until the onion is softened. Drain the potatoes and put in a large serving bowl with 4 chopped plum tomatoes. Add the onion mixture with a handful of chopped flat leaf parsley. Season, toss to mix well, and serve warm or at room temperature.

Thai Massaman Butternut Squash Curry

Serves 4

2 tablespoons vegetable oil

2 tablespoons Thai massaman curry paste

6 shallots, thinly sliced

3 inch length of trimmed lemon grass stalk, finely chopped

6 green cardamom pods

2 teaspoons black mustard seeds

1¾ lb butternut squash, peeled, seeded, and cut into ½ inch cubes

1 cup hot vegetable stock

1 (14 fl oz) can coconut milk

juice of 1 lime

To garnish

small handful of Thai basil leaves or mint leaves

red chile slivers

To serve (optional)

lime wedges

- Heat the oil in a heavy saucepan, add the curry paste, shallots, lemon grass, cardamom, and mustard seeds, and cook over medium heat for 1–2 minutes, until fragrant.

- Add the pumpkin and pour over the stock and coconut milk. Bring to a simmer, then cook for 10–12 minutes or until the pumpkin is tender.

- Remove from the heat and stir in the lime juice. Ladle into warm bowls, sprinkle with Thai basil or mint leaves and red chile slivers, and serve with lime wedges for squeezing over the curry and with steamed jasmine rice, if desired.

Thai Massaman Vegetable Stir-Fry

Heat 2 tablespoons sunflower oil in a large wok or skillet until hot, add 1 (16 oz) package stir-fry vegetables and 1 tablespoon massaman curry paste, and stir-fry over high heat for 1–2 minutes. Pour in 1 cup canned coconut milk and stir-fry for an additional 3–4 minutes or until the vegetables are tender. Serve with rice or noodles.

Spicy Roast Thai Massaman

Vegetables Cut ½ peeled and seeded butternut squash, 2 cored and seeded red bell peppers, and 1 large eggplant into ¾ inch cubes and place in an ovenproof dish. Mix together 2 tablespoons Thai massaman curry paste and 1 cup canned coconut milk in a bowl. Pour the mixture over the vegetables, toss to mix well, and season with salt. Place in a preheated oven, at 400°F, for 20–25 minutes or until tender. Sprinkle with a small handful of Thai basil or mint leaves and serve with steamed rice.

HOT-VEGE-FYO

QuickCook

Beans, Peas, and Grains

Recipes listed by cooking time

30

Edamame, Ginger, and
Chile Rice   232

Herbed Chicken Rice
with Vietnamese-Style
Sauce   234

Spicy Shrimp and Tofu
Vegetables   236

Spicy Green Bean and Pesto
Pasta Gratin   238

Spicy Black Bean,
Scallion, and
Noodle Omelet   240

Carrot and Black Bean
Curry   242

Spicy Asparagus and Smoked
Salmon Risotto   244

Harissa Tabbouleh with
Roasted Vegetables   246

Spicy Roasted Veg Couscous
with Cashews and Feta   248

Spicy Pork with Crispy
Noodles   250

Spiced Bean and Red
Pepper Pilaf   252

Spicy Lentil and Carrot
Soup with Caramelized
Onions   254

Spicy Rice Noodle
Omelet   256

Chile Green Lentil and Lima
Bean Pasta   258

Spicy Coconut Shrimp with
Angel-Hair Pasta   260

Spicy Tuna, Tomato, and
Olive Pasta Casserole   262

Spiced Rice and Yellow
Lentils   264

Spicy Shrimp and Pea Pilaf 266

Spiced Fava Bean and
Dill Pilaf   268

Chile and Zucchini
Pennette   270

Chile and Butternut
Squash Risotto   272

Spicy Chickpea Curry   274

Burmese Coconut Chicken
and Rice Noodle Curry   276

Spicy Quinoa, Fava Bean,
and Avocado Salad   278

20

Warm Edamame, Ginger,
Chile, and Noodle Salad   232

Vietnamese Chicken,
Herb, and Rice Soup   234

Spicy Shrimp and
Vegetable Noodles   236

Spicy Green Bean, Potato,
and Pesto Linguine   238

Warm Spicy Black
Bean, Scallion, and
Noodle Salad   240

Spicy Carrot and Black
Bean Noodles   242

Spicy Smoked Salmon, Pea
and Asparagus Pasta   244

Harissa Vegetable Stew
with Bulgur Wheat   246

Spicy Veg and Cashew Stew
with Feta and Couscous 248

Spicy Pork and Noodle
Omelet   250

Spicy Bean and Red
Pepper Curry   252

Spicy Lentil and
Carrot Dal   254

Singapore Rice Noodles   256

Green lentil and Lima Bean
Pilaf with Chile Dressing 258

10

Spiced Shrimp, Coconut, and Rice Noodle Soup 260

Spicy Tuna, Tomato, and Olive Pasta 262

Spicy Vegetable and Lentil Stew 264

Spicy Shrimp, Pea, and Rice Soup 266

Spicy Fava Bean and Dill Pasta 268

Zucchini and Chile Pasta Salad 270

Butternut Squash and Chile Pasta 272

Spicy Chickpea Soup 274

Broiled Coconut Chicken with Spicy Rice Noodles 276

Spicy Quinoa and Fava Bean Broth 278

Edamame, Ginger, Chile, and Noodle Broth 232

Vietnamese Chicken, Herb, and Rice Salad 234

Spicy Shrimp and Vegetable Rice 236

Spicy Green Bean and Pesto Pasta Salad 238

Spicy Black Bean and Scallion Salad 240

Spicy Carrot and Black Bean Salad 242

Spicy Smoked Salmon, Asparagus and Pasta Salad 244

Moroccan Vegetable Couscous Salad 246

Spicy Veg, Cashew, and Feta Couscous Salad 248

Spicy Pork and Noodle Stir-Fry 250

Spicy Bean and Bell Pepper Salad 252

Spicy Lentil and Carrot Salad 254

Spicy Rice Noodle Soup 256

Green Lentil and Lima Bean Salad with Chile Dressing 258

Spicy Shrimp and Coconut Noodle Soup 260

Spicy Tuna, Tomato, and Olive Pasta Salad 262

Spicy Rice and Lentil Soup 264

Spicy Shrimp and Pea Stir-Fried Rice 266

Spicy Fava Bean and Dill Rice Salad 268

Chile and Zucchini Stir-Fry Noodles 270

Chile, Butternut Squash, and Rice Broth 272

Spicy Hummus 274

Spicy Coconut Chicken and Rice Noodles 276

Spicy Avocado and Fava Bean Bruschettas 278

Warm Edamame, Ginger, Chile, and Noodle Salad

Serves 4

8 oz dried soba noodles

1⅔ cups frozen, shelled edamames

6 scallions, thinly sliced diagonally

2 tablespoons sesame seeds

1 inch piece of fresh ginger root

1 red chile, finely chopped

1 tablespoon toasted sesame oil

3 tablespoons mirin

3 tablespoons light soy sauce

1 teaspoon honey

salt

chopped cilantro leaves, to garnish

· Cook the noodles and edamames in a large saucepan of lightly salted, boiling water for 4–5 minutes, or according to the package directions. Drain well, then return to the pan and add the scallions. Cover and keep warm.

· Heat a skillet until hot, add the sesame seeds, and dry-fry over medium heat until lightly golden, then remove from the pan and set aside.

· Peel and grate the ginger root into a bowl, then stir in the remaining ingredients and mix well. Pour the dressing over the noodle mixture and toss to mix well.

· Ladle into warm bowls, sprinkle with the sesame seeds and chopped cilantro, and serve.

 Edamame, Ginger, Chile, and Noodle Broth Put 3½ cups hot vegetable stock, 1 teaspoon peeled and grated fresh ginger root, 1 chopped red chile, and 6 finely sliced scallions in a saucepan and bring to a boil, then add 12 oz store-bought precooked soba noodles and 1⅓ cups frozen, shelled edamames. Bring back to a boil, then season and serve sprinkled with chopped cilantro leaves and a drizzle of sesame oil.

 Edamame, Ginger and Chile Rice Heat 2 tablespoons sunflower oil in a heavy saucepan, add 8 sliced scallions, 2 teaspoons peeled and chopped fresh ginger root, and 2 finely chopped red chiles, and cook, stirring, over low heat for 1–2 minutes, then add 2 cups long-grain rice and cook, stirring to coat the rice, for an additional 1–2 minutes. Stir in 3 cups hot vegetable stock and 1⅓ cups frozen, shelled edamames and bring to a boil. Cover tightly, reduce the heat to low, and cook, undisturbed, for 12–15 minutes or until the liquid is absorbed and the rice and beans are tender. Remove from the heat and let stand for 10 minutes. When ready to serve, fluff up the rice with a fork. Serve sprinkled with ¼ cup toasted sesame seeds and with Japanese-style pickles, if desired.

HOT-PULS-SYE

Herbed Chicken Rice with Vietnamese-Style Sauce

Serves 4

2 cups long-grain rice, rinsed and drained

3½ cups good-quality chicken stock

12 oz boneless, skinless chicken thighs, sliced

6 shallots, finely sliced

2 red chiles, finely sliced

2 teaspoons peeled and grated fresh ginger root

handful of chopped mint leaves

handful of chopped cilantro

8 scallions, finely sliced, to garnish

For the Vietnamese-style sauce

2 garlic cloves, chopped

1 red chile, chopped

1 lime

3–4 tablespoons Thai fish sauce

1–2 tablespoons water

- To make the Vietnamese-style sauce, put the garlic and red chile in a mortar and mash with the pestle to form a paste. Squeeze the juice of the lime into the paste, then remove the pulp and add it to the mixture. Mash to a paste again, then stir in enough fish sauce and water to dilute. Set aside.

- Put the rice in a heavy saucepan, then stir in the stock, chicken, shallots, red chiles, and ginger and bring to a boil. Cover tightly, reduce the heat to low, and cook, undisturbed, for 12–15 minutes or until the liquid is absorbed, the rice is tender, and the chicken is cooked all the way through.

- Remove the pan from the heat and stir in the herbs and scallions. Cover and let stand for a few minutes.

- Ladle into warm bowls and serve with the Vietnamese-style sauce spooned over or in a bowl on the side.

Vietnamese Chicken, Herb, and Rice Salad

Put 3½ cups cooked long-grain rice, 12 oz store-bought, cooked chicken breasts, skin removed and shredded, 1 shredded cucumber, 1 finely chopped red chile, and a small handful each of chopped mint and cilantro in a large salad bowl. Make the Vietnamese-style sauce as above, then spoon 2 tablespoons of the sauce over the salad. Toss to mix well and serve.

Vietnamese Chicken, Herb, and Rice Soup

Heat 1 tablespoon sunflower oil in a heavy saucepan, add 1 chopped onion, 2 chopped garlic cloves, 1 teaspoon peeled and grated fresh ginger root, a ¾ inch length of trimmed lemon grass stalk, finely chopped, and 1 finely chopped red chile, and cook over low heat, stirring occasionally, for 4–5 minutes, until the onion is softened. Stir in 3¾ cups hot chicken stock and ½ cup long-grain rice and bring to a boil, then cook, uncovered, for 10–12 minutes or until the rice is tender. Stir in 12 oz store-bought, cooked chicken breasts, skin removed and shredded, and a small handful of chopped mint leaves. Serve immediately.

 # Spicy Shrimp and Vegetable Noodles

Serves 4

2 tablespoons sunflower oil

12 oz raw, peeled jumbo shrimp

6 scallions, cut diagonally into
  ¾ inch lengths

2 garlic cloves, crushed

1 red chile, finely chopped

1 teaspoon grated fresh ginger root

1 red bell pepper, cored, seeded,
  and finely chopped

1 carrot, peeled and cut into thin
  matchsticks

⅔ cup frozen peas

1 lb fresh egg noodles

2 tablespoons hot chili sauce

1 tablespoon dark soy sauce

3 tablespoons sweet chili sauce

chopped cilantro leaves, to
  garnish

- Heat the oil in a large wok or skillet until hot, add the shrimp, scallions, garlic, red chile, and ginger, and stir-fry over high heat for 4–5 minutes or until the shrimp turn pink.

- Add the red bell pepper, carrot, and peas and stir-fry over medium-high heat for an additional 3–4 minutes. Stir in the noodles, hot chili sauce, soy sauce, and sweet chili sauce and continue to stir-fry for 3–4 minutes or until the noodles are piping hot.

- Divide among warm bowls, sprinkle with chopped cilantro, and serve immediately.

 ### Spicy Shrimp and Vegetable Rice

Heat 2 tablespoons sunflower oil in a large wok or skillet until hot, add a 1 (12 oz) package stir-fry vegetables, thawed if frozen, and stir-fry over high heat for 2–3 minutes, then add 3½ cups cooked egg-fried rice, 10 oz cooked, peeled shrimp, 2 tablespoons hot chili sauce, and ½ cup Chinese stir-fry sauce and stir-fry for an additional 1–2 minutes or until the rice is piping hot. Serve immediately.

 ### Spicy Shrimp and Tofu Vegetables

Heat 2 tablespoons sunflower oil in a large wok or skillet until hot, add 2 chopped shallots, 2 sliced red chiles, 2 teaspoons grated fresh ginger root, 2 teaspoons grated garlic, 1 teaspoon crushed Szechuan peppercorns, and a pinch of salt, and stir-fry over medium-high heat for 1 minute. Add 5 oz diced firm tofu and stir-fry for an additional 2 minutes, then transfer to a plate. Heat another 2 tablespoons sunflower oil in the wok until hot, add 1 peeled carrot, cut into matchsticks, 2 cored and seeded red bell peppers, sliced, and 3 cups diagonally halved snow peas, and stir-fry over high heat for 2–4 minutes or until starting to wilt, then add 2 tablespoons sweet chili sauce, 1 tablespoon hot chili sauce, ¼ cup light soy sauce, and 2 tablespoons Chinese rice wine. Return the tofu to the wok with 10 oz cooked, peeled shrimp, toss to mix well, and heat through until piping hot. Drizzle with 1 tablespoon sesame oil and serve with cooked noodles.

20 Spicy Green Bean, Potato, and Pesto Linguine

Serves 4

2 white round potatoes, peeled and cut into small cubes
2 cups trimmed, halved green beans
12 oz dried linguine
2 red chiles, finely chopped
1 (6½ oz) jar green pesto
salt and pepper
grated pecorino cheese, to serve

- Cook the potatoes in a large saucepan of lightly salted, boiling water for 10–12 minutes or until just tender, adding the beans 4 minutes before the end of the cooking time. Drain well, then return to the pan.

- Meanwhile, cook the pasta in a separate saucepan of boiling water according to the package directions until al dente, then drain and add to the potatoes and beans.

- Mix together the red chiles and pesto in a bowl, then season well. Spoon into the pasta mixture and toss to mix well.

- Spoon into warm bowls and serve with grated pecorino cheese to sprinkle with.

---

10 Spicy Green Bean and Pesto Pasta Salad Cook 10 oz fresh penne and 5 cups trimmed green beans in a large saucepan of lightly salted, boiling water for 2–4 minutes, or according to the pasta package directions, until tender. Drain, then refresh under cold running water and drain again. Put the pasta and beans in a large salad bowl and add 1 sliced red onion and 12 halved cherry tomatoes. Mix together 2 finely chopped red chiles and 1 (6½ oz) jar green pesto in a bowl. Pour the dressing over the salad, season, and toss to mix well before serving.

30 Spicy Green Bean and Pesto Pasta Gratin Cook 12 oz dried penne in a large saucepan of lightly salted, boiling water according to the package directions until al dente, adding 4 cups trimmed, chopped green beans 2 minutes before the end of the cooking time. Meanwhile, mix together 2 finely chopped red chiles, 1 (6½ oz) jar green pesto, 1 cup mascarpone cheese, and 2 lightly beaten eggs. Drain the pasta and beans, then put in a lightly greased, shallow ovenproof dish. Pour the pesto mixture over the pasta and beans and toss to mix well. Sprinkle with 1 cup dried bread crumbs and place in a preheated oven, at 400°F, for 10–15 minutes or until piping hot. Serve with an arugula salad.

HOT-PULS-GYS

Warm Spicy Black Bean, Scallion, and Noodle Salad

Serves 4

8 oz dried egg noodles

6 scallions

2 (15 oz) cans black beans, rinsed
  and drained

1 inch piece of fresh ginger root

2 red chiles, finely diced

1 tablespoon sesame oil

1–2 teaspoons chile oil

3 tablespoons sweet chili sauce

3 tablepoons light soy sauce

1 teaspoon honey

salt

chopped cilantro leaves,
  to garnish

- Cook the noodles in a large saucepan of lightly salted, boiling water according to the package directions. Drain well, then return to the pan and cover. Thinly slice the scallions diagonally and add to the noodles with the black beans and toss to mix well.

- Peel and grate the ginger root into a bowl, then stir in the remaining ingredients and mix well. Pour the dressing over the noodle mixture and toss to mix well. Cook over low heat for a few minutes, until warmed through.

- Ladle into warm bowls, sprinkle with chopped cilantro leaves, and serve.

Spicy Black Bean and Scallion Salad

Put (3 oz) package mixed salad leaves, 1 (15 oz) can black beans, rinsed and drained, 6 sliced scallions, 2 finely diced red chiles, and a small handful of chopped cilantro leaves in a large salad bowl. Pour ⅔ cup store-bought French salad dressing and 2 tablespoons sweet chili sauce over the salad, toss to mix well, and serve with warm bread rolls.

Spicy Black Bean, Scallion, and

Noodle Omelet Cook 8 oz dried egg noodles according to the package directions, then drain and set aside. Meanwhile, heat 2 tablespoons sunflower oil in medium ovenproof skillet, add 2 finely diced red chiles, 8 sliced scallions, and 2 finely chopped garlic cloves, and cook over medium heat for 2–4 minutes, then add 1 (15 oz) can black beans, rinsed and drained. Meanwhile, lightly beat 6 eggs in a bowl and stir in a small handful of chopped cilantro leaves and season. Add the drained noodles to the skillet and stir to mix well. Pour the egg mixture over the noodles and cook over medium heat for 8–10 minutes or until the bottom is set, then place the skillet under a preheated medium-hot broiler and cook for 2–4 minutes or until the top is lightly golden and set. Serve warm or at room temperature, cut into wedges.

HOT-PULS-TYL

Carrot and Black Bean Curry

Serves 4

2 cups vegetable stock, plus extra
   if needed
4 large carrots, peeled and cut
   into ½ inch dice
1 (15 oz) can black beans, rinsed
   and drained
4 plum tomatoes
2 tablespoons sunflower oil
2 teaspoons cumin seeds
1 teaspoon fennel seeds
2 shallots, finely chopped
2 red chiles, finely chopped
1 teaspoon grated fresh ginger root
3 garlic cloves, finely chopped
1 teaspoon ground turmeric
1 teaspoon garam masala
juice of 1 lime
¼ cup finely chopped
   cilantro leaves
steamed rice, to serve

- Pour the stock into a saucepan and bring to a boil, add the carrots, reduce the heat, and simmer for 8 minutes or until tender. Stir in the black beans and simmer for an additional 2 minutes. Drain and set aside, reserving the stock.

- Meanwhile, put the tomatoes in a heatproof bowl and pour over boiling water to cover. Let stand for 5 minutes, then plunge into cold water and drain. Cut a cross at the stem end of each tomato and peel off the skins. Coarsely chop and set aside.

- Heat the oil in a heavy saucepan, add the cumin seeds, fennel seeds, shallots, red chiles, ginger, and garlic, and cook, stirring, over medium heat for 3–4 minutes, until the shallots are softened. Add the tomatoes and ½ cup of the reserved stock, reduce the heat to low, and cook, stirring, for about 2 minutes. Stir in the turmeric and cook for an additional 2 minutes. Stir in the reserved carrot and beans and simmer for 3–4 minutes, adding more stock if the curry looks dry.

- Remove from the heat and stir in the garam masala, lime juice, and cilantro. Ladle into warm bowls and serve with steamed rice.

Spicy Carrot and Black Bean Salad

Heat a skillet until hot, add 2 teaspoons cumin seeds, and dry-fry until browned, then remove from the skillet and set aside. Put 2 large, peeled and shredded carrots and 2 (15 oz) cans black beans, rinsed and drained, in a salad bowl. Stir in 1 finely chopped red chile, the juice of 2 limes, and the toasted cumin seeds. Season, then stir in ¼ cup finely chopped cilantro. Toss to mix, then serve.

Spicy Carrot and Black Bean Noodles

Prepare 12 oz egg noodles according to the package directions. Meanwhile, heat 2 tablespoons sunflower oil in a large wok or skillet until hot, add 2 finely chopped red chiles, 1 finely chopped onion, 2 chopped garlic cloves, and 1 teaspoon peeled and grated fresh ginger root, and stir-fry over medium heat for 4–5 minutes, until softened. Add 2 large, peeled and shredded carrots and stir-fry for an additional 2–4 minutes, then stir in 1 (15 oz) can black beans, rinsed and drained, the prepared egg noodles, and 2 tablespoons oyster sauce. Stir to mix well and heat through until piping hot. Season well and serve immediately.

Spicy Smoked Salmon, Pea and Asparagus Pasta

Serves 4

12 oz dried bucatini, linguine, or
  spaghetti
8 oz asparagus tips, halved
  lengthwise
1 tablespoon butter
1 tablespoon olive oil
1 red chile, finely chopped
1 teaspoon dried red pepper flakes
2 garlic cloves, finely chopped
2 shallots, finely chopped
1 cup crème fraîche
8 oz smoked salmon, coarsely
  chopped
3½ oz frozen peas
¼ cup finely chopped dill
salt and pepper
green salad, to serve

- Cook the pasta in a large saucepan of lightly salted, boiling water according to the package directions until al dente, adding the asparagus 2 minutes before the end of the cooking time.

- Heat the butter and oil in a large skillet, add the red chile, red pepper flakes, garlic, and shallots, and cook over medium heat for 2–3 minutes.

- Drain the pasta and asparagus, then add to the skillet with the crème fraîche, smoked salmon, peas, and chopped dill and heat through until piping hot, then season.

- Serve in warm bowls with a crisp green salad.

 Spicy Smoked Salmon, Asparagus, and Pasta Salad Cook 10 oz fresh penne, 3½ oz frozen peas and 12 oz asparagus tips in a large saucepan of lightly salted, boiling water according to the pasta package directions, until the pasta is al dente. Drain, refresh under cold running water, and drain again. Put in a salad bowl with 12 oz chopped smoked salmon. Mix together 1 teaspoon dried red pepper flakes, 1 teaspoon medium curry powder, and ¾ cup store-bought French salad dressing in a bowl. Pour the dressing over the pasta, toss, and serve.

Spicy Asparagus, Pea, and Smoked Salmon Risotto Heat 2 tablespoons sunflower oil and 2 tablespoons butter in a heavy saucepan, add 1 chopped onion, 2 finely chopped red chiles, and 2 chopped garlic cloves, and cook for 2–3 minutes, until beginning to soften. Add 1½ cups risotto rice and 12 oz asparagus tips and stir for 1–2 minutes, until the rice is well coated, then add ⅔ cup dry white wine and simmer for 1 minute, stirring continuously. Reduce the heat, then add 5 cups hot vegetable stock, one ladleful at a time, stirring continuously until each ladleful is absorbed, and cook until the rice is tender but still firm (al dente). Add in 3½ oz frozen peas and stir in 8 oz coarsely chopped smoked salmon, then remove the pan from the heat and stir in 1 cup grated Parmesan cheese and the finely grated rind of 1 lemon. Season well and serve.

30 Harissa Tabbouleh with Roasted Vegetables

Serves 4

1 zucchini, cut into bite-size pieces

2 red bell peppers, cored, seeded, and cut into bite-size pieces

1 yellow bell pepper, cored, seeded, and cut into bite-size pieces

¼ cup olive oil

3 garlic cloves, crushed

1 red chile, finely chopped

2 tablespoons harissa paste

1 cup bulgur wheat

2½ cups hot vegetable stock

juice of 1 lemon

⅓ cup finely chopped cilantro leaves

⅓ cup finely chopped mint leaves

- Put the zucchini and bell peppers in a roasting pan. Mix together the oil, garlic, red chile, and harissa in a bowl, then pour the mixture over the vegetables and toss to coat evenly. Place in a preheated oven, at 400°F, for 20 minutes or until softened and the vegetables are just beginning to char at the edges.

- Meanwhile, put the bulgur wheat in a large, heatproof bowl and pour the stock over the grains, then cover tightly with plastic wrap and let stand for 15 minutes, until the grains are tender but still have a little bite.

- Let the bulgur wheat cool slightly, then add the roasted vegetables, lemon juice, and chopped herbs and toss to mix well. Serve warm or at room temperature.

 Moroccan Vegetable Couscous Salad

Put 1 (1 lb) package store-bought, fresh Moroccan-style couscous salad in a large bowl with 1 (3 oz) package mixed salad greens, 2 (7 oz) jars roasted red peppers in olive oil, drained, and a small handful each of chopped cilantro and mint leaves. Season, then toss to mix well and serve.

 Harissa Vegetable Stew with Bulgur Wheat Put 1 cup bulgur wheat in a large, heatproof bowl and pour 2½ cups water over the grains, then cover tightly with plastic wrap and let stand for 15 minutes, until the grains are tender. Meanwhile, heat 2 tablespoons olive oil in a heavy saucepan, add 1 chopped onion, 2 chopped garlic cloves, 2 cored, seeded, and finely chopped red bell peppers, and 1 finely chopped zucchini, and cook over medium heat for 1–2 minutes. Add 2 cups hot vegetable stock and 1 tablespoon harissa paste and bring to a boil, then reduce the heat and cook for 10–15 minutes or until the vegetables are tender. Season and stir in 2 tablespoons each of finely chopped cilantro and mint leaves. Serve with the cooked bulgur wheat.

30 Spicy Roasted Veg Couscous with Cashews and Feta

Serves 4

2 red bell peppers, cored, seeded, and cut into ¾ inch pieces
1 yellow bell pepper, cored, seeded, and cut into ¾ inch pieces
1 zucchini, cut into ¾ inch cubes
2 large red onions, thickly sliced
¼ cup olive oil
1 cup couscous
½ cup cashew nuts
handful of chopped mint
handful of chopped cilantro
6–8 preserved lemons, halved
1⅓ cups crumbled feta cheese
salt and pepper

For the dressing

juice of 1 orange
⅓ cup extra-virgin olive oil
1 teaspoon sweet smoked paprika
1 red chile, finely chopped
1 teaspoon ground cumin
1 teaspoon mild curry powder

- Put the vegetables on a large baking sheet, then drizzle with the oil and season well. Place in a preheated oven, at 400°F, for 12–15 minutes or until softened and the vegetables are just beginning to char at the edges.

- Meanwhile, put the couscous in a large, heatproof bowl and season well. Pour over enough boiling water to just cover, then cover with plastic wrap and let stand for 8–10 minutes, or according to the package directions, until the water is absorbed.

- To make the dressing, mix together all the ingredients in a bowl and season well, then set aside.

- To toast the cashew nuts, heat a skillet until hot, add the nuts, and dry-fry over medium heat until lightly brown, then remove from the skillet and set aside.

- Gently fork the couscous to separate the grains and place in a large, shallow serving dish, then fold in the roasted vegetables, herbs, and preserved lemons. Pour the dressing over the couscous and toss to mix well. Sprinkle with the toasted cashew nuts and the feta cheese and serve.

 Spicy Veg, Cashew, and Feta Couscous Salad Put 1 (1 lb) package store-bought, fresh spicy vegetable couscous salad in a large bowl with ½ cup each of chopped mint and cilantro leaves and 6 sliced scallions. Add 1 cup crumbled feta cheese and ½ cup cashew nuts, toasted as above. Season, then toss to mix well and serve.

 Spicy Veg and Cashew Stew with Feta and Couscous Heat 2 tablespoons olive oil in a heavy saucepan, add 2 coarsely chopped red onions, 1 finely chopped garlic clove, 2 sliced red chiles, 1 coarsely diced zucchini, 1 cored, seeded, and diced red bell pepper, and 1 cored, seeded, and diced yellow bell pepper, and cook over medium heat for 2–4 minutes, until softened. Add 1 (14½ oz) can diced tomatoes and 1 cup hot vegetable stock and bring to a boil, then reduce the heat to medium and cook for 15 minutes or until the vegetables are tender. Season, remove from the heat, and stir in 1 cup cashew nuts, toasted as above, and crumble ⅔ cup feta cheese over the stew. Stir in a small handful each of mint and cilantro, then serve with couscous.

Spicy Pork with Crispy Noodles

Serves 4

sunflower oil, for deep-frying
8 oz rice vermicelli noodles,
  broken into pieces
12 oz ground pork
3 garlic cloves, finely chopped
2 scallions, finely chopped,
  plus 2 scallions, finely shredded
3 tablespoons lime juice
2 tablespoons Thai fish sauce
⅓ cup sweet chili sauce
1 tablespoon hot chili sauce
1 tablespoon tomato paste
1 teaspoon dried red pepper flakes
4 oz firm tofu, cut into ½ inch dice
2 cups chopped cilantro leaves
  and stems
½ cup bean sprouts
2–3 Thai chiles, finely sliced

- Fill a large wok or deep saucepan one-quarter full with sunflower oil and heat until 350–375°F, or until a cube of bread browns in 30 seconds. Add the noodles, in batches if necessary, and deep-fry in the oil for 30–40 seconds or until they puff up and are lightly golden. Remove with a slotted spoon and drain on paper towels.

- Carefully pour all but 2 tablespoons of the oil out of the wok, add the pork, and stir-fry over high heat for 4–5 minutes or until it is browned and cooked all the way through, then transfer to a plate and keep warm.

- Reduce the heat to medium-low, add the garlic and scallions, and stir-fry for 1–2 minutes. Stir in the lime juice, sauces, tomato paste, and red pepper flakes, reduce the heat to low, and simmer for 3–4 minutes or until syrupy. Stir half of the fried rice noodles into the sauce and toss to coat evenly. Stir in the pork and the remaining noodles and heat through.

- Divide the mixture among large serving plates, top with the tofu, shredded scallions, chopped cilantro, bean sprouts, and Thai chiles, and serve immediately.

 ### Spicy Pork and Noodle Stir-Fry

Prepare 12 oz egg noodles according to package directions. Meanwhile, heat 2 tablespoons sunflower oil in a wok or skillet until hot, add 1 finely chopped red chile and 12 oz ground pork, and stir-fry over high heat for 1–2 minutes or until browned. Add ¾ cup sweet chile stir-fry sauce and the egg noodles and stir-fry for a few minutes until piping hot and the pork is cooked through.

 ### Spicy Pork and Noodle Omelet

Prepare 8 oz egg noodles according to the package directions. Meanwhile, heat 2 tablespoons sunflower oil in medium ovenproof skillet, add 8 sliced scallions, 2 finely chopped red chiles, 2 chopped garlic cloves, and 8 oz ground pork, and cook over high heat for 2–4 minutes or until the pork is browned and cooked through. Add the noodles and stir to mix well. Meanwhile, beat together 4 extra-large eggs, 1 tablespoon hot chili sauce, and 2 tablespoons sweet chili sauce in a bowl, then pour into the skillet. Cook for 6–8 minutes, until the bottom is beginning to set, then place the skillet under a preheated medium-hot broiler and cook for 2–4 minutes or until the top is golden and set. Serve warm or at room temperature, cut into wedges.

HOT-PULS-JYY

Spicy Bean and Bell Pepper Salad

Serves 4

1 (15 oz) can red kidney beans
1 (15 oz) can cannellini beans
1 (15 oz) can lima beans
1 red bell pepper
1 green pepper
1 yellow bell pepper
1 small red onion, finely diced
2 red chiles, finely diced
2 celery sticks, finely diced
small handful of chopped cilantro
   leaves, to garnish
salt and pepper

For the dressing

⅓ cup extra-virgin olive oil
juice of 1 large lemon
2 tablespoons cider vinegar
1 teaspoons honey

- Rinse and drain the canned beans and put in a large bowl. Core, seed, and finely dice the bell peppers, then add to the bowl along with the onion, chiles, and celery.

- Mix together all the dressing ingredients in a small bowl. Pour the dressing over the salad, season, and toss to mix well.

- Sprinkle with chopped cilantro leaves and serve with toasted ciabatta bread or steamed rice, if desired.

Spicy Bean and Red Pepper Curry

Heat 2 tablespoons olive oil in a large skillet, add 2 chopped red chiles, 1 chopped red onion, 2 chopped garlic cloves, and 2 cored, seeded, and coarsely chopped red bell peppers, and cook over medium heat, stirring, for 4–5 minutes. Stir in 1 tablespoon curry powder and 1 cup canned coconut milk and bring to a boil. Add 2 cups rinsed and drained, mixed canned beans, reduce the heat to medium, and cook for 8 minutes. Stir in a handful of chopped cilantro and serve.

 ### Spiced Bean and Red Pepper Pilaf

Heat 2 tablespoons sunflower oil in a heavy saucepan, add 1 chopped onion, and cook, stirring, for 1–2 minutes. Stir in 2 teaspoons cumin seeds, 2 sliced red chiles, 1 cinnamon stick, 1 tablespoon mild curry powder, 2 cored, seeded, and diced red bell peppers, and 2 cups rinsed and drained, mixed canned beans, and cook for an additional 1–2 minutes, then stir in 1⅓ cups long-grain rice and 2¾ cups hot vegetable stock and bring to a boil. Cover tightly, reduce the heat to low, and cook, undisturbed, for 15–20 minutes or until the liquid is absorbed and the rice is tender. Remove from the heat and let stand for a few minutes before serving.

HOT-PULS-NOU

30 Spicy Lentil and Carrot Soup with Caramelized Onions

Serves 4

2 tablespoons sunflower oil

1 garlic clove, finely chopped

1 teaspoon grated fresh ginger root

1 red chile, finely chopped

1 onion, finely chopped

1 tablespoon sweet smoked paprika, plus extra to garnish

5 cups peeled and finely chopped carrots (about 1½ lb)

¾ cup rinsed and drained red split lentils

⅔ cup light cream

4 cups hot vegetable stock

½ cup crème fraîche or sour cream

small handful of chopped cilantro leaves

salt and pepper

For the caramelized onions

1 tablespoon butter

1 tablespoon olive oil

1 onion, thinly sliced

- Heat the sunflower oil in a heavy saucepan, add the garlic, ginger, red chile, onion, and smoked paprika, and cook, stirring, over medium-high heat for 1–2 minutes. Add the carrots, lentils, cream, and stock and bring to a boil, then reduce the heat to medium and simmer, uncovered, for 15–20 minutes.

- Meanwhile, to make the caramelized onions, heat the butter and olive oil in a skillet, add the onion, and cook over low heat for 12–15 minutes or until caramelized and golden brown. Drain on paper towels and keep warm.

- Using an electric immersion blender, blend the lentil mixture in the pan until smooth, then season well.

- Ladle into bowls, add a spoonful of crème fraiche, and sprinkle with chopped cilantro leaves and the caramelized onions. Sprinkle with a little smoked paprika before serving.

 Spicy Lentil and Carrot Salad

Put 2 (15 oz) cans green lentils, rinsed and drained, 2 peeled and shredded carrots, 1 finely chopped red chile, 4 sliced scallions, and a large handful of chopped cilantro leaves in a salad bowl. Pour ⅔ cup store-bought French salad dressing over the salad and add 1 teaspoon sweet smoked paprika. Season, toss to mix, and serve.

 Spicy Lentil and Carrot Dal

Put ¾ cup rinsed and drained red split lentils, 2 peeled and finely diced carrots, 1 chopped onion, 2 teaspoons peeled and grated fresh ginger root, 2 teaspoons grated garlic, 2 teaspoons cumin seeds, 2 teaspoons black mustard seeds, and 1 tablespoon medium or hot curry powder in a saucepan, then pour in 3½ cups hot vegetable stock and bring to a boil. Reduce the heat to medium and cook, uncovered, for 12–15 minutes or until thickened and the lentils are just tender. Season, stir in a small handful of chopped cilantro leaves, and serve with steamed rice or bread.

Singapore Rice Noodles

Serves 4

8 oz dried rice noodles
¼ cup vegetable oil
1 lb raw, peeled jumbo shrimp
4 oz bacon pieces
3 garlic cloves, crushed
1 red chile, thinly sliced, plus extra
to garnish
1 teaspoon grated fresh ginger root
1 onion, thinly sliced
1 large carrot, peeled and cut into
thin sticks
3 cups thinly sliced sugarsnap peas
½ cup bean sprouts
6 scallions, finely sliced diagonally
1–2 tablespoons medium or hot
curry powder
2 tablespoons water
⅓ cup dark soy sauce
pepper
lime wedges, to serve

- Cook the noodles following the package directions, then drain and set aside.

- Heat 2 tablespoons of the oil in a large wok or skillet until hot, add the shrimp and bacon piees, and stir-fry over high heat for 4–5 minutes or until the shrimp turn pink and the bacon is lightly golden. Use a slotted spoon to transfer the shrimp and bacon to a plate and keep warm. Rinse out the wok or skillet and wipe dry with paper towels.

- Heat the remaining oil in the wok or skillet until hot, add the garlic, red chile, and ginger, and stir-fry over high heat for 30 seconds or until lightly browned, then add the onion and vegetables and stir-fry for an additional 3–4 minutes, until just beginning to soften, then add the curry powder and continue to stir for an additional 1 minute.

- Add the drained noodles and measured water and toss well, then stir in the soy sauce, season with pepper, and stir-fry for 1 minute. Toss the shrimp and bacon through the mixture and heat through until piping hot.

- Divide the noodles among warm shallow bowls or plates, sprinkle with extra sliced red chiles, and serve with lime wedges to squeeze over the shrimp.

Spicy Rice Noodle Soup Put 10 oz fresh rice noodles, 1 tablespoon tom yum paste, and 3½ cups hot vegetable stock in a saucepan and bring to a boil, then cook for 2–2 minutes. Stir in 12 oz cooked, peeled shrimp and cook for an additional 1 minute or until piping hot. Serve immediately.

Spicy Rice Noodle Omelet Beat together 6 eggs, 6 finely sliced scallions, and 1 tablespoon medium or hot curry powder in a bowl, then season well. Heat 2 tablespoons olive oil in a large ovenproof skillet, add 8 oz peeled, jumbo shrimp, and stir-fry over high heat for 4–5 minutes or until the shrimp turn pink. Add 10 oz fresh rice noodles and pour the egg mixture over the shrimp and noodles. Cook over medium heat for 10–12 minutes or until the bottom is set, then place the skillet under a preheated medium-hot broiler and cook for 4–5 minutes or until the top is golden and set. Let cool, then serve cut into wedges with a green salad.

HOT-PULS-PIV

Green Lentil and Lima Bean Salad with Chile Dressing

Serves 4

1 (15 oz) can green lentils, rinsed and drained

1 (15 oz) can lima beans, rinsed and drained

1 red onion, finely sliced

12 cherry tomatoes, halved

1 cup flat-leaf parsley, coarsely chopped

For the dressing

⅓ cup extra-virgin olive oil

2 red chiles, minced

2 tablespoons red wine vinegar

1 teaspoon Dijon or whole-grain mustard

1 teaspoon honey

½ garlic clove, crushed

- Put the lentils and lima beans in a large serving bowl, then add the onion, cherry tomatoes, and parsley.

- Mix together all the dressing ingredients in a small bowl, then pour over the salad, toss to mix well, and serve.

---

2 **Green Lentil and Lima Bean Pilaf with Chile Dressing** Cook 1⅓ cups long-grain rice in a large saucepan of lightly salted, boiling water according to the package directions. Meanwhile, make the Green Lentil and Lima Bean Salad with Chile Dressing as above. Drain the rice, then stir into the lentil salad and toss to mix well. Serve warm or at room temperature.

3 **Chile Green Lentil and Lima Bean Pasta** Cook 12 oz orzo pasta in a large saucepan of lightly salted, boiling water according to the package directions until just al dente, then drain and return to the pan. Cover and keep warm. Meanwhile, heat 2 tablespoons sunflower oil in a large skillet, add 1 sliced red onion, 2 sliced red chiles, and 2 sliced garlic cloves and cook over medium heat, stirring occasionally, for 5–6 minutes, until softened. Stir in 1 (15 oz) can green lentils, rinsed and drained, 1 (15 oz) can lima beans, rinsed and drained, ¾ cup hot vegetable stock, and the prepared orzo and bring to a boil, then reduce the heat to medium, cover, and cook for 5–6 minutes, stirring occasionally. Season, then stir in a small handful of chopped flat-leaf parsley and serve.

Spiced Shrimp, Coconut, and Rice Noodle Soup

Serves 4

1 tablespoon sunflower oil

6 pink shallots, finely sliced

1 red chile, finely sliced, plus extra slivers to garnish

1 green chile, finely sliced

1 cinnamon stick

1 star anise

2 inch piece of fresh ginger root, peeled and thinly sliced

3 inch length of trimmed lemon grass stalk, finely chopped

1¾ cup hot fish stock

2 tablespoons Thai fish sauce

1 tablespoon brown sugar

12 oz raw, peeled jumbo shrimp

6 baby bok choy, halved or quartered

1 (14 fl oz) can coconut milk

juice of 2 limes

8 oz dried flat rice noodles

sliced scallions, to garnish

· Heat the oil in a saucepan, add the shallots, chiles, cinnamon stick, star anise, and ginger, and cook gently for 2 minutes. Add the lemon grass and stock and bring to a simmer.

· Stir in the fish sauce, sugar, and shrimp and simmer for 5–6 minutes or until the shrimp turn pink and are cooked through. Add the bok choy, coconut milk, and lime juice and heat through until the bok choy wilts.

· Cook the noodles according to the package directions, then drain. Divide the noodles among warm bowls and ladle the shrimp mixture over the noodles. Sprinkle with slivered red chiles and scallions and serve immediately.

 Spicy Shrimp and Coconut Noodle Soup Put 2½ cups hot vegetable stock, 1 tablespoon medium curry paste, and 1 (14 fl oz) can coconut milk in a saucepan and bring to a boil. Add 10 oz fresh rice noodles and 12 oz cooked, peeled shrimp and cook for 1–2 minutes or until piping hot. Remove from the heat and squeeze the juice of 1 lime over the soup. Serve immediately.

 Spicy Coconut Shrimp with Angel-Hair Pasta Cook 12 oz angel-hair pasta in a large saucepan of lightly salted, boiling water according to the package directions. Heat 1 tablespoon sunflower oil in a heavy saucepan, add 1 chopped onion, 2 chopped red chiles, and 2 chopped garlic cloves, and cook over low heat, stirring occasionally, for 6–8 minutes, until softened. Add 1 lb raw, peeled jumbo shrimp to the onions, increase the heat to medium, and cook for 5–6 minutes or until they turn pink and are cooked through. Stir in 1 cup coconut milk and a small handful each of chopped cilantro and Thai basil leaves. Drain the pasta, then add to the shrimp mixture. Season, toss to mix well, and serve immediately.

Spicy Tuna, Tomato, and Olive Pasta

Serves 4

12 oz dried penne
2 (12 oz) cans tuna chunks in
water, drained
2 red chiles, finely chopped
1 teaspoon dried red pepper flakes
2 cups pitted ripe black olives
1 cup sun-dried tomatoes in oil
salt and pepper
chopped flat-leaf parsley,
to garnish

- Cook the pasta in a large saucepan of lightly salted, boiling water according to the package directions until al dente.

- Meanwhile, put the tuna in a large bowl and coarsely flake with a fork, then add the red chiles, red pepper flakes, olives, and tomatoes with their oil.

- Drain the pasta, add to the tuna mixture, and toss to mix well, then season.

- Spoon into warm bowls, sprinkle with chopped parsley, and serve.

 Spicy Tuna, Tomato, and Olive Pasta Salad Cook 10 oz fresh penne in a large saucepan of lightly salted, boiling water according to the package directions, until al dente. Drain, then refresh under cold running water and drain again. Meanwhile, put 2 (13 oz) cans tuna in water, drained, in a salad bowl and coarsely flake with a fork, then add 2 cups pitted ripe black olives, 2 coarsely chopped plum tomatoes, 1 finely chopped red chile, and a small handful of chopped flat-leaf parsley. Add the drained pasta, then drizzle with 1 tablespoon chile oil and 2 tablespoons extra-virgin olive oil and squeeze the juice of 1 lemon over the salad. Season, toss to mix well, and serve.

Spicy Tuna, Tomato, and Olive Pasta Casserole Cook 12 oz dried fusilli in a large saucepan of lightly salted, boiling water according to the package directions until al dente. Meanwhile, heat 2 tablespoons olive oil in a large skillet, add 3 cups halved, small button mushrooms, 2 finely chopped red chiles, and 1 sliced bunch of scallions, and cook over medium heat for 5 minutes or until softened. Stir in 1 cup cream cheese with garlic and herbs, ¼ cup heavy cream, 12 halved cherry tomatoes, and 2 cups pitted ripe black olives and gently heat through, stirring occasionally, until the cream cheese and cream have combined to make a sauce. Drain and flake 1 (13 oz) can tuna in water. Drain the pasta, then mix with the tuna and creamy sauce. Transfer to an ovenproof dish and sprinkle with ¾ cup shredded sharp cheddar cheese. Place in a preheated oven, at 350°F, for 10 minutes or until lightly browned. Serve immediately with a green salad.

HOT-PULS-MED

30 Spiced Rice and Yellow Lentils

Serves 4

3 tablespoons sunflower oil
1 onion, finely chopped
1 teaspoon ground turmeric
1 tablespoon cumin seeds
1 dried red chile
1 cinnamon stick
3 whole cloves
½ teaspoon crushed
 cardamom seeds
1¼ cups long-grain rice
⅔ cup yellow split lentils, rinsed
 and drained
2½ cups hot vegetable stock
⅓ cup finely chopped
 cilantro leaves
salt and pepper

To serve (optional)
pickles
poppadums
plain yogurt

- Heat the oil in a heavy saucepan, add the onion, and cook over medium heat for 1–2 minutes, then add the spices and cook for an additional 2–3 minutes, until fragrant. Add the rice and lentils and stir to coat well for 1–2 minutes.

- Pour in the stock, add the cilantro, and season well. Bring to a boil, then reduce the heat to low, cover tightly, and cook for 10 minutes. Remove from the heat and let stand, covered, for 10 minutes.

- Spoon into bowls and serve with pickles, poppadums, and yogurt, if desired.

Spicy Rice and Lentil Soup

Put 2 (14½ oz) cans lentil soup, 2 teaspoons mild curry paste, and 1⅓ cups cooked long-grain rice in a saucepan and bring to a boil, then reduce the heat to medium and cook for 2–4 minutes or until piping hot. Serve with spoonfuls of yogurt and warm crusty bread.

Spicy Vegetable and Lentil Stew

Heat 2 tablespoons sunflower oil in a saucepan, add 1 chopped onion, 2 teaspoons peeled and grated fresh ginger root, 2 teaspoons grated garlic, 2 finely chopped red chiles, and 1 tablespoon medium curry paste, and cook for 2–3 minutes, then stir in 2 (14½ oz) cans lentil soup and 1 (16 oz) package frozen mixed vegetables. Bring to a boil, then reduce the heat to medium-low and cook for 6–8 minutes or until piping hot. Serve with crusty bread or steamed rice.

HOT-PULS-MON

30 Spicy Shrimp and Pea Pilaf

Serves 4

1 tablespoon sunflower oil
1 tablespoon butter
1 large onion, finely chopped
2 garlic cloves, finely chopped
1 tablespoon medium or hot
 curry paste
1¼ cups long-grain rice
2½ cups hot fish stock or
 vegetable stock
2 cups frozen peas
finely grated rind and juice
 of 1 large lime
½ cup finely chopped cilanto
12 oz cooked, peeled shrimp
salt and pepper

- Heat the oil and butter in a heavy saucepan, add the onion, and cook over medium heat for 2–3 minutes, until softened. Stir in the garlic and curry paste and cook for an additional 1–2 minutes, until fragrant, then add the rice and stir to coat well.

- Stir in the stock, peas, and lime rind, then season well and bring to a boil. Cover tightly, then reduce the heat to low and cook for 12–15 minutes or until the liquid is absorbed and the rice is tender.

- Remove the pan from the heat and stir in the lime juice, cilantro, and shrimp. Cover and let the shrimp heat through for a few minutes before serving.

 Spicy Shrimp and Pea Stir-Fried Rice

Heat 2 tablespoons sunflower oil in a large wok or skillet until hot, add 1 tablespoon medium curry paste, 12 oz cooked, peeled shrimp, 1⅓ cups frozen peas, and 3½ cups cooked long-grain rice, and stir-fry over high heat for 4–5 minutes or until piping hot. Remove from the heat, season, and stir in ⅓ cup chopped cilantro leaves. Serve immediately.

 Spicy Shrimp, Pea, and Rice Soup

Heat 1 tablespoon butter in a saucepan, add 1 tablespoon mild curry powder, and stir for 20–40 seconds, then add 6 sliced scallions, 1 chopped garlic clove, and 1 teaspoon peeled and grated fresh ginger root and cook for an additional 1–2 minutes. Pour in 3½ cups hot fish stock and bring to a boil, then cook, uncovered, for 4–5 minutes. Add 12 oz raw, peeled jumbo shrimp, 1⅓ cups frozen peas and ⅔ cup cooked long-grain rice. Bring back to a boil, then reduce the heat to medium and cook for 5–6 minutes, until the shrimp turn pink and the rice and peas are tender. Season and remove from the heat, then stir in ¼ cup finely chopped cilantro leaves and serve.

30 Spiced Fava Bean and Dill Pilaf

Serves 4

2 cups shelled fava beans
4 tablespoons butter
2 red chiles, finely chopped
1 tablespoon cumin seeds
2 cloves
6 green cardamom pods
1 cinnamon stick
¼ cup red split lentils, rinsed
   and drained
1⅓ cups long-grain rice
6 finely sliced scallions
⅓ cup finely chopped dill
salt and pepper

- Cook the fava beans in a saucepan of boiling water for 1–2 minutes. Drain, then put in a bowl of cold water and let the beans cool slightly. Drain again, then slip off and discard the skins and set the beans aside.

- Melt the butter in a saucepan over low heat, add the red chiles and spices and stir for 1 minute, then add the lentils and rice and continue to stir until well coated.

- Pour over enough water to come about ¾ inch above the level of the rice. Season well and bring to a boil. Stir once, then reduce the heat to low, cover tightly, and cook gently for 8–10 minutes. Remove from the heat and let stand, covered, for 10–12 minutes or until the liquid is absorbed and the rice is tender.

- Stir the fava beans, scallions, and dill through the rice, then spoon into a bowls and serve.

 Spicy Fava Bean and Dill Rice Salad

Blanch and skin 2⅔ cups shelled fava beans as above. Meanwhile, heat a skillet until hot, add 1 tablespoon cumin seeds, and dry-fry over medium heat until browned, then let cool. Put 3½ cups cooked rice, 2 finely chopped red chiles, the toasted cumin seeds, 6 finely sliced scallions, and the fava beans in a large bowl. Pour ⅔ cup store-bought fresh vinaigrette over the salad and sprinkle with a small handful of chopped dill. Season, toss to mix, well and serve.

 Spicy Fava Bean and Dill Pasta

Cook 12 oz dried penne in a large saucepan of lightly salted, boiling water according to the package directions until al dente, adding 1⅓ cups shelled fava beans 2–4 minutes before the end of the cooking time. Meanwhile, heat 1 tablespoon butter in a skillet, add 6 finely sliced scallions, 2 finely chopped red chiles, and 2 finely chopped garlic cloves, and cook over low heat for 2–4 minutes, until softened. Add 1 cup crème fraîche or sour cream and heat through for a few minutes, until piping hot.

Drain the pasta and fava beans, return to the pan and stir in the crème fraiche mixture. Season, toss to mix well, and sprinkle with a small handful of chopped dill before serving.

HOT-PULS-SAH

30 Chile and Zucchini Pennette

Serves 4

1 tablespoon butter
1 tablespoon olive oil
2 red chiles, finely chopped
2 garlic cloves, finely chopped
4 scallions, minced
3 zucchini, coarsely grated
finely grated rind of 1 lime
⅔ cup cream cheese
12 oz dried pennette or other
  short pasta shapes
small handful of flat-leaf parsley,
  chopped
salt and pepper

- Heat the butter and oil in a large skillet, add the red chiles, garlic, scallions, and zucchini, and cook over medium-low heat for 10 minutes or until softened.

- Reduce the heat to low, add the lime rind, and gently cook for 3–4 minutes, then add the cream cheese and mix together until the cheese melts. Season to taste.

- Meanwhile, cook the pasta in a large saucepan of lightly salted, boiling water according to the package directions until al dente.

- Drain the pasta and stir into the zucchini mixture with the parsley. Spoon into warm bowls and serve.

 Chile and Zucchini Stir-Fry Noodles

Heat 2 tablespoons olive oil in a large skillet, add 6 sliced scallions, 2 crushed garlic cloves, 1 chopped red chile, and 2 shredded zucchini, and cook over high heat for 4–5 minutes, until softened. Add 1¼ lb fresh egg noodles and ¼ cup light soy sauce and toss to mix well. Stir-fry for 1–2 minutes or until piping hot. Serve immediately.

 Zucchini and Chile Pasta Salad

Cook 12 oz dried pennette in a large saucepan of lightly salted, boiling water according to the package directions until al dente. Drain the pasta, rinse under cold running water, and drain again, then let cool for 10 minutes. Put 2 shredded zucchini, 4 sliced scallions, ¼ cup each of coarsely chopped cilantro and mint leaves, and 12 halved cherry tomatoes in a large salad bowl, then add the cooled pasta. Beat together 2 finely chopped red chiles, 2 crushed garlic cloves, ⅓ cup extra-virgin olive oil, the juice of 1 lemon, and 1 teaspoon honey in a bowl, then season well. Pour the dressing over the salad, toss to mix well, and serve.

HOT-PULS-GEH

30 Chile and Butternut Squash Risotto

Serves 4

4 tablespoon butter
1 tablespoon olive oil
1 onion, minced
2 garlic cloves, finely chopped
2 red chiles, finely chopped
2 cups peeled, seeded, and diced
  butternut squash
1½ cups risotto rice
4¼ cups hot vegetable stock
1 cup finely grated Parmesan
  cheese, plus extra to serve
salt and pepper
chopped flat-leaf parsley,
  to garnish

- Heat the butter and oil in medium saucepan, add the onion, garlic, red chiles, and butternut squash, and cook over medium heat for 3–4 minutes, until softened. Add the rice and stir for 1 minute or until the grains are well coated.

- Add 1 ladle of hot stock and simmer, stirring until it has been absorbed. Repeat with another ladle of stock, then continue to add the stock at intervals and cook as before, for an additional 18–20 minutes or until the liquid has been absorbed and the rice is tender but still firm (al dente). Reserve 1 ladle of stock.

- When cooked, stir in the reserved stock and Parmesan, season, and mix well. Remove from the heat, cover, and let stand for 2 minutes.

- Spoon into warm bowls, sprinkle with chopped parsley, and serve with extra grated Parmesan.

 Chile, Butternut Squash, and Rice Broth Heat 1 tablespoon butter in a saucepan, add 1 chopped red chile, and cook, stirring, for 1 minute, then add 2 (15 oz) cans of vegetable and butternut squash soup and 1⅓ cups cooked white rice and bring to a boil. Reduce the heat to medium and cook gently for 2–4 minutes or until piping hot. Serve immediately.

 Butternut Squash and Chile Pasta Cook 3 cups peeled, seeded, and diced butternut squash in a large saucepan of lightly salted, boiling water for 10 minutes, then add 12 oz thin spaghetti and cook according to package directions, until the squash is tender and the pasta is al dente. Drain well, then return to the saucepan and add 2 tablespoons chile oil and 1 cup grated Parmesan cheese. Toss to mix well, spoon into warm bowls, sprinkle with a small handful of chopped flat-leaf parsley, and serve.

HOT-PULS-RER

30 Spicy Chickpea Curry

Serves 4

2 tablespoons sunflower oil
4 garlic cloves, minced
2 teaspoons peeled and finely
    grated fresh ginger root
1 large onion, coarsely grated
1–2 green chiles, finely sliced
1 teaspoon hot chili powder
1 tablespoon ground cumin
1 tablespoon ground coriander
3 tablespoons plain yogurt,
    plus extra, beatened, to serve
2 teaspoons garam masala
2 cups water
2 teaspoons tamarind paste
2 teaspoons medium or hot
    curry powder
2 (15 oz) cans chickpeas, rinsed
    and drained
chopped cilantro leaves, to
    garnish
lemon wedges, to serve
    (optional)

- Heat the oil in a large, heavy skillet, add the garlic, ginger, onion, and green chiles, and cook over medium heat, stirring occasionally, for 5–6 minutes, until the onion is lightly golden. Add the chili powder, cumin, ground coriander, yogurt, and garam masala and cook for an additional 1–2 minutes.

- Stir in the measured water and bring to a boil. Add the tamarind paste, curry powder, and chickpeas and bring back to a boil, then reduce the heat to medium and cook, uncovered, for 15–20 minutes or until the sauce is thickened.

- Ladle into warm bowls, drizzle with the extra beatened yogurt, and sprinkle with chopped cilantro. Serve with lemon wedges for squeezing over the chickpeas, if desired.

10 Spicy Hummus

Put 2 (15 oz) cans chickpeas, rinsed and drained, 1 tablespoon medium or hot curry powder, 1 teaspoon garlic paste, the juice of 1 lemon, and 1¾ cups crème fraîche or sour cream in a food processor or blender, then season and blend until fairly smooth. Serve with toasted pita bread and a chopped salad.

20 Spicy Chickpea Soup

Heat 2 tablespoons sunflower oil in a saucepan, add 1 chopped onion, and cook, stirring, for 1–2 minutes, until softened. Add 1 tablespoon medium or hot curry powder and 2½ cups hot vegetable stock and bring to a boil, then add 1 (15 oz) can chickpeas, rinsed and drained, and 1 cup light cream. Bring back to a boil, then reduce the heat to medium and cook for 4–5 minutes or until piping hot. Season, stir in ¼ cup chopped cilantro leaves, and serve with crusty bread.

Burmese Coconut Chicken and Rice Noodle Curry

Serves 4

1¾ lb boneless, skinless chicken
  thighs, cut into bite-size pieces
2 large onions, coarsely chopped
5 garlic cloves, coarsely chopped
1 teaspoon peeled and finely
  grated fresh ginger root
2 tablespoons sunflower oil
½ teaspoon Burmese shrimp paste
1 (14 fl oz) can coconut milk
2 tablespoons hot curry powder
8 oz dried flat rice noodles
salt and pepper
lime wedges, to serve

To garnish

chopped cilantro leaves
finely chopped red onion
fried garlic slivers
sliced red chiles

- Season the chicken pieces and set aside. Put the onion, garlic, and ginger in a food processor or blender and blend to a smooth paste, adding a little water, if needed.

- Heat the oil in a large saucepan, add the onion mixture and shrimp paste, and cook, stirring, over high heat for 4–5 minutes. Add the chicken, reduce the heat to medium, and cook, stirring, for 1–2 minutes, until browned.

- Stir in the coconut milk and curry powder and bring to a boil, then cover, reduce the heat, and simmer for 15–20 minutes, stirring occasionally.

- Meanwhile, cook the noodles according to the package directions, then drain and divide among large, warm bowls.

- Ladle the curry over the noodles, sprinkle with chopped cilantro, chopped red onion, fried garlic slivers, and sliced red chiles, then serve with lime wedges to squeeze over the curry.

 Spicy Coconut Chicken and Rice Noodles Heat 2 tablespoons sunflower oil in a large wok until hot, add 8 chopped scallions, 2 chopped garlic cloves, and 1 tablespoon hot curry powder, and stir-fry over high heat for 1–2 minutes. Stir in 12 oz fresh rice noodles, 1¼ lb store-bought, cooked skinless chicken breasts, and 1 cup canned coconut milk and stir-fry for an additional 1–2 minutes or until piping hot. Serve immediately with lime wedges.

 Broiled Coconut Chicken with Spicy Rice Noodles Mix together 2 tablespoons medium or hot curry powder, ½ cup canned coconut milk, and the juice of 1 lime in a small bowl, then brush over 4 large, boneless chicken breasts with skin. Cook under a preheated medium broiler for 6–8 minutes on each side or until cooked through. Meanwhile, prepare 12 oz dried rice noodles according to the package directions, then drain. Put the noodles in a bowl, then add 2 tablespoons extra-virgin olive oil, the juice of 1 lime, and 1 finely chopped red chile, season, and toss to mix well. Divide the noodles among warm plates, top with the broiled chicken, and serve immediately.

HOT-PULS-DEP

Spicy Quinoa, Fava Bean, and Avocado Salad

Serves 4

1 cup quinoa
3½ cups hot vegetable stock
3 cups shelled fava beans
1 tablespoon cumin seeds
3 lemons
2 ripe avocados
2 garlic cloves, crushed
2 red chiles, finely chopped
2 cups thickly sliced radishes
small handful of chopped cilantro
   leaves
⅓ cup extra-virgin olive oil
salt and pepper

- Put the quinoa in a strainer and rinse well, then put in medium saucepan and add the stock. Bring to a boil, then reduce the heat to medium and simmer for 10–12 minutes, uncovered, until the germ separates and most of the stock has been absorbed. Drain well, then let cool.

- Meanwhile, cook the fava beans in a saucepan of boiling water for 1–2 minutes. Drain, then put in a bowl of cold water, and let the beans cool slightly. Drain again, then slip off and discard the skins and set the beans aside.

- Heat a skillet until hot, add the cumin seeds, and dry-fry over medium heat until lightly brown, then remove from the skillet and set aside. When cooled, lightly crush the seeds.

- Remove the peel and pith from the lemons and cut each one into segments, discarding any seeds, then put into a large bowl. Squeeze any remaining juices into the bowl.

- Peel, pit, and thickly slice the avocados, add to the bowl ,and toss in the lemon juice. Add the drained quinoa, fava beans, toasted cumin seeds, and the remaining ingredients, then season. Toss to mix well and serve.

---

1 **Spicy Avocado and Fava Bean Bruschettas** Blanch and skin ⅔ cup shelled fava beans as above. Peel, pit, and chop 2 avocados, then put in a blender with the skinned fava beans, 2 chopped red chiles, ¼ cup chopped flat-leaf parsley, ¼ cup olive oil, and the juice of 1 lemon. Season, then blend until smooth. Spread onto toasted ciabatta slices and serve, drizzled with a little extra olive oil.

2 **Spicy Quinoa and Fava Bean Broth** Put ⅓ cup quinoa and 2½ cups water in a saucepan and bring to a boil, then reduce the heat to medium and simmer, uncovered, for 8–10 minutes, until the germ separates and most of the liquid has been absorbed. Drain well, then return to the saucepan and add 3½ cups hot vegetable stock, 3 cups shelled fava beans, 1 tablespoon chile oil, and 1 tablespoon hot curry powder. Season, then bring to a boil, stirring frequently, and cook for 2–4 minutes or until piping hot. Remove from the heat, stir in a small handful of chopped cilantro leaves, and serve.

Index

Page references in *italics* indicate photographs.

angel-hair pasta: Spicy Coconut Shrimp with Angel-Hair Pasta 260
arugula
  Chicken Salad with Chile & Arugula Pesto 30
  Chicken with Chile & Arugula Pesto Linguine 30
  Grilled Chicken with Chile & Arugula Pesto 30, 31
  Hot & Spicy Steak & Arugula Ciabattas 86, 87
  Spiced Crayfish & Arugula Sandwiches 152, 153
  Spicy Steak, Potato & Arugula Salad 86
asparagus
  Spicy Asparagus & Smoked Salmon Risotto 244
  Spicy Smoked Salmon & Asparagus Pasta 244, 245
  Spicy Smoked Salmon, Asparagus & Pasta Salad 244
avocados
  Island-Spiced Corn with Avocado & Tomato 188, 189
  Spicy Avocado & Fava Bean Bruschettas 278
  Spicy Quinoa, Fava Bean & Avocado Salad 278, 279
  Spicy Corn, Avocado & Tomato Pasta 188
  Spicy Corn, Avocado & Tomato Salad 188

baked beans: Spicy Sausage & Bean Stew 98
beans
  Chorizo Sausage, Paprika & Bean Stew 92, 93
  Pan-Fried Chorizo, Paprika & Beans 92
  Quick Chorizo, Paprika and Bean Soup 92
  Spicy Bean & Bell Pepper Salad 252, 253
  Spicy Bean & Red Pepper Curry 252
  Spicy Bean & Red Pepper Pilaf 252
  see also baked beans; black beans; edamame; fava beans; green beans
beef
  African Curried Beef & Mango Chutney Casserole 76, 77
  Beef & Mixed Peppercorn Pilaf 94
  Beef & Mixed Peppercorn Stroganoff 94, 95

Beef Meatball Curry 96
Chinese Beef, Tofu & Vegetable Noodles 78
Chinese Beef, Tofu & Vegetable Salad 78
Chinese Beef with Tofu & Vegetables 78, 79
Curried Beef & Black Bean Stir-Fry 120
Curried Beef & Mango Chutney Rolls 76
Curried Beef & Mango Chutney Wraps 76
Hot & Spicy Steak & Arugula Ciabattas 86, 87
Quick Spiced Beef & Mushroom Pie 94
Spicy Beef Enchilada Wraps 104, 105
Spicy Beef Enchiladas 104
Spicy Beef Meatballs with Mint Relish 96, 97
Spicy Enchilada Beef Rice 104
Spicy Meatball Heroes 96
Spicy Spaghetti and Meat Sauce 86
Spicy Steak, Potato & Arugula Salad 86
Jamaican Curried Beef & Black Bean Stew 120, 121
beets
  Creamy Beet, Green Bean & Tomato Curry 184, 185
  Curried Beet, Green Bean & Tomato Broth 184
  Curried Beet, Green Bean & Tomato Rice 184
bell peppers
  Butternut Squash & Red Pepper Curry 212, 213
  Chinese Monkfish & Bell Pepper Stir-Fry 144
  Curried Butternut Squash & Red Pepper Soup 212
  Curried Roasted Butternut Squash & Red Peppers 212
  Harissa-Spiced Turkey & Bell Pepper Kebabs 32, 33
  Malaysian Red Pepper & Cabbage Stir-Fry 222, 223
  Piquant Chicken & Bell Pepper Brochettes 36, 37
  Piquant Chicken & Bell Pepper Stew 36
  Piquant Chicken & Roasted Pepper Salad 36
  Pork, Red Pepper & Pea Curry 90, 91
  Spicy Bean & Bell Pepper Salad 252, 253
  Spicy Bean & Red Pepper Curry 252
  Spicy Bean & Red Pepper Pilaf 252

Spicy Cabbage & Red Pepper Salad 222
Spicy Cabbage & Red Pepper Stew 222
Spicy Monkfish & Bell Pepper Kebabs 144
Spicy Monkfish & Bell Pepper Stew 144, 145
Turkey, Bell Pepper & Harissa Stir-Fry 32
black beans
  Carrot & Black Bean Curry 242, 243
  Curried Beef & Black Bean Pilaf 120
  Curried Beef & Black Bean Stir-Fry 120
  Jamaican Curried Beef & Black Bean Stew 120, 121
  Spicy Black Bean & Scallion Salad 240
  Spicy Black Bean, Scallion & Noodle Omelet 240
  Spicy Carrot & Black Bean Noodles 242
  Spicy Carrot & Black Bean Salad 242
  Warm Spicy Black Bean, Scallion & Noodle Salad 240, 241
bok choy: Spicy Tofu with Bok Choy & Scallions 220, 221
bulgur wheat: Harissa Vegetable Stew with Bulgur Wheat 246
butternut squash
  Butternut Squash & Chile Pasta 272
  Butternut Squash & Red Pepper Curry 212, 213
  Chile & Butternut Squash Risotto 272, 273
  Chile, Butternut Squash & Rice Broth 272
  Curried Butternut Squash & Red Pepper Soup 212
  Curried Roast Butternut Squash & Red Peppers 212
  Thai Massaman Butternut Squash Curry 226, 227

cabbage
  Malaysian Red Pepper & Cabbage Stir-Fry 222, 223
  Spiced Red Cabbage & Carrot Salad 196, 197
  Spicy Cabbage & Carrot Casserole 196
  Spicy Cabbage & Carrot Stir-Fry 196
  Spicy Cabbage & Red Pepper Salad 222
  Spicy Cabbage & Red Pepper Stew 222
calves' liver
  Curried Calves' Liver with Caramelized Onions 82

Curried Calves' Liver with Herbed Salad 82, 83
Warm Curried Calves' Liver Salad 82
carrots
Carrot & Black Bean Curry 242, 243
Carrot, Pea & Potato Curry 204, 205
Spiced Carrot & Green Bean Slaw 198
Spiced Carrot & Green Bean Stew 198, 199
Spiced Red Cabbage & Carrot Salad 196, l 197
Spicy Cabbage & Carrot Casserole 196
Spicy Cabbage & Carrot Stir-Fry 196
Spicy Carrot & Black Bean Noodles 242
Spicy Carrot & Black Bean Salad 242
Spicy Carrot & Green Bean Soup 198
Spicy Lentil & Carrot Dal 254
Spicy Lentil & Carrot Salad 254
Spicy Lentil & Carrot Soup with Caramelized Onions 254, 255
Spicy Pea, Carrot & Potato Frittata 204
Spicy Pea, Carrot & Potato Stir-Fry 204
cashew nuts
Spicy Roasted Veg Couscous with Cashews & Feta 248, 249
Spicy Veg & Cashew Stew with Feta & Couscous 248
Spicy Veg, Cashew & Feta Couscous Salad 248
cauliflower
Spicy Mushroom, Cauliflower & Chickpea Rice 200
Spicy Mushroom, Cauliflower & Chickpea Stew 200, 201
cheese
Spicy Roasted Veg Couscous with Cashews & Feta 248, 249
Spicy Spinach, Tomato & Cottage Cheese Salad 202
Spinach, Tomato & Paneer Curry 202, 203
see also cottage cheese; feta cheese; goat cheese
chicken
Broiled Chicken with Chile, Lemon & Tarragon Butter 26
Broiled Chicken with Curry Mayonnaise 66
Broiled Coconut Chicken with Spicy Rice Noodles 276
Broiled Rose Harissa Chicken 54
Broiled Thai Green Chicken 46
Burmese Coconut Chicken & Rice Noodle Curry 276, 277
Chicken & Mango Curry 34

Chicken, Chile & Rosemary Soup 60, 61
Chicken, Lemon & Tarragon Risotto 26, 27
Chicken, Mushroom & Spinach Salad with Spicy Yogurt Dressing 58
Chicken Salad with Chile & Arugula Pesto 30
Chicken, Shrimp & Lemon Grass Cakes 64, 65
Chicken, Shrimp & Lemon Grass Skewers 64
Chicken, Shrimp & Lemon Grass Stir-Fry 64
Chicken with Chile & Arugula Pesto Linguine 30
Cold Roast Chicken with Spicy Salsa Verde 28, 29
Creamy Chicken, Chile & Rosemary Pasta 60
Curried Chicken & Grape Salad 66, 67
Curried Chicken & Peas 62, 63
Curried Chicken Pasta Salad 66
Fruity Chicken Moroccan Stew 40
Green Chicken Skewers with Cucumber & Chile Dip 24, 25
Grilled Chicken with Chile & Arugula Pesto 30, 31
Herbed Chicken Rice with Vietnamese-Style Sauce 234, 235
Pan-fried Chicken with Spicy Salsa Verde 28
Piquant Chicken & Bell Pepper Brochettes 36, 37
Piquant Chicken & Bell Pepper Stew 36
Piquant Chicken & Roasted Pepper Salad 36
Poached Chicken with Spicy Salsa Verde 28
Quick Chicken & Pea Curry 62
Quick Rose Harissa & Chicken Sauté 54
Quick Thai Green Chicken Curry 50
Rose Harissa & Chicken Meatball Moroccan Stew 54, 55
Rosemary & Chile-Stuffed Chicken 60
Spiced Chicken, Mushroom & Spinach Pilaf 58
Spiced Chicken Stew with Preserved Lemon 42, 43
Spicy Chicken & Fruit Couscous Salad 40
Spicy Chicken & Mango Noodles 34, 35
Spicy Chicken & Mango Kebabs 34
Spicy Chicken & Pea with Pasta 62
Spicy Chicken & Preserved Lemon Skewers 42

Spicy Chicken, Apricot & Cranberry Couscous 40, 41
Spicy Chicken, Mushroom & Spinach Crepes 58, 59
Spicy Coconut Chicken & Rice Noodles 276
Spicy Lemon Chicken Salad 42
Spicy Vietnamese Chicken 44, 45
Sweet & Spicy Chicken & Pea Rice 52
Sweet & Spicy Chicken Drumsticks 52
Sweet & Spicy Chicken Noodles 52, 53
Thai Green Chicken Curry 46, 47
Thai Green Chicken Fried Rice 50
Thai Green Chicken Stir-Fry 46
Thai Green Coconut-Stuffed Chicken 50, 51
Vietnamese Broiled Chicken 44
Vietnamese Chicken, Herb & Rice Salad 234
Vietnamese Chicken, Herb & Rice Soup 234
Vietnamese Chicken Soup 44
Warm Green Chicken & Rice Salad 24
chickpeas
Lamb Chops with Spicy Chickpeas & Spinach 88, 89
Spicy Chickpea Curry 274, 275
Spicy Chickpea Soup 274
Spicy Lamb, Spinach & Chickpea Rice 88
Spicy Lamb, Spinach & Chickpea Salad 88
Spicy Mushroom & Chickpea Soup 200
Spicy Mushroom, Cauliflower & Chickpea Rice 200
Spicy Mushroom, Cauliflower & Chickpea Stew 200, 201
chorizo sausages
Chorizo Sausage, Paprika & Bean Stew 92, 93
Chorizo, Spinach & Egg Salad with Paprika Croutons 106, 107
Pan-Fried Chorizo, Paprika & Beans 92
Quick Chorizo, Paprika and Bean Soup 92
Spicy Chorizo & Spinach Egg-Fried Rice 106
Spicy Chorizo & Spinach Frittata 106
chow mein: Chinese Turkey Chow Mein 70, 71
chowder: Spicy Clam & Coconut Chowder 154
ciabattas
Hot & Spicy Steak & Arugula Ciabattas 86, 87
Spicy Meatball Heroes 96

Turkey Ciabattas with Harissa Mayo 32

cilantro 8, 9
Chile & Cilantro Crab Cakes 134, 135
Crab, Chile & Cilantro Pasta 134
Grilled Piri Piri Squid with Mint & Cilantro 140, 141
Pan-Fried Scallops with Chile, Cilantro & Coconut 166
Scallop, Chile, Cilantro & Coconut Pasta 166
Warm Crab, Chile & Cilantro Rice Salad 134

clams
Chile & Garlic-Braised Clams 130
Chile Spaghetti with Vodka 130, 131
Clam & Chile Rice 130
Coconut Spiced Clams 154, 155
Spicy Clam & Coconut Chowder 154
Spicy Clam Omelet 154

coconut
Indonesian Okra with Coconut 210, 211
Mango & Coconut Curry 186, 187
Spiced Mango & Coconut Salad 186
Spiced Okra, Tomato & Coconut 218, 219
Spicy Fried Okra with Coconut 218
Spicy Herb & Coconut Salmon Packages 128, 129
Spicy Mango & Coconut Rice 186

coconut milk 9
Broiled Coconut Chicken with Spicy Rice Noodles 276
Burmese Coconut Chicken & Rice Noodle Curry 276, 277
Caribbean Crayfish & Coconut Curry 152
Coconut Spiced Clams 154, 155
Crayfish, Vegetable & Coconut Stir-Fry 152
Pan-Fried Scallops with Chile, Cilantro & Coconut 166
Scallop, Chile, Cilantro & Coconut Pasta 166
Spiced Coconut & Okra Rice 210
Spiced Shrimp, Coconut & Rice Noodle Soup 260, 261
Spicy Clam & Coconut Chowder 154
Spicy Coconut Chicken & Rice Noodles 276
Spicy Coconut Shrimp with Angel-Hair Pasta 260
Spicy Coconut Soup with Deep-Fried Okra 210
Spicy Shrimp & Coconut Noodle Soup 260
Thai Green Coconut-Stuffed Chicken 50, 51

Tomato, Coconut & Okra Curry 218
cod
Baked Tamarind Fish with Cherry Tomatoes 136
Broiled Tomato & Tamarind Fish 136
Tomato & Tamarind Fish Curry 136, 137

corn
Island-Spiced Corn with Avocado & Tomato 188, 189
Spicy Corn, Avocado & Tomato Pasta 188
Spicy Corn, Avocado & Tomato Salad 188

couscous
Moroccan Couscous Salad 192
Moroccan Vegetable Couscous Salad 246
Moroccan Vegetable Stew with Couscous 192, 193
Spicy Chicken & Fruit Couscous Salad 40
Spicy Chicken, Apricot & Cranberry Couscous 40, 41
Spicy Roasted Veg Couscous with Cashews & Feta 248, 249
Spicy Veg & Cashew Stew with Feta & Couscous 248
Spicy Veg, Cashew & Feta Couscous Salad 248

crab
Chile & Cilantro Crab Cakes 134, 135
Crab, Chile & Cilantro Pasta 134
Warm Crab, Chile & Cilantro Rice Salad 134

crayfish
Caribbean Crayfish & Coconut Curry 152
Crayfish, Vegetable & Coconut Stir-Fry 152
Spiced Crayfish & Arugula Sandwiches 152, 153

crepes: Spicy Chicken, Mushroom & Spinach Crepes 58, 59
cucumbers: Green Chicken Skewers with Cucumber & Chile Dip 24, 25

dal: Spicy Lentil & Carrot Dal 254
duck
Broiled Thai Red Duck 48
Duck & Vegetable Tikka Stir-Fry 68
Duck Tikka Kebabs 68, 69
Mango & Duck Curry 56
Spicy Mango & Duck Noodles 56
Spicy Mango & Duck Salad 56, 57
Thai Red Duck Curry 48, 49
Thai-Style Red Duck Salad 48
Tikka-Spiced Duck Omelet 68

edamame
Edamame, Ginger & Chile Rice 232
Edamame, Ginger, Chile & Noodle Broth 232
Warm Edamame, Ginger, Chile & Noodle Salad 232, 233

egg noodles
Chile & Zucchini Stir-Fry Noodles 270
Chinese Turkey & Noodle Salad 70
Chinese Turkey Chow Mein 70, 71
Spicy Black Bean, Scallion & Noodle Omelet 240
Spicy Carrot & Black Bean Noodles 242
Spicy Chicken & Mango Noodles 34, 35
Spicy Ham & Pea Noodles 108
Spicy Mango & Duck Noodles 56
Spicy Pork & Noodle Omelet 250
Spicy Pork & Noodle Stir-Fry 250
Spicy Pork, Vegetable & Noodle Stir-Fry 114
Spicy Shrimp & Vegetable Noodles 236, 237
Spicy Sweet Potato & Litchi Noodles 190
Sticky Spicy Pork with Vegetable Noodles 114, 115
Sweet & Spicy Chicken Noodles 52, 53
Sweet Chile Veal & Scallion Noodles 116
Warm Spicy Black Bean, Scallion & Noodle Salad 240, 241

eggplants
Chile, Eggplant & Tomato Sauté 180
Deep-Fried Spiced Baby Eggplant 216, 217
Eggplant, Tomato & Chile Curry 180, 181
Eggplant, Tomato & Chile Salad 180
Spiced Baby Eggplants with Chile & Herbs 216

eggs
Chorizo, Spinach & Egg Salad with Paprika Croutons 106, 107
Curried Smoked Mussel Omelet 132
Green Bean, Chile & Egg-Fried Rice 206
Laksa Salmon & Shrimp Omelet 142
Spicy Black Bean, Scallion & Noodle Omelet 240
Spicy Chorizo & Spinach Egg-Fried Rice 106
Spicy Clam Omelet 154
Spicy Eggs with Merguez Sausages & Tomato 103, 103
Spicy Pork & Noodle Omelet 250
Spicy Rice Noodle Omelet 256

Spicy Scrambled Eggs with Merguez
   Sausages 102
Spicy Thai Scrambled Eggs 118
enchiladas
   Spicy Beef Enchilada Wraps 104, 105
   Spicy Beef Enchiladas 104
   Spicy Enchilada Beef Rice 104

fava beans
   Spiced Fava Bean & Dill Pilaf 268, 269
   Spicy Avocado & Fava Bean
      Bruschettas 278
   Spicy Fava Bean & Dill Pasta 268
   Spicy Fava Bean & Dill Rice Salad 268
   Spicy Quinoa & Fava Bean Broth 278
   Spicy Quinoa, Fava Bean & Avocado
      Salad 278, 279
feta cheese
   Spicy Roasted Veg Couscous with
      Cashews & Feta 248, 249
   Spicy Veg & Cashew Stew with Feta &
      Couscous 248
   Spicy Veg, Cashew & Feta Couscous
      Salad 248
fish: see cod; halibut; lemon sole;
   mackerel; flounder; monkfish; salmon;
   trout; tuna; white fish
flounder
   Baked Tamarind Fish with Cherry
      Tomatoes 136
   Broiled Tomato & Tamarind Fish 136
   Pan-Fried Fish with Mustard & Curry
      Leaves 162
   Tomato & Tamarind Fish Curry 136,
      137

garbanzo beans: see chickpeas
ginger 8
   Edamame, Ginger & Chile Rice 232
   Edamame, Ginger, Chile & Noodle
      Broth 232
   Warm Edamame, Ginger, Chile &
      Noodle Salad 232, 233
goat cheese
   Chile, Cherry Tomato & Goat Cheese
      Pasta 182
   Chile, Cherry Tomato & Goat Cheese
      Salad 182
   Chile, Cherry Tomato & Goat Cheese
      Tart 182, 183
gratins
   Chile Tomato & Shrimp Gratin 168
   Spicy Lobster Gratin 156
   Spicy Shrimp & Tomato Gratin 146
green beans
   Chinese-Style Green Beans with Chile
      206, 207
   Creamy Beet, Green Bean & Tomato
      Curry 184, 185

Curried Beet, Green Bean & Tomato
   Broth 184
Curried Beet, Green Bean & Tomato
   Rice 184
Five-Spice Pork Chops with Green
   Beans 122, 123
Green Bean, Chile & Egg-Fried Rice
   206
Spiced Carrot & Green Bean Slaw 198
Spiced Carrot & Green Bean Stew
   198, 199
Spiced Green Bean & Chile Pilaf 206
Spicy Carrot & Green Bean Soup 198
Spicy Green Bean & Pesto Pasta Gratin
   238
Spicy Green Bean & Pesto Salad 238
Spicy Green Bean, Potato & Pesto
   Linguine 238, 239
green lentils
   Chile Green Lentil & Lima Bean Pasta
      258
   Green Lentil & Lima Bean Pilaf with
      Chile Dressing 258
   Green Lentil & Lima Bean Salad with
      Chile Dressing 258, 259

halibut
   Baked Tamarind Fish with Cherry
      Tomatoes 136
   Broiled Tomato & Tamarind Fish 136
   Casseroled Mustard & Curry Leaf
      Fish 162
   Goan Fish Curry 158
   Goan Fish Cakes 158
   Goan Fried Fish 158, 159
   Mustard & Curry Leaf Halibut 162,
      163
   Tomato & Tamarind Fish Curry 136,
      137
ham
   Spicy Ham & Pea Noodles 108
   Spicy Ham & Pea Risotto 108, 109
   Spicy Ham & Pea Tortilla 108
harissa paste
   Harissa Tabbouleh with Roasted
      Vegetables 246, 247
   Harissa Vegetable Stew with Bulgur
      Wheat 246
   Harissa-Spiced Turkey & Bell Pepper
      Kebabs 32, 33
   Turkey Ciabattas with Harissa Mayo 32
   Turkey, Bell Pepper & Harissa Stir-
      Fry 32

Italian sausages
   Spicy Sausage & Tomato Casserole
      110
   Spicy Sausage & Tomato Pasta 110,
      111

kebabs
   Duck Tikka Kebabs 68, 69
   Moroccan Kebabs 192
   Spicy Lamb & Herb Kebabs 100, 101
   Spicy Monkfish & Bell Pepper Kebabs
      144
   Sumac, Chile & Lemon-Spiced
      Monkfish Kebabs 170, 171
   Veal & Scallion Kebabs with Sweet Chili
      Dip 116, 117

lamb
   Broiled Spicy Lamb Cutlets 112
   Broiled Tandoori Lamb Chops 84, 85
   Lamb Chops with Spicy Chickpeas &
      Spinach 88, 89
   Spiced Lamb Pilaf 100
   Spicy Lamb & Herb Kebabs 100, 101
   Spicy Lamb & Vegetable Curry 112
   Spicy Lamb & Vegetable Stew 112,
      113
   Spicy Lamb, Spinach & Chickpea Rice
      88
   Spicy Lamb, Spinach & Chickpea
      Salad 88
   Spicy Lamb Stir-Fry 100
   Tandoori Lamb Wraps 84
   Tandoori Roasted Rack of Lamb 84
lemon grass 8
   Burmese Lemon Grass & Chile Pork
      80, 81
   Chicken, Shrimp & Lemon Grass Cakes
      64, 65
   Chicken, Shrimp & Lemon Grass
      Skewers 64
   Chicken, Shrimp & Lemon Grass Stir-
      Fry 64
   Pork Chops with Lemon Grass &
      Chile 80
   Pork, Lemon Grass & Chile Stir-Fry
      80
   Shrimp, Lemon Grass & Mango 164
   Shrimp, Lemon Grass & Mango Curry
      164, 165
   Shrimp, Lemon Grass & Mango Rice
      164
Lemon Sole with Spicy Salsa 138, 139
lemons
   Broiled Chicken with Chile, Lemon &
      Tarragon Butter 26
   Chicken, Lemon & Tarragon Baguettes
      26
   Chicken, Lemon & Tarragon Risotto
      26, 27
   Quick Turkey, Chile & Lemon Rice
      38
   Sumac, Chile & Lemon-Spiced
      Monkfish Kebabs 170, 171
   Turkey, Chile & Lemon Stir-Fry 38

lentils
  Chile Green Lentil & Lima Bean Pasta 258
  Green Lentil & Lima Bean Pilaf with Chile Dressing 258
  Green Lentil & Lima Bean Salad with Chile Dressing 258, 259
  Spiced Rice & Yellow Lentils 264, 265
  Spicy Lentil & Carrot Dal 254
  Spicy Lentil & Carrot Salad 254
  Spicy Lentil & Carrot Soup with Caramelized Onions 254, 255
  Spicy Rice & Lentil Soup 264
  Spicy Vegetable & Lentil Stew 264
lima beans
  Chile Green Lentil & Lima Bean Pasta 258
  Green Lentil & Lima Bean Pilaf with Chile Dressing 258
  Green Lentil & Lima Bean Salad with Chile Dressing 258, 259
lobster
  Creamy Spiced Lobster Tail 156, 157
  Spicy Lobster Bisque 156
  Spicy Lobster Gratin 156

mackerel
  Mackerel & Rice Noodle Stir-Fry 174
  Turmeric Mackerel Curry 174
  Turmeric Mackerel Skewers with Chile Rice Noodles 174, 175
mangoes
  Chicken & Mango Curry 34
  Mango & Duck Curry 56
  Shrimp, Lemon Grass & Mango 164
  Shrimp, Lemon Grass & Mango Curry 164, 165
  Shrimp, Lemon Grass & Mango Rice 164
  Spiced Mango & Coconut Salad 186
  Spicy Chicken & Mango Noodles 34, 35
  Spicy Chicken & Mango Kebabs 34
  Spicy Mango & Coconut Rice 186
  Spicy Mango & Duck Noodles 56
  Spicy Mango & Duck Salad 56, 57
meatballs
  Beef Meatball Curry 96
  Spicy Beef Meatballs with Mint Relish 96, 97
  Spicy Meatball Heroes 96
merguez sausages
  Merguez Sausage & Tomato Tortilla 102
  Spicy Eggs with Merguez Sausages & Tomato 102, 103
  Spicy Scrambled Eggs with Merguez Sausages 102

mint
  Grilled Piri Piri Squid with Mint & Cilantro 140, 141
  Grilled Spicy Zucchini with Tomato & Mint 214
  Middle Eastern Zucchini, Tomato & Mint Curry 214, 215
  Spicy Beef Meatballs with Mint Relish 96, 97
  Spicy Zucchini, Tomato & Mint Salad 214
  Tandoori Jumbo Shrimp Skewers with Mint & Yogurt Dip 148, 149
monkfish
  Chinese Monkfish & Bell Pepper Stir-Fry 144
  Spicy Monkfish & Bell Pepper Kebabs 144
  Spicy Monkfish & Bell Pepper Stew 144, 145
  Sumac & Lemon Monkfish Stew 170
  Sumac, Chile & Lemon-Spiced Monkfish Kebabs 170, 171
mushrooms
  Chicken, Mushroom & Spinach Salad with Spicy Yogurt Dressing 58
  Curried Mushrooms & Tomatoes 208, 209
  Quick Spiced Beef & Mushroom Pie 94
  Spiced Chicken, Mushroom & Spinach Pilaf 58
  Spicy Chicken, Mushroom & Spinach Crepes 58, 59
  Spicy Mushroom & Chickpea Soup 200
  Spicy Mushroom & Tomato Rice 208
  Spicy Mushroom & Tomato Stir-Fry 208
  Spicy Mushroom, Cauliflower & Chickpea Rice 200
  Spicy Mushroom, Cauliflower & Chickpea Stew 200, 201
mussels
  Creamy Curried Mussel Pilaf 132
  Creamy Curried Mussel Soup 132, 133
  Curried Smoked Mussel Omelet 132

noodles see egg noodles; rice noodles; rice vermicelli noodles; soba noodles

okra
  Indonesian Okra with Coconut 210, 211
  Spiced Coconut & Okra Rice 210
  Spiced Okra, Tomato & Coconut 218, 219
  Spicy Coconut Soup with Deep-Fried Okra 210

  Spicy Fried Okra with Coconut 218
  Tomato, Coconut & Okra Curry 218
olives
  Spicy Tuna, Tomato & Olive Pasta 262, 263
  Spicy Tuna, Tomato & Olive Pasta Casserole 262
  Spicy Tuna, Tomato & Olive Pasta Salad 262
omelets
  Curried Smoked Mussel Omelet 132
  Laksa Salmon & Shrimp Omelet 142
  Spicy Black Bean, Scallion & Noodle Omelet 240
  Spicy Clam Omelet 154
  Spicy Pork & Noodle Omelet 250
  Spicy Rice Noodle Omelet 256
  Tikka-Spiced Duck Omelet 68
orzo: Chile Green Lentil & Lima Bean Pasta 258

paneer: Spinach, Tomato & Paneer Curry 202, 203
pasta see angel-hair pasta; bucatini; fusilli; linguine; orzo; penne; pennette; spaghetti
peas
  Carrot, Pea & Potato Curry 204, 205
  Curried Chicken & Peas 62, 63
  Pork, Red Pepper & Pea Curry 90, 91
  Quick Chicken & Pea Curry 62
  Spicy Chicken & Pea with Pasta 62
  Spicy Ham & Pea Noodles 108
  Spicy Ham & Pea Risotto 108, 109
  Spicy Ham & Pea Tortilla 108
  Spicy Pea, Carrot & Potato Frittata 204
  Spicy Pea, Carrot & Potato Stir-Fry 204
  Spicy Shrimp & Pea Pilaf 266, 267
  Spicy Shrimp & Pea Stir-Fried Rice 266
  Spicy Shrimp, Pea & Rice Soup 266
  Sweet & Spicy Chicken & Pea Rice 52
penne
  Chile, Cherry Tomato & Goat Cheese Pasta 182
  Creamy Chicken, Chile & Rosemary Pasta 60
  Curried Chicken Pasta Salad 66
  Spicy Corn, Avocado & Tomato Pasta 188
  Spicy Fava Bean & Dill Pasta 268
  Spicy Green Bean & Pesto Pasta Gratin 238
  Spicy Sausage & Tomato Pasta 110, 111
  Spicy Smoked Salmon, Asparagus & Pasta Salad 244

Spicy Tuna, Tomato & Olive Pasta 262, 263
Spicy Tuna, Tomato & Olive Pasta Salad 262
pennette
Chile & Zucchini Pennette 270, 271
Zucchini & Chile Pasta Salad 270
pesto
Chicken Salad with Chile & Arugula Pesto 30
Chicken with Chile & Arugula Pesto Linguine 30
Grilled Chicken with Chile & Arugula Pesto 30, 31
Spicy Green Bean & Pesto Pasta Gratin 238
Spicy Green Bean & Pesto Salad 238
Spicy Green Bean, Potato & Pesto Linguine 238, 239
pilafs
Beef & Mixed Peppercorn Pilaf 94
Creamy Curried Mussel Pilaf 132
Curried Beef & Black Bean Pilaf 120
Green Lentil & Lima Bean Pilaf with Chile Dressing 258
Spiced Fava Bean & Dill Pilaf 268, 269
Spiced Chicken, Mushroom & Spinach Pilaf 58
Spiced Green Bean & Chile Pilaf 206
Spiced Lamb Pilaf 100
Spicy Bean & Red Pepper Pilaf 252
Spicy Shrimp & Pea Pilaf 266, 267
pomegranates: Cumin Potatoes with Pomegranate Seeds 194, 195
pork
Broiled Spicy Pork 114
Burmese Lemon Grass & Chile Pork 80, 81
Chorizo Sausage, Paprika & Bean Stew 92, 93
Chorizo, Spinach & Egg Salad with Paprika Croutons 106, 107
Curried Pork Chops 90
Five-Spice Pork Chops with Green Beans 122, 123
Pan-Fried Chorizo, Paprika & Beans 92
Pork Chops with Lemon Grass & Chile 80
Pork, Lemon Grass & Chile Stir-Fry 80
Pork, Red Pepper & Pea Curry 90, 91
Quick Chorizo, Paprika & Bean Soup 92
Spicy Chorizo & Spinach Egg-Fried Rice 106
Spicy Chorizo & Spinach Frittata 106
Spicy Pork & Noodle Omelet 250
Spicy Pork & Noodle Stir-Fry 250
Spicy Pork & Vegetable Broth 122
Spicy Pork & Vegetable Stir-Fry 122

Spicy Pork with Crispy Noodles 250, 251
Spicy Pork, Vegetable & Noodle Stir-Fry 114
Spicy Sausage Salad 98
Sticky Spicy Pork with Vegetable Noodles 114, 115
Thai Green Pork Rice 118
Thai Pork Noodle Salad 118, 119
Vietnamese-Style Pork Baguettes 90
pork sausages: Spicy Chili Sausages in Rolls 98, 99
potatoes
Carrot, Pea & Potato Curry 204, 205
Cumin Potatoes with Pomegranate Seeds 194, 195
Cumnin Potato Curry 194
Roasted Cumin Potato Wedges 194
Spanish Potatoes with Spicy Tomatoes 224, 225
Spicy Green Bean, Potato & Pesto Linguine 238, 239
Spicy Pea, Carrot & Potato Frittata 204
Spicy Pea, Carrot & Potato Stir-Fry 204
Spicy Potato & Tomato Stir-Fry 224
Spicy Steak, Potato & Arugula Salad 86
Spicy Warm Potato & Tomato Salad 224
Yellow Fish, Potato & Tomato Curry 172, 173

quinoa
Spicy Quinoa & Fava Bean Broth 278
Spicy Quinoa, Fava Bean & Avocado Salad 278, 279

raisins: Fruity Chicken Moroccan Stew 40
rice noodles
Broiled Coconut Chicken with Spicy Rice Noodles 276
Burmese Coconut Chicken & Rice Noodle Curry 276, 277
Chinese Beef, Tofu & Vegetable Noodles 78
Mackerel & Rice Noodle Stir-Fry 174
Singapore Rice Noodles 256, 257
Spiced Shrimp, Coconut & Rice Noodle Soup 260, 261
Spicy Coconut Chicken & Rice Noodles 276
Spicy Rice Noodle Omelet 256
Spicy Rice Noodle Soup 256
Spicy Shrimp & Coconut Noodle Soup 260
Thai Fish Ball Noodles 150

Turmeric Mackerel Skewers with Chile Rice Noodles 174, 175
rice vermicelli noodles: Spicy Pork with Crispy Noodles 250, 251
risottos
Chicken, Lemon & Tarragon Risotto 26, 27
Chile & Butternut Squash Risotto 272, 273
Spicy Asparagus & Smoked Salmon Risotto 244
Spicy Ham & Pea Risotto 108, 109
rosemary
Chicken, Chile & Rosemary Soup 60, 61
Creamy Chicken, Chile & Rosemary Pasta 60
Rosemary & Chile-Stuffed Chicken 60

salads
Chicken, Mushroom & Spinach Salad with Spicy Yogurt Dressing 58
Chicken Salad with Chile & Arugula Pesto 30
Chile, Cherry Tomato & Goat Cheese Salad 182
Chinese Beef, Tofu & Vegetable Salad 78
Chinese Turkey & Noodle Salad 70
Chorizo, Spinach & Egg Salad with Paprika Croutons 106, 107
Curried Calves' Liver with Herbed Salad 82, 83
Curried Chicken & Grape Salad 66, 67
Curried Chicken Pasta Salad 66
Eggplant, Tomato & Chile Salad 180
Fish & Spicy Salsa Salad 138
Green Lentil & Lima Bean Salad with Chile Dressing 258, 259
Moroccan Couscous Salad 192
Moroccan Vegetable Couscous Salad 246
Piquant Chicken & Roasted Pepper Salad 36
Shrimp, Tomato & Chile Salad 168
Spiced Mango & Coconut Salad 186
Spiced Red Cabbage & Carrot Salad 196, 197
Spicy Bean & Bell Pepper Salad 252, 253
Spicy Black Bean & Scallion Salad 240
Spicy Cabbage & Red Pepper Salad 222
Spicy Carrot & Black Bean Salad 242
Spicy Corn, Avocado & Tomato Salad 188
Spicy Fava Bean & Dill Rice Salad 268
Spicy Green Bean & Pesto Salad 238
Spicy Lamb, Spinach & Chickpea Salad 88

Spicy Lemon Chicken Salad 42
Spicy Lentil & Carrot Salad 254
Spicy Mango & Duck Salad 56, 57
Spicy Quinoa, Fava Bean & Avocado
 Salad 278, 279
Spicy Salmon & Herb Salad 128
Spicy Sausage & Tomato Salad 110
Spicy Sausage Salad 98
Spicy Shrimp & Tomato Salad 146
Spicy Smoked Salmon, Asparagus &
 Pasta Salad 244
Spicy Steak, Potato & Arugula Salad 86
Spicy Sweet Potato & Litchi Salad 190
Spicy Tuna, Tomato & Olive Pasta
 Salad 262
Spicy Veg, Cashew & Feta Couscous
 Salad 248
Spicy Warm Potato & Tomato Salad
 224
Spicy Zucchini, Tomato & Mint Salad
 214
Thai Pork Noodle Salad 118, 119
Thai-Style Red Duck Salad 48
Vietnamese Chicken, Herb & Rice
 Salad 234
Warm Crab, Chile & Cilantro Rice Salad
 134
Warm Curried Calves' Liver Salad 82
Warm Edamame, Ginger, Chile &
 Noodle Salad 232, 233
Warm Green Chicken & Rice Salad 24
Warm Spicy Black Bean, Scallion &
 Noodle Salad 240, 241
Zucchini & Chile Pasta Salad 270
salmon
 Broiled Hot, Sweet & Sour Salmon 160
 Fish & Spicy Salsa Salad 138
 Hot & Sour Fish Soup 160
 Hot Salmon & Shrimp Laksa Rice 142
 Hot, Sweet & Sour Salmon 160, 161
 Laksa Salmon & Shrimp Omelet 142
 Shrimp & Salmon Laksa 142, 143
 Spicy Asparagus & Smoked Salmon
  Risotto 244
 Spicy Fish & Tomato Soup 172
 Spicy Herb & Coconut Salmon
  Packages 128, 129
 Spicy Salmon & Herb Rice 128
 Spicy Salmon & Herb Salad 128
 Spicy Smoked Salmon & Asparagus
  Pasta 244, 245
 Spicy Smoked Salmon, Asparagus &
  Pasta Salad 244
 Spicy Yellow Fish & Tomato Rice 172
 Yellow Fish, Potato & Tomato Curry
  172, 173
sausages
 Chorizo Sausage, Paprika & Bean Stew
  92, 93

Chorizo, Spinach & Egg Salad with
 Paprika Croutons 106, 107
Merguez Sausage & Tomato Tortilla
 102
Pan-Fried Chorizo, Paprika & Beans 92
Quick Chorizo, Paprika and Bean Soup
 92
Spicy Chili Sausages in Rolls 98, 99
Spicy Chorizo & Spinach Egg-Fried
 Rice 106
Spicy Chorizo & Spinach Frittata 106
Spicy Eggs with Merguez Sausages &
 Tomato 102, 103
Spicy Sausage & Bean Stew 98
Spicy Sausage & Tomato Casserole 110
Spicy Sausage & Tomato Pasta 110,
 111
Spicy Sausage & Tomato Salad 110
Spicy Sausage Salad 98
Spicy Scrambled Eggs with Merguez
 Sausages 102
scallions
 Japanese-Style Tofu with Scallions
  202
 Spicy Black Bean & Scallion Salad 240
 Spicy Black Bean, Scallion & Noodle
  Omelet 240
 Spicy Tofu & Scallion Stir-Fry 220
 Spicy Tofu with Bok Choy & Scallions
  220, 221
 Sweet Chile Veal & Scallion Noodles
  116
 Veal & Scallion Kebabs with Sweet Chili
  Dip 116, 117
 Warm Spicy Black Bean, Scallion &
  Noodle Salad 240, 241
scallops
 Pan-Fried Scallops with Chile, Cilantro
  & Coconut 166
 Scallop, Chile, Cilantro & Coconut
  Pasta 166
 Scallop Molee 166, 167
seafood
 Piri Piri Squid & Seafood Salad 140
 see also clams; crab; crayfish; lobster;
  mussels; scallops; shrimp; squid
shrimp
 Chicken, Shrimp & Lemon Grass Cakes
  64, 65
 Chicken, Shrimp & Lemon Grass
  Skewers 64
 Chicken, Shrimp & Lemon Grass Stir-
  Fry 64
 Chile Tomato & Shrimp Gratin 168
 Garlicky Chile & Tomato Shrimp 168,
  169
 Hot Salmon & Shrimp Laksa Rice 142
 Laksa Salmon & Shrimp Omelet 142
 Shrimp & Salmon Laksa 142, 143

Shrimp & Tomato Curry 146, 147
Shrimp, Lemon Grass & Mango 164
Shrimp, Lemon Grass & Mango Curry
 164, 165
Shrimp, Lemon Grass & Mango Rice
 164
Shrimp, Tomato & Chile Salad 168
Spiced Shrimp, Coconut & Rice Noodle
 Soup 260, 261
Spicy Coconut Shrimp with Angel-Hair
 Pasta 260
Spicy Shrimp & Coconut Noodle Soup
 260
Spicy Shrimp & Pea Pilaf 266, 267
Spicy Shrimp & Pea Stir-Fried Rice
 266
Spicy Shrimp & Tofu Vegetables 236
Spicy Shrimp & Tomato Gratin 146
Spicy Shrimp & Tomato Salad 146
Spicy Shrimp & Vegetable Noodles
 236, 237
Spicy Shrimp & Vegetable Rice 236
Spicy Shrimp, Pea & Rice Soup 266
Tandoori Jumbo Shrimp Skewers with
 Mint & Yogurt Dip 148, 149
Tandoori Shrimp Biryani 148
Tandoori Shrimp Stir-Fry 148
preserved lemons
 Spiced Chicken Stew with Preserved
  Lemon 42, 43
 Spicy Chicken & Preserved Lemon
  Skewers 42
 Spicy Lemon Chicken Salad 42
 Sumac & Lemon Monkfish Stew 170
soba noodles
 Edamame, Ginger, Chile & Noodle
  Broth 232
 Warm Edamame, Ginger, Chile &
  Noodle Salad 232, 233
soups
 Chicken, Chile & Rosemary Soup 60,
  61
 Creamy Curried Mussel Soup 132,
  133
 Curried Butternut Squash & Red
  Pepper Soup 212
 Hot & Sour Fish Soup 160
 Quick Chorizo, Paprika and Bean Soup
  92
 Quick Thai Fish Ball Soup 150
 Spiced Shrimp, Coconut & Rice Noodle
  Soup 260, 261
 Spicy Carrot & Green Bean Soup 198
 Spicy Chickpea Soup 274
 Spicy Coconut Soup with Deep-Fried
  Okra 210
 Spicy Fish & Tomato Soup 172
 Spicy Lentil & Carrot Soup with
  Caramelized Onions 254, 255

Spicy Mushroom & Chickpea Soup 200

Spicy Shrimp & Coconut Noodle Soup 260

Spicy Shrimp, Pea & Rice Soup 266

Spicy Rice & Lentil Soup 264

Spicy Rice Noodle Soup 256

Spicy Spinach & Tomato Soup with Crème Fraîche 202

Vietnamese Chicken, Herb & Rice Soup 234

Vietnamese Chicken Soup 44

spaghetti
  Butternut Squash & Chile Pasta 272
  Chile Spaghetti with Vodka 130, 131
  Spicy Spaghetti and Meat Sauce 86

spicy salsa verde
  Cold Roasted Chicken with Spicy Salsa Verde 28, 29
  Pan-Fried Chicken with Spicy Salsa Verde 28
  Poached Chicken with Spicy Salsa Verde 28

spinach
  Chicken, Mushroom & Spinach Salad with Spicy Yogurt Dressing 58
  Chorizo, Spinach & Egg Salad with Paprika Croutons 106, 107
  Lamb Chops with Spicy Chickpeas & Spinach 88, 89
  Spicy Chicken, Mushroom & Spinach Crepes 58, 59
  Spiced Chicken, Mushroom & Spinach Pilaf 58
  Spicy Chorizo & Spinach Egg-Fried Rice 106
  Spicy Chorizo & Spinach Frittata 106
  Spicy Lamb, Spinach & Chickpea Rice 88
  Spicy Lamb, Spinach & Chickpea Salad 88
  Spicy Spinach & Tomato Soup with Crème Fraîche 202
  Spicy Spinach, Tomato & Cottage Cheese Salad 202
  Spinach, Tomato & Paneer Curry 202, 203

squid
  Crispy Fried Piri Piri Squid 140
  Grilled Piri Piri Squid with Mint & Cilantro 140, 141
  Piri Piri Squid & Seafood Salad 140

stews
  Chorizo Sausage, Paprika & Bean Stew 92, 93
  Fruity Chicken Moroccan Stew 40
  Harissa Vegetable Stew with Bulgur Wheat 246

Jamaican Curried Beef & Black Bean Stew 120, 121

Moroccan Vegetable Stew with Couscous 192, 193

Rose Harissa & Chicken Meatball Moroccan Stew 54, 55

Spanish Turkey Stew with Lemon & Chile 38, 39

Spiced Carrot & Green Bean Stew 198, 199

Spiced Chicken Stew with Preserved Lemon 42, 43

Spicy Cabbage & Red Pepper Stew 222

Spicy Lamb & Vegetable Stew 112, 113

Spicy Monkfish & Bell Pepper Stew 144, 145

Spicy Mushroom, Cauliflower & Chickpea Stew 200, 201

Spicy Sausage & Bean Stew 98

Spicy Veg & Cashew Stew with Feta & Couscous 248

Spicy Vegetable & Lentil Stew 264

Sumac & Lemon Monkfish Stew 170

stir-fries
  Chicken, Shrimp & Lemon Grass Stir-Fry 64
  Chile & Zucchini Stir-Fry Noodles 270
  Chinese Monkfish & Bell Pepper Stir-Fry 144
  Crayfish, Vegetable & Coconut Stir-Fry 152
  Curried Beef & Black Bean Stir-Fry 120
  Duck & Vegetable Tikka Stir-Fry 68
  Green Chicken Stir-Fry 24
  Mackerel & Rice Noodle Stir-Fry 174
  Malaysian Red Pepper & Cabbage Stir-Fry 222, 223
  Pork, Lemon Grass & Chile Stir-Fry 80
  Spicy Cabbage & Carrot Stir-Fry 196
  Spicy Lamb Stir-Fry 100
  Spicy Mushroom & Tomato Stir-Fry 208
  Spicy Pea, Carrot & Potato Stir-Fry 204
  Spicy Pork & Noodle Stir-Fry 250
  Spicy Pork & Vegetable Stir-Fry 122
  Spicy Pork, Vegetable & Noodle Stir-Fry 114
  Spicy Potato & Tomato Stir-Fry 224
  Spicy Shrimp & Pea Stir-Fried Rice 266
  Spicy Tofu & Scallion Stir-Fry 220
  Tandoori Shrimp Stir-Fry 148
  Thai Green Chicken Stir-Fry 46
  Thai Massaman Vegetable Stir-Fry 226

Turkey, Chile & Lemon Stir-Fry 38

Turkey, Bell Pepper & Harissa Stir-Fry 32

sumac
  Sumac & Chile Fish Rolls with Lemon Mayo 170
  Sumac & Lemon Monkfish Stew 170
  Sumac, Chile & Lemon-Spiced Monkfish Kebabs 170, 171

sweet chili sauce
  Veal & Scallion Kebabs with Sweet Chili Dip 116, 117

sweet potatoes
  Spicy Sweet Potato & Litchi Noodles 190
  Spicy Sweet Potato & Litchi Salad 190
  Sweet Potato & Litchi Curry 190, 191

tamarind paste 10
  Baked Tamarind Fish with Cherry Tomatoes 136
  Broiled Tomato & Tamarind Fish 136
  Tomato & Tamarind Fish Curry 136, 137

tandoori paste
  Broiled Tandoori Lamb Chops 84, 85
  Tandoori Jumbo Shrimp Skewers with Mint & Yogurt Dip 148, 149
  Tandoori Lamb Wraps 84
  Tandoori Shrimp Biryani 148
  Tandoori Shrimp Stir-Fry 148
  Tandoori Roasted Rack of Lamb 84

tarragon
  Broiled Chicken with Chile, Lemon & Tarragon Butter 26
  Chicken, Lemon & Tarragon Baguettes 26
  Chicken, Lemon & Tarragon Risotto 26, 27

Thai basil 8

Thai massaman curry paste
  Spicy Roasted Thai Massaman Vegetables 226
  Thai Massaman Butternut Squash Curry 226, 227
  Thai Massaman Vegetable Stir-Fry 226

tikka paste
  Duck & Vegetable Tikka Stir-Fry 68
  Duck Tikka Kebabs 68, 69
  Tikka-Spiced Duck Omelet 68

tofu
  Chinese Beef, Tofu & Vegetable Salad 78
  Chinese Beef with Tofu & Vegetables 78, 79
  Japanese-Style Tofu with Scallions 220
  Spicy Shrimp & Tofu Vegetables 236

Spicy Tofu & Scallion Stir-Fry 220
Spicy Tofu with Bok Choy & Scallions
220, 221
tomatoes
Baked Tamarind Fish with Cherry
Tomatoes 136
Broiled Tomato & Tamarind Fish 136
Chile, Eggplant & Tomato Sauté 180
Chile, Cherry Tomato & Goat Cheese
Pasta 182
Chile, Cherry Tomato & Goat Cheese
Salad 182
Chile, Cherry Tomato & Goat Cheese
Tart 182, 183
Chile Tomato & Shrimp Gratin 168
Creamy Beet, Green Bean & Tomato
Curry 184, 185
Curried Beet, Green Bean & Tomato
Broth 184
Curried Beet, Green Bean & Tomato
Rice 184
Curried Mushrooms & Tomatoes 208,
209
Eggplant, Tomato & Chile Curry 180,
181
Eggplant, Tomato & Chile Salad 180
Garlicky Chile & Tomato Shrimp 168,
169
Grilled Spicy Zucchini with Tomato &
Mint 214
Island-Spiced Corn with Avocado &
Tomato 188, 189
Merguez Sausage & Tomato Tortilla
102
Middle Eastern Zucchini, Tomato &
Mint Curry 214, 215
Shrimp & Tomato Curry 146, 147
Shrimp, Tomato & Chile Salad 168
Spanish Potatoes with Spicy Tomatoes
224, 225
Spiced Okra, Tomato & Coconut 218,
219
Spicy Corn, Avocado & Tomato Pasta
188
Spicy Corn, Avocado & Tomato Salad
188

Spicy Eggs with Merguez Sausages &
Tomato 102, 103
Spicy Fish & Tomato Soup 172
Spicy Mushroom & Tomato Rice 208
Spicy Mushroom & Tomato Stir-Fry
208
Spicy Potato & Tomato Stir-Fry 224
Spicy Sausage & Tomato Casserole
110
Spicy Sausage & Tomato Pasta 110,
111
Spicy Sausage & Tomato Salad 110
Spicy Shrimp & Tomato Gratin 146
Spicy Shrimp & Tomato Salad 146
Spicy Spinach & Tomato Soup with
Crème Fraîche 202
Spicy Spinach, Tomato & Cottage
Cheese Salad 202
Spicy Tuna, Tomato & Olive Pasta
262, 263
Spicy Tuna, Tomato & Olive Pasta
Casserole 262
Spicy Tuna, Tomato & Olive Pasta
Salad 262
Spicy Warm Potato & Tomato Salad
224
Spicy Yellow Fish & Tomato Rice 172
Spicy Zucchini, Tomato & Mint Salad
214
Spinach, Tomato & Paneer Curry 202,
203
Tomato & Tamarind Fish Curry 136,
137
Tomato, Coconut & Okra Curry 218
Yellow Fish, Potato & Tomato Curry
172, 173
tortillas
Merguez Sausage & Tomato Tortilla
102
Spicy Beef Enchilada Wraps 104, 105
Spicy Ham & Pea Tortilla 108
trout: Fish & Spicy Salsa Salad 138
tuna
Spicy Tuna, Tomato & Olive Pasta
262, 263

Spicy Tuna, Tomato & Olive Pasta
Casserole 262
Spicy Tuna, Tomato & Olive Pasta
Salad 262
turkey
Chinese Turkey & Noodle Salad 70
Chinese Turkey Chow Mein 70, 71
Glazed Chinese-Style Turkey Cutlets
70
Harissa-Spiced Turkey & Bell Pepper
Kebabs 32, 33
Quick Turkey, Chile & Lemon Rice 38
Spanish Turkey Stew with Lemon &
Chile 38, 39
Turkey, Bell Pepper & Harissa Stir-
Fry 32
Turkey Ciabattas with Harissa Mayo
32

veal
Sweet Chile Veal & Scallion Noodles
116
Sweet Chile Veal & Scallion Rice 116
Veal & Scallion Kebabs with Sweet Chili
Dip 116, 117

white fish
Mexican Fish & Salsa Casserole 138
Thai Fish Ball Curry 150, 151
Thai Fish Ball Noodles 150
also see cod; flounder; halibut
yellow split lentils: Spiced Rice & Yellow
Lentils 264, 265

zucchini
Chile & Zucchini Pennette 270, 271
Chile & Zucchini Stir-Fry Noodles
270
Grilled Spicy Zucchini with Tomato &
Mint 214
Middle Eastern Zucchini, Tomato &
Mint Curry 214, 215
Spicy Zucchini, Tomato & Mint Salad
214
Zucchini & Chile Pasta Salad 270

Acknowledgments

Executive editor: Eleanor Maxfield
Editor: Joanne Wilson
Copy-editor: Jo Murray
Art Director: Jonathan Christie
Design: www.gradedesign.com
Art Direction: Juliette Norsworthy & Tracy Killick
Photographer: Craig Robertson
Home economist: Emma Lewis
Stylist: Isabel De Cordova
Production: Peter Hunt